Virginia Shade

An African American History of Falmouth, Virginia

NORMAN SCHOOLS

iUniverse, Inc.
Bloomington

Virginia Shade
An African American History of Falmouth, Virginia

Copyright © 2010, 2012 by Norman Schools.
Cover Design by Dale Glasgow

Cover Image: Emancipation.
Columbia holding the Emancipation Proclamation, carte de visite photograph c.1863, by John P. Soule, from a painting by the artist, G.G. Fish. Courtesy Library of Congress

All rights reserved. No part of this book may be used or reproduced by any means, graphic, electronic, or mechanical, including photocopying, recording, taping or by any information storage retrieval system without the written permission of the publisher except in the case of brief quotations embodied in critical articles and reviews. It is expressly conveyed to the reader that it is entirely unintentional to defame, purge, humiliate and or hurt someone's person or feelings as a result of them reading and or acting upon any or all of the information in this book.

iUniverse books may be ordered through booksellers or by contacting:

iUniverse
1663 Liberty Drive
Bloomington, IN 47403
www.iuniverse.com
1-800-Authors (1-800-288-4677)

Because of the dynamic nature of the Internet, any web addresses or links contained in this book may have changed since publication and may no longer be valid. The views expressed in this work are solely those of the author and do not necessarily reflect the views of the publisher, and the publisher hereby disclaims any responsibility for them.

ISBN: 978-1-4759-0810-7 (sc)
ISBN: 978-1-4759-0809-1 (hc)
ISBN: 978-1-4759-0808-4 (ebk)

Library of Congress Control Number: 2012906182

Printed in the United States of America

iUniverse rev. date: 07/03/2012

CONTENTS

Acknowledgements..xv
Foreword...xvii
Preface..xxi
Introduction...xxiii

Part I: Colonial Falmouth

Gathering Shards...2
A Considerable Trade 3
Hogtown..4
Charms 6
The King's Highway..7
King Carter's Cure..8
Rather Die Free Men Than Live Slaves...............................9
Over Time...11
The Native and The Dragon 13

Part II: The Federal Period Through The Antebellum Years

The Abolitionist Hymn..17
The Fatal Christmas Party 17
A Tisket, A Tasket, A Red and Yellow Basket 19
Don't Sell Lucy...21
Saved by the Horn..23
Separate and Unequal..24
A Fable..26
A Course Man and His Cart..27
African Princess..28
Beautiful Clear Water from the Spring 29
Sunday Morning Sunshine 31
Turn the Pot Upside Down...32

Holler	33
Clearing the Way	36
The Wood-Cellar	37
Such an Offence	37
The Observer	39
Blood Money	41
Time of Fire	44
Aunt Nancy and Benjamin	45
A Trembling Man	46
Is a Slave	48
The Father's Letter	52
It Was Exile	54
An Ex-Slave's Letter	56
The Underground Railroad	61
A Choice	65
A Kiss	68
An Ancient and a Modern Compromise	72

Part III: The Civil War

A Prophet	77
Though it Cost My Life	78
Orderly and Obedient	81
Our First Fallen	82
Freedom's Price	84
Judgment Day	85
Bless You Honey	87
The Crossing	88
As Good Abolitionist as Any of You	89
They Took the Nurse Girl	91
Elizah Followed by a "B"	94
April Wind	94
The Camp	96
Hoe Cakes and Other Luxuries	99
Black Dispatches	102
Jeff Davis and His Coachman	105
The Beating	109
A Good Laugh	111

Jubilo	113
Cooks and Hostlers	114
The Birthday Party	117
It Didn't Belong Here	119
Independence Day	120
Canaan's Freedom Wagons	121
The Fugitive Slave of the Boston Riots	123
A Small Candy-Shop and Sixty Dollars	126
The Train Ride to Freedom	128
When I Can Read My Title Clear	131
An Old Hoe	134
The Doctor's Coach Driver	135
Together They Went to War	136
Return to Slavery and a Return to Freedom	138
The Black Scout of the Rappahannock	139
The Unsung Hero of the Aboveground Railroad	142
Zion	144
Ten Thousand to the Land of Freedom	145
A Great Battle	148
Watch Night	149
How We Got Over	151
The Faithful Servant	153
Rebel Negro Pickets and the Teamsters' Duel	155
A Brave Act	158
Saluted by Death and Kissed by Immortality	159
A Clothes-Line Telegraph	160
The Blight	164
The Madness	166
Comfortable Quarters	167
The Divine Idea	168
The God of Battles	170
A Wail from the House of Bondage	171
Writing on the Wall	173
Testimonies Concerning Slavery	177
Then I Laid My Burden Down	179
With Malice Toward None	180
O Captain! My Captain!	182

Part IV: Falmouth After The War

Not Yet Man 187
And Not This Man 188
The Freedmen's Bureau 190
Gathering Bones 194
The Look of Freedom 196
The Congregation 198
The Union Branch of the True Vine 199
New Freedom 202
A Bush Arbor 203
Old Path 205
Little Shiloh 206
Not Here 207
Letter from Virginia 208
A Certain Youth 210

Part V: The Late 19th And Early 20th Century

Lucas is Walking Tonight 215
The Confederate Secretary of War and an Ex-Slave 218
From Slave to a Contraband, from a Contraband to a Citizen 220
Her Master was a Rebel Congressman 222
Incident at Spout Hill and the Colored Belle of Falmouth 223
An African American Cemetery 225
A True Soul 225
Born in Virginia 228
A Beacon Light in Falmouth 232
Uncle Jim 233
Pap Lucas 235
The Stud 237
Yes and No 237
Know Their Place 238
Color 239
A Hilly Relationship 242
Pick it Up, Brother 243
The Faithful Friend 245
Evil Spirits 247

The Gate Posts 249
Early 1920s and 30s photographs 250

Part VI: The Modern Era

The Best Place...256
Goosey Goose 259
The AMOCO Connection..259
Carlton Slave Graveyard 261
Behold, I Show You a Mystery..262
A New Century 264
Epilogue...265
   A Secret..265
   Civil Liberty..265
Appendix A: Train Ride to Freedom in Conway's Own Words 267
Appendix B: Names of the Conway Colony Freedom Seekers 273
Appendix C: Letter from Virginia...277
Appendix D: African Americans from Falmouth of the late-19th to
   mid-20th centuries, with Comments from Oral History...........280
Appendix E: Moncure Conway After the American Civil War......290
Appendix F: Union Branch of the True Vine Covenant 293
Notes 295
Bibliography..343
Index..357

This book is dedicated to the descendants of the Conway Colony in Yellow Springs, Ohio, whose ancestors as slaves from Falmouth, Virginia, emancipated themselves and founded in 1863 the First Anti-Slavery Baptist Church of Yellow Springs.

And so our parents and grandparents have, more often than not anonymously, handed down the spark of freedom, "the seed of the flower they themselves never hoped to see, or like a sealed letter they could not plainly read."

_____Alice Walker

ACKNOWLEDGEMENTS

I have entered the undertaking of this work with all humility, knowing full well that I write of history belonging to another people. It is my sincerest hope that these stories will be enjoyed, will enlighten, and perhaps, will reconcile. If my hope is fulfilled, it will be to the credit of the many people who collaborated with me in this endeavor.

With much gratitude I thank John d'Entremont, the biographer of Moncure Daniel Conway. Through his passion for and knowledge of Virginia history, he brought Conway alive for me, and conveyed Conway's relevance in the light of modern times. It was his elegant reference to "Concord light and Virginia shade" which inspired the title of this book.

I am also indebted to Frank White, a noted African American historian of Stafford County, who located and made contact with the Conway Colony descendants in Yellow Springs, Ohio. He was largely responsible for their return visits to Falmouth, Virginia, and for my opportunities to learn about their family histories.

Jean McKee is a fifth-generation descendant and historian of the Conway Colony in Yellow Springs. She graciously shared her research and identified many of the original members of the Conway Colony.

James K. Bryant, II, Ph.D. contributed the Foreword to this work. A scholar of African American studies, he has been a friend of Conway House for over a decade. I have been enriched and inspired by his friendship.

Tanya Gossett served as my general editor. Eleya Frields did the copy editing and proofreading. To both I am much indebted for taking on the monumental task of putting my poor efforts into a polished and finished form.

Albert Z. Conner has an exceptional analytical mind and I thank him for the many times he collaborated with me on some particular topic. I admire his sincere interest in history and his deep reverence for those who lived it.

John Hennessy, Chief Historian of the Fredericksburg and Spotsylvania National Military Park, has a tremendous passion for

African American history in the region. His zeal is another inspiration for this book.

Longtime Falmouth resident Herbert Brooks graciously shared his vast knowledge of the community with me. His stories of old Falmouth are as enchanting as he is himself. Another Falmouth resident, Marion Brooks Robinson, also shared her fascinating knowledge of Falmouth's history. I am especially appreciative for her account of the slave Lucas in the vignette, "Lucas is Walking Tonight."

I am grateful to Jerrilynn Eby MacGregor, author and historian, for unreservedly sharing her personal local history collection and for her eagerness to assist me with my research.

Kathy Olmstead, longtime friend and expert in the field of genealogical research, gave much of her time providing valuable assistance.

Wayne Morris has a remarkable knowledge of the early frontier. He provided the history of the fur and skin trade in Virginia, for which I am most appreciative.

I would like to thank especially Scott Sanders, archivist at Antioch College in Yellow Springs, Ohio, and Paula Royster, director of the Center for African American Genealogical Research, Inc., for their assistance.

My gratitude extends to Gari Melchers Home and Studio in Falmouth, Virginia, and Joanna Catron, curator, for allowing the use of the three paintings: *Color*, *Ironing*, and *Uncle Jim*. Uncle Jim's grandson, James Lucas, graciously provided his important collection of photographs.

The book was also made possible by the contributions of the following persons: Jerome Baker, Linwood Bourne, Jr., Robert and Aline Burton, Marcia Chaves, Gloria Chittum, Jane Conner, Janet Cox, Marjorie Dawson, Janet Edson, Larry Evans, Ruth Coder Fitzgerald, Dennis Gannon, Tim Garrett, Ben Greenbaum, Shirley Heim, Kirby Kendall, Jr., Barbara Kirby, L. Reginald Lucas, Ralph MacKenzie, Eric Mink, Bonnie and D.P. Newton, Megan Orient, Roger Poindexter, Jr., Dave Rider, Frank Ruiz, Billy Shelton, Glenna Graves Shiflett, Louellen Whitefeather Silver, Paul Sopko, Jim Thomas, Lawrence Wheeler, April Wegner, and Gene Wiles.

Finally, to my wife, Lenetta, whose encouragement prompted the writing of this book, I commend and thank her for her patience and collaboration.

FOREWORD

It was a little more than 11 years ago that Lenetta and Norman Schools first invited me to their historic home in Falmouth, Virginia. At the time, I was still a historian with the National Park Service and was invited to make a few remarks for the dedication and unveiling of a painted portrait of Moncure Daniel Conway, who had resided in the Schools' home 150 years before. Finding it a pleasure and a privilege to be a part of a momentous occasion for Falmouth, I was humbled by the presence of both Conway's great-grand niece and a descendant of the former Conway Family slaves who had left the South for Ohio in 1862 with Conway as their personal escort. This event clearly showed that history continued to live, grow, and evolve through the lives and memories of those in the past, bearing fruit in the hearts and minds of those descendants in our present.

Falmouth and the surrounding environs of Stafford County, Virginia, offer a unique crossroads of American history and culture, particularly the African-American component, from the early colonial days through present times. By 1860, slightly more than 42% of Stafford County's population was of African descent. The unassuming village of Falmouth at the edge of the Rappahannock River would be the testing grounds for acquainting fugitive slaves with the Union Army and freedom as well as educating white Union soldiers on the realities of slavery and slave life. Slavery, a complex institution involving human relationships, had been a major component in antebellum Virginia society. Dr. W.E.B. Du Bois wrote in 1908 that it was difficult to form a clear picture of the antebellum life of African-Americans characterized by slavery "between the Southern apologist and his picture of cabin life, with idyllic devotion and careless toil, and that of the abolitionist with his tale of family disruption and cruelty . . ." Somewhere in the middle, Du Bois argued, could be found a reasonable statement of "average truth."[1] Slaves indeed had experiences ranging from cruel tyrants for masters to benevolent owners with affectionate and genuine concern for the welfare of "their people." In this search for truth, it becomes increasingly clear that two distinct worlds had emerged in the antebellum period: a black world and a white world.

"If scholars want to know the hearts and secret thoughts of slaves," wrote the late scholar John W. Blassingame, "they must study the testimony of the blacks."[2] Norman Schools presents this current volume as "vignettes" of the African-American experience in Falmouth to give readers the often-overlooked "rare" voice and memory of African-Americans before and after Emancipation. The oral traditions through story-telling, song, and practiced cultural traditions remain important sources that help improve our understanding of African-American history and heritage. The Union soldiers stationed in Falmouth during the Civil War served as ambassadors to the "Gateway to Freedom," encouraging young Fredericksburg slave John Washington in crossing the Rappahannock to freedom just as they had assisted Andrew Weaver, who had been a slave at J. Horace Lacy's Chatham Manor next door to the Conway House. Both Washington and Weaver worked as camp servants for Union forces. Weaver eventually enlisted into the 23rd U.S. Colored Infantry that saw limited action in neighboring Spotsylvania County in the spring of 1864. Other Falmouth residents of African descent felt the pangs of loyalty and community attachment despite living under a system of oppression, demonstrating the many shades of what freedom meant among Falmouth's African-American population.

Dr. Blassingame also reminded us that since slaves did not know the hearts and secret thoughts of their masters, the testimony of white residents as shown through *Virginia Shade* needs to be examined. "Neither the whites nor the blacks had a monopoly on truth," Blassingame continued, "had rented the veil cloaking the life of the other, or had seen clearly the pain and joy bounded by color and caste."[3]

---

[1] W.E.B. Du Bois, ed., *The Negro American Family* (Atlanta, GA: Atlanta University Press, 1908), 9.

[2] John W. Blassingame, ed. *Slave Testimony: Two Centuries of Letters, Speeches, Interviews, and Autobiographies* (Baton Rouge, LA: Louisiana State University Press, 1977, 1999), lxv.

[3] Blassingame, ed., *Slave Testimony*, lxv.

It is within this framework young Moncure Daniel Conway began to symbolize the struggling conscience of the nation in the mid-19th Century. The United States unsuccessfully attempted to live up to its ideals of freedom and liberty while sanctioning an institution contrary to those very ideals. For Conway, his only weapons were the power of the pen and a cache of moral fortitude and courage. The greatest threat to his own person was not only physical harm to his personal being, but alienation and ostracism from his own family, his beloved Virginia, his nation, his religious affiliations, and perhaps his own sense of self in these contradictory struggles.

Almost six years ago, Norman and Lenetta Schools opened their home again for a major celebration in Falmouth in honor of the Conway House becoming a recognized site of the National Park Service's Underground Railroad Network to Freedom. A large gathering of local residents and a larger representation of the descendants of the former Conway slaves who moved to Ohio in 1862 attended this memorable event. Speeches were made by the congressional representative for the district that included Falmouth, officials from the National Park Service, and state and local officials. Prayers were offered by the pastors and ministers of the local churches. Remarks were made by members of the Stafford County Historical Society and other historical organizations. I, again, was more than happy to provide some brief remarks, this time as an Associate Professor of History and Chair for the History Department at Shenandoah University. My humble words could never measure up to the other speakers nor capture the pride of a shared heritage displayed by the participants—both black and white—on that joyous day.

Falmouth continues to be our "Gateway to Freedom" in war and peace. The historical record and memory are key tools to ensure that freedom is what we all strive to achieve and maintain. *Virginia Shade* and the African-American experience is a continuous reminder that freedom has to be cultivated, respected, and practiced among us for it to flourish and spread for all who call themselves Americans.

James K. Bryant, II, Ph.D.
Stephens City, Virginia
2012

PREFACE

I have researched Falmouth's history and the life of Moncure Daniel Conway for the past ten years. During that time I have accumulated bits and pieces of Falmouth's African American history as I ran across them. They have provided the basis for this book.

The form I have chosen is a compilation of vignettes, the intent being not to produce an in-depth work but rather one which takes the reader on a journey. The vignettes of Falmouth's earliest history tend to be more matter of fact, while those of later periods are more narrative. I have included historic quotes where possible and have tried to avoid cluttering them up with 21st century commentary. Today's reader may find aspects of these stories ironic, perhaps even chilling. But also woven throughout *Virginia Shade* is a theme of reconciliation, through which I hope the reader will discover the human nature of both enslaved and enslaver.

Early source material on African Americans in Falmouth is scarce. *Virginia Shade* draws heavily on the autobiography of Moncure Daniel Conway and significantly focuses on Falmouth during the Civil War. I endeavored to place Falmouth and certain important national figures together in a historical context. In some small measure, I hope this work may inspire others to continue the search for stories of Falmouth's distinctive history.

This book would not be possible without those African Americans, known and unknown, whose courageous lives make up our treasured past. The author wishes this work will humbly pay homage to some of those lives and extends a thank you to the interested reader. May you enjoy traveling back in time under the *Virginia Shade*.

Norman Sschools
Falmouth, VA
March 2012

INTRODUCTION

Falmouth's African American history has been largely lost to time; indeed it has been all but forgotten and ignored from the town's inception through the beginning of the 21st century. This could be said for the most part to include all of Falmouth history (black and white). It is sad to contemplate what has been lost and will never come to light again; the more to cherish and respect what is known. The African American thread is more closely woven throughout Falmouth's history than has been acknowledged or researched. Since Falmouth's beginning, African American history has been suppressed by the dogmas of southern society and swept away by the winds of war and time.

Falmouth offers a unique study in African American history. Part of the nation's oldest English colony (being approximately 110 miles from Jamestown where Africans were first brought to Virginia in 1619), Falmouth is situated at the fall line of the Rappahannock River. Captain John Smith explored this area in 1608, and received a hostile welcome from local American Indians. The town's commercial history began with the fur and skin trade, followed by the tobacco trade. The Virginia General Assembly established Falmouth in 1727, and the town quickly evolved into an international shipping port, important enough to be made an official tobacco inspection station of the colony.

Although the river port eventually silted in, its fall line provided a resource of water power to sustain a thriving milling industry. Throughout each phase of Falmouth's development and prosperity, slave labor played an essential role. Falmouth's African American history offers a window into the lives of men, women, and children who had to adapt, survive, and have faith to endure a broad range of social pressures, opportunities, and disadvantages.

One son of Falmouth saw things differently than his contemporaries. Moncure Daniel Conway, the most radical abolitionist produced by the south, grew up in Falmouth, but was forced to leave because of his outspoken views on universal freedom and equality of man. From London in 1864, Conway published his *Testimonies Concerning Slavery*, which opens a window onto the peculiar institution of slavery based on his observations while growing up in Falmouth. We are fortunate today to have Conway's insights, which provide a compassionate accounting of black history during the mid-19th century. Conway will serve a role as observer and witness in many of the forthcoming vignettes.

In 2012, the population of historic Falmouth remains small, with no African Americans. Today as the Falmouth Historic District suffers from economic decline, its greatest resource is its rich history. African Americans can be proud to claim their part of that history.

PART I

COLONIAL FALMOUTH

Before there was a town, there was a river, a valley, and the falls. Below the falls, the river flowed east into a great bay named Chesapeake. The region was populated by native people only. Then, in 1608, white men came by boat and set up crosses of wood and brass and cut their names upon trees to signify possession had been taken by English authority. Under this authority appeared a people of black skin taken from another continent and brought to this place without their consent. So began the African American history of Falmouth, Virginia.

GATHERING SHARDS

The African American history of Falmouth begins at the Falls of the Rappahannock, before the town had its name. The land about the fall line, which divides the coastal plain from the Piedmont of Virginia, was inhabited by Native Americans. At the river, where the falls disallowed easy navigation, the Indians gathered to barter "trade material." Captain John Smith sailed up to the falls in 1608. By his own account, Smith and his band of explorers received a hostile reception by the local residents.[1] To discover how and when African Americans entered upon the historical stage at the Falls, we must turn to the clay of the earth and what archeologists term "material culture."

After the first African Americans arrived at Jamestown, Virginia, in 1619, there began a blending of European, African, and Native American cultures. This cultural interaction produced distinctive earthenware vessels which archeologists and scholars have termed Colono Ware. These earthenware pots were hand made using techniques shared between Native Americans and African Americans. European forms were combined with those used by Nigerian and Ghanaian potters. Colono Ware was unglazed but "burnished" using a West African pottery technique. As based on archeological findings, "Evidence of plantation manufacture of Colono Ware in Virginia is rare; suggesting that much of it was manufactured by Native Americans and traded."[2]

At a river's fall line, seasonal runs of anadromous fish as well as plants and animals could be exploited for food. Fall lines were places of cultural contact between different peoples.[3] While we do not know exactly when African Americans first appeared at the Falls, we can trace their influence through material culture. Along with Native American potsherds found at the Falls, one shard of Colono Ware was also unearthed.[4] Perhaps this shard was from a pot used as a Native American trade item or made by one of the earliest African Americans living at the Falls.

Less likely to boil over and put out the fire, Colono Ware had an advantage over metal pots for the slow cooking of meats and vegetables. Colono Ware vessels were also used in medicinal and religious rituals. African American women made and used Colono Ware under the stressful conditions of slavery. Maintaining African traditional ideology was seen as a "very important element required in maintaining health, controlling one's body, and protecting one's self against enemies."[5] Given the growth of the African American population of Falmouth throughout the Colonial period, more shards of Colono Ware may yet be found by the archeologist's trowel.

Gather the pieces that nothing be lost; that we might tell generations what history cost.

_____Author Unknown

A Considerable Trade

One of the earliest commercial enterprises in Virginia had its beginnings in the 17th century as the fur and skin trade. By 1642, garments made of deer skin were popular in England and on the Continent. From the Falls of the Rappahannock River, caravans and pack trains of horses loaded with trade items sallied into the interior to barter with Native Americans for skins and furs, then returned with the prizes to the Falls for shipment to Europe.

These ventures were operated by merchants or wealthy landowners who could afford to financially back such an enterprise. Others were adventuresome individuals such as Cadwallader Jones, "one of the principals of the trade," whose enterprise was headquartered at the Falls.[6] From the Falls, traders started out on Indian trails which "served as important links in trade among the various Indian tribes and confederacies and served as such in the later English trade with the Indians of the Rappahannock Valley and with the regions beyond the Blue Ridge Mountains."[7] Pack trains of up to 200 horses traveled as far south as Alabama and as far north as the Great Lakes.[8] Trade goods included items such as guns, ammunition, axes, knives, scissors, liquor, blankets, shirts, coarse cloth, beads, bracelets, trinkets, and utensils.

Needless to say these enterprises required men who were daring, brave, and physically fit to serve as horse packers for caravans traveling through the hostile interior. While few records exist, we do know that ". . . traders went out with a few white, black, or Indian servants and employees" and that Cadwallader Jones did a "considerable trade" from his headquarters at the Falls.[9]

At the Falls, ships were loaded with hogsheads each containing 300 or more deerskins.[10] Labor was required to pack the skins into hogsheads and load vessels for shipment. Skins were not fully dressed when shipped; final dressing would be preformed after arrival in foreign markets. The African American servants and employees who "went out" from the Falls no doubt returned by shaded trails with many an adventuresome story and wild tale.

Hogtown

Falmouth became a town by Act of the General Assembly of Virginia in 1727. It encompassed fifty acres regularly laid off in streets, squares, and lots. As an official tobacco inspection station situated at the fall line of the Rappahannock River, it attracted international shipping and became an important export center. At the Port of Falmouth, ships could be seen displaying the flags of foreign countries. A citizen of Falmouth described the commotion:

> At the head of navigation of the Rappahannock river [sic] its situation made it formally the market of all that section of the country lying above it between the Blue Ridge Mountains and Tidewater . . . in those days Falmouth had a regular trade with foreign countries . . . Wagon trains, miles in length, loaded with grain, were frequently seen approaching it from the mountains, merchant ships anchored at its wharf to purchase flour and other products, and sea captains and sailors moved constantly through its streets. Its storage capacity was not equal to its trade, and hogsheads of sugar and molasses lined its streets . . .[11]

Transporting a hogshead. "Rolling roads" brought hogsheads containing tobacco, weighing an average 1,000 pounds, to the Port of Falmouth and its warehouses. Courtesy LOC

During the Colonial period Falmouth was nicknamed "Hogtown" due to the large number of hogs which ran freely about in its streets until gathered later for shipment. The name stuck and Falmouth was referred to as Hogtown well into the 20th century.[12] By 1812, the town's Trustees were concerned about hogs "going at large." They created an ordinance for the police officer to capture any loose hogs and advertise for the owners to come forward. If the owner was not a town resident, he was to pay 50 cents per hog and 12 ½ cents per day for storage. Hogs not claimed within ten days were sold at auction.

At one time there were a couple of distilleries in Falmouth which threw out their old mash. The hogs running loose would root through and consume the discarded mash. The name Hogtown was further compelled upon the town as groups of drunken hogs stumbled along its streets.[13]

Since vessels entered port at Falmouth, this offered the opportunity for slaves to make an escape to freedom either by jumping ship or boarding one. A reward notice for a slave named Ned states at Falmouth he had "run away from the sloop *Susannah*, Capt. John Dow . . ." Another slave from Culpeper County named Natt was the subject of a reward notice in which his owner stated, "As I expect he will endeavor to get on board some vessel . . . I traced him to the town of Falmouth yesterday evening."[14] Both notices have toward the end the typical warning found on such notices forewarning all masters of vessels from harboring or secreting runaway slaves at their peril.

By March 30, 1728, the town of Fredericksburg had been created on the opposite side of the river one mile below Falmouth. Ruth Coder Fitzgerald, the area's foremost authority on African American history, has written, "As the colony grew, Falmouth and Fredericksburg, situated on the Rappahannock River at the limits of inland navigation, became important seaports. Seagoing ships lined the wharves, and slaves busily unloaded and loaded supplies at these trading centers. Human cargo from newly arrived slave ships disembarked as well, and slave auctions could be held anywhere a crowd would gather."[15] The Rappahannock River has since silted in where once a thriving port existed with its stone wharf and large iron rings for mooring ships. In Falmouth today these lie buried deep beneath the sand.[16]

Charms

A Falmouth resident related that its folklore "was mostly of the familiar kind,—one or two houses 'haunted,' an occasional ghost reported . . . A horsehair left in a tub of rain-water would turn to a snake: a snake could charm a bird into his mouth: any deficiency of milk in a cow was ascribed to the 'cowsucker' (black snake)." Below Falmouth was reported "a phantom scow floating on the river with negroes singing and dancing on it . . . Various herbs were used to cure warts, the herb after application being always buried." And, the "belief in witchcraft prevailed . . ."[17]

Enslaved African Americans were thrust into a dehumanizing and demoralizing situation. Lost was their ability to control one's own self destiny. In this presumably powerless condition, slaves attached special meaning to even small items as a way of gaining supernatural advantage over enemies, sickness, slave owners, and overseers. African Americans in Falmouth kept charms in the form of beads or a small silver coin with a hole pierced for wearing around the neck, ankle, or for sewing onto a garment. A piece of silver worn next to the skin would bring good luck or prevent harm. Blue beads were used for adornment and as amulets for protection against illness and misfortune. Reflective of West African culture, belief in the evil eye was prevalent among slaves and the color blue was considered a potent form of spiritual protection.

Left or lost, these little charms have been found in yards or gardens in Falmouth, but their exact meaning can only be speculated upon. The talismans embodied resistance to slavery by psychological and social means. Though elderly female slaves were often considered of lesser value by owners and overseers, their knowledge of charms may have given them an authoritative role as conjurer or healer. Males finding the physical demands of slavery overwhelming due to an injury, sickness, or infirmity of age may have used charms to bestow powers of strength, skill, and wisdom. Charms certainly would have represented spiritual beliefs. They served as small reminders of freedom. Perhaps they offered a brief respite to carry one's soul into the clouds and stars which moved in their own freedom; but a freedom denied to those enslaved.

THE KING'S HIGHWAY

In 1660, King Charles II envisioned linking the English Crown's colonies in America. The King's Highway, which very often followed old Indian trails, became the first major north-south route throughout the colonies. By 1735, the King's Highway was an established route of more than 1,300 miles. It ran from Boston to Charles Towne, South Carolina, and took two months to travel. Later the road was extended to Savannah, Georgia. In the northern colonies, the King's Highway included the Boston Post Road and the Great Coastal Road. In Virginia, it was also called the Potomac Path or the Potomac Trail between Alexandria and Fredericksburg.[18]

Historian Fairfax Harrison has written that by 1664, "The Potomac Path—The oldest white man's road in northern Virginia is, like his land, a conquest of a pre-existing Indian trail . . . In the surviving records of the Stafford Court we can see it being gradually converted into a road, extending upward to the 'freshes' [creeks]." This suggests that by that date, a "road" passed north of the Falls and through the future town of Falmouth, then continued north to Potomac and Aquia Creeks.[19] In laying out the streets of the town in 1728, Falmouth's colonial founders named the first street along the town's waterfront King's Street, perhaps to honor their sovereign and to acknowledge the importance of the Crown's existing thoroughfare.[20]

Usually lying in obscurity, original segments of the King's Highway still exist today, sometimes with names such as King's Road, King's Street, or King Street. In Falmouth, the street along the waterfront is named King Street, changed only slightly from the 18th century spelling of King's Street.[21] This street led colonial travelers to or from the ferry crossing as they continued their journeys on the King's Highway. Today, the ferry crossing is long gone. Beyond the ferry's historic location, King Street becomes River Road, which leads to the Chatham Bridge further down the river.

During the 17th and 18th centuries, Virginia law required landowners to contribute annually to maintaining the King's Highway. ". . . all male labouring persons, being tithable, shall when required, attend the surveyor and assist him in laying out, clearing, and repairing the roads in his precinct, except such who are masters of two or more tithable male labouring servants or slaves, who are hereby declared exempted from personal service or attendance."[22] Slave owners met the requirements of the law by sending their chattel in their place. Much of the work on the King's Highway was preformed by slaves.

And there in the King's Highway sat and sits a figure, veiled and bowed, by which the traveler's footsteps hasten as they go.

———————W.E.B. Du Bois

KING CARTER'S CURE

Like King's Street, the other streets in Falmouth that were laid out east-to-west, parallel to the river, were originally given names associated with the British monarchy, such as Prince, Caroline, Ann, and Amelia. On the west edge of the town, the first street running north-to-south was named for Falmouth's senior trustee, Robert Carter. He was the

Virginia Colony's most powerful figure. Carter was agent for Lord Fairfax, proprietor of the entire Northern Neck of Virginia. Known as "King" Carter, he was the leading influence behind the General Assembly's Act creating Falmouth Towne. Carter purchased enormous amounts of land along the upper stretches of the Rappahannock River in what are now Stafford and King George counties. By having a town with a wharf and warehouses centrally located, the worth of his property holdings would substantially increase.

King Carter's son Charles was one of the other trustees of the town. Historian Jerrilynn Eby MacGregor notes that, "Charles Carter seems to have pretty much run the town for years and years. Not until after his death in 1764 were the Scots merchants able to take over many of the trustees' positions."[23] King Carter's son Landon owned several lots in town, as did his son-in-law, Mann Page. The second north-to-south street laid out was named Page Street. Carter Street is now West Cambridge and Page Street is now Gordon.[24]

The Carters were the early economic dynasty in Falmouth and their slaves likely labored in the port town. King Carter, who owned numerous slaves, had a special way of discouraging runaways. In 1723, he successfully petitioned the General Assembly to legally grant him the power of dismembering.[25] His slaves would have understood that if they were to be captured after running away, they would have their toes cut off. Carter himself stated, "I have cured many a negro from running away by this means."[26]

RATHER DIE FREE MEN THAN LIVE SLAVES

African American author Anita Wills wrote, "Virginia was part of the Upper South, and the darling of Europe. Her tobacco was the finest in the world, and made landless Europeans into the Landed Gentry of Virginia. The slaves who cultivated the tobacco were despised by the people who benefited from their labor."[27]

Falmouth Towne had a host of tobacco merchants known as "factors." One such factor was Cuninghame and Company of Glasgow, Scotland, which traded in Virginia and Maryland. Its operational headquarters was in Falmouth. The Cuninghame firm became extremely wealthy because it was able to successfully compete with the larger British trading firms. It accomplished this by operating stores that "staked out" smaller planters for the growing season with an agreement to buy crops at a set price at harvest. The Scottish store system was well adapted to the needs of the less wealthy planter class because it enabled them to live between tobacco harvests and to buy more slaves to extend cultivation. It also locked in Cuninghame's crop futures, which allowed the firm to compete with the wealthy tobacco barons and large river plantations. The arrangement worked so well it gained the firm sizable profits.[28]

Tobacco and store goods were not the firm's only commodities. Letters of instruction from the company's Falmouth headquarters store indicates that Falmouth served as a port of entry for African slaves. Once there, the slaves would be disbursed among the other factors, who in turn would sell them. One letter inquired, "Have you as yet disposed of the two negroes and for how much?" Another letter dated November 30, 1767, was written from Falmouth to a factor at Fauquier Court House.

> At present you have no proper place for the reception of negroes or servants, which may be sent up to you for sale, you will on receipt of this, get a log house built for that purpose. Let it be about 10 feet square, made of strong logs, with a chimney at one end, and place it in some convenient place close to the road. I leave the construction of it to you and hope you will continue it so that there will be no danger of servants or slaves making their escape out of it. You will go as frugally to work on it as possible, and I imagine at this time of the year you may have it done cheaper than at any other time.
>
> The sooner you get this done the better, as I expect to receive a few negro men and women soon, which probably may be sent up to you for sale. You will therefore on receipt of this make it your business to acquaint the people who have got money that you expect some likely slaves to dispose of soon.[29]

As the letter clearly indicates the perceived need for a slave pen, there is little doubt that such a building also existed in Falmouth by 1767. The "superintending factor" directly responsible to William Cuninghame in Glasgow was James Robinson. He employed fourteen slaves in the operation of the Falmouth store: five as house servants, one to load and unload ships, one as a carpenter, four to man a sloop, and three as crew of a schooner. From Falmouth in 1775, Superintendent Robinson sent a letter to Messrs. Cuninghame & Co. stating his fears that the American colonies intended to revolt against the British Crown, an event that would affect the firm's trade.[30] The letter to Scotland quoted the colonists as saying, ". . . we will rather die free men than live slaves." Superintendent Robinson was quoting "A Declaration of the Causes and Necessity of Taking Up Arms," passed by representatives of the United Colonies of North-America, meeting in Philadelphia on July 6, 1775.[31] The slogan will appear again during the Civil War on the regimental flag of the 3rd United States Colored Troops.

As long as one man is a slave in this land, we are all slaves.

_____Moncure Conway

OVER TIME

The King's Highway crossed the Rappahannock River at the Falmouth Ferry. During the Revolutionary War, the wagon train of the French Expeditionary Force used the Falmouth Ferry on their way to Yorktown. In 1782, French troops returning north used the ferry again and encamped just above Falmouth.[32] A captured slave notice in the *Virginia Gazette*, September 28, 1782, states that "A YOUNG likely Negro Man . . . he calls himself William Lucas, and says that he was with the French army at Falmouth in their march northward, and got separated from them by accident . . . [He] has with him some shoemakers tools and professes himself a shoemaker; he is very well made, active, dances well and plays on the fiddle, has remarkable bad teeth." The notice asks that the slave's owner "prove his property, pay charges and take him away."[33]

The Rappahannock Forge, also known as Hunter's Iron Works, was situated along the Rappahannock River and just above the town of Falmouth. The height of productive activity at this forge was between the turbulent years 1770 and 1784. Part of the work force was slave labor. By a surviving notice we know at least one slave named Moses was a "run away from Rappahannock Forge" in 1777.[34] The 1783 personal property tax record for James Hunter counted his slaves as chattel along with livestock. That year Hunter paid taxes on 260 slaves, 43 cattle, and 81 horses.[35]

During the American Revolutionary War, the forge was a vital source of weapons and camp utensils for General Washington's Continental Army. The African Americans who produced these war materials at the forge contributed to winning our nation's independence and individual freedom. Yet the First Constitutional Convention failed to extend this freedom to African Americans. Historian and author, Jerrilynn Eby MacGregor, provides an account of the Rappahannock Forge in latter years:

> The forge property was occupied by Union Troops during the War Between the States. How many, if any of Hunter's buildings were still standing at that time is unknown. Any structures on the site were destroyed or dismantled and utilized as bridge building material, all but erasing the last traces of Hunter's complex. Over time, the trees grew up along the riverbank and hillside and "the greatest iron works that is upon the Continent" was largely forgotten.[36]

Over time the King's Highway was forgotten. Over time the trees and vegetation overtook the once prominent industrial Hunter's complex and concealed the contributions of the enslaved African Americans who had been instruments of freedom for others. Like the ironworks, Falmouth's slaves continued on as if vines entwined their hands in bondage, the thickets shaded freedom from the light of day, and the shadows wove together over their very souls.

THE NATIVE AND THE DRAGON

John DeBaptiste was a native of African descent from the Island of St. Kitts, more formally known as Saint Christopher Island, in the West Indies. During the Revolutionary War, he served as a sailor on board the ship *Dragon*, commissioned by George Washington. In 1777, the vessel was built in Fredericksburg by Washington's brother-in-law, Fielding Lewis. During the war, *Dragon* patrolled the Rappahannock River and parts of the Chesapeake Bay. Upon the wars end "the [Virginia] General Assembly granted immediate emancipation to any Negro slave who had served in the Revolutionary War."[37] It is unclear if serving in the Virginia Navy brought John DeBaptiste his freedom. What is known is that he owned much property and operated the ferry at Falmouth as a free black from 1792 until his death in 1804.[38]

The labor intensive farming of sugar cane on St. Kitts and other West Indian islands led to the large-scale importation of African slaves. The story of how John DeBaptiste came to Virginia would bear much interest. Since Falmouth was an international port, ships trading in the West Indies would be a familiar sight in the Rappahannock. Why the West Indian native chose to stay in Falmouth after the Revolutionary War, is unknown. But clearly this prominent black citizen possessed excellent seamanship skills and a love of the water. His son, George DeBaptiste, served in the War of 1812.[39]

The Grave of John DeBaptist.
Photograph by Berry Fitzgerald, courtesy of Ruth Coder Fitzgerald

   An ancient and ornate carved stone marks John DeBaptiste's grave in the Union Church Cemetery, the town's "Revolutionary burying-ground." G. MacLaren Bryden, a historian of early Virginia church history, visited the cemetery in 1916 and recorded its description as "an old overgrown graveyard."[40] Remaining that way for many years, the cemetery must have been an eerie sight. During the early 1920s and 1930s, a group of young white men in Falmouth formed the "Graveyard Convention." Initiation into this group demanded a "proven" venture into the Union Church Cemetery at midnight "when most of the ghosts were walking."[41]
   Initiates were challenged to chip off a piece of the DeBaptiste gravestone at midnight and present it the following day as proof of their courage. Why DeBaptiste's gravestone was selected is unknown and can only be pondered. Was it because he was African American? Because the mysterious Isle of St. Kitts was associated with superstition

and possibly voodoo? Because of the grave's location in the cemetery? Or because the marker itself was ornate and well known? According to oral history related by the Payne family of Falmouth, a lad by the name of Burley Payne is known to have been at least one of the culprits.[42] How many there were who could not meet the initiation criteria is a humorous thought. Today, evidence of the Graveyard Convention's rite is plain: chips of stone are missing from the DeBaptiste marker's lower edge and upper right corner.

PART II

THE FEDERAL PERIOD THROUGH THE ANTEBELLUM YEARS

At Yorktown, the American forces and French allies under Comte de Rochambeau deal a death-blow to British authority. When the Treaty of Paris ended the Revolutionary War in 1783, the Federal Period ushered in the promise of a new nation founded on liberty and equality. However, African Americans were not included. The Constitution of the new United States upheld slavery and withheld the full rights of citizenship from free blacks. The tensions of inequality would continue to build for seven decades.

In 1811, a commissioner appointed by the Trustees of Falmouth was asked to make a "report on all lots, buildings, slaves, horses, mules, barns, wagons, drays, and carts." Slaves were considered no more than property. By 1860, the Trustees had declared that no slave, free Negro or mulatto "not belonging to the Town should be allowed to visit or loiter about the town on Sunday . . . this ordinance does not prohibit those Negroes having wives in Town from visiting them provided they have a pass." When slaves were separated from family members by "hiring out" or simply belonging to another master, a pass was necessary to visit one's own wife. Falmouth slaves would endure this ordinance and other restrictions on their personal liberty. What was not accomplished for all Americans in the First Constitutional Convention would have to wait until the duration of another period, the Antebellum, came to a close as the nation tore itself asunder.

The Abolitionist Hymn

We ask not that the slave should lie
As lies his master, at his ease,
Beneath a silken canopy,
Or in the shade of blooming trees.

We ask not "eye for eye," that all
Who forge the chain and ply the whip
Should feel their torture, while the slave
Should wield the scourge of mastership.

We mourn not that man should toil,
'Tis nature's need, 'tis God's decree;
But let the hand that tills the soil,
Be, like the wind that fans it, free.

_____Anonymous

The Fatal Christmas Party

Just below the town of Falmouth and situated on the heights above the Rappahannock River is the Chatham estate and mansion. Construction on this Georgian-style manor house began in 1768 and was completed in 1771. "The design of the house bespeaks the elegance and dignity of the Virginia plantation era at its height."[43]

Chatham Manor, the Fitzhugh estate.
Courtesy LOC

On January 4, 1805, the Fredericksburg *Virginia Herald* reported "on Wednesday last the negroes belonging to Wm. Fitzhugh, esq. on his estate at Chatham, opposite this town, after enjoying their usual relaxation from labor during the Christmas holidays, being ordered, by their overseer, Mr. Stark, to go back to work . . . was seized by them, tied up and severely whipped. . . ." This incident is further related by noted author Ruth Coder Fitzgerald.

> Early in January 1805, slaves belonging to William Fitzhugh, of Chatham, in Stafford County, refused to return to their jobs after the Christmas holidays. When ordered back to work by the overseer, Mr. Starke, they tied him up and severely whipped him. He escaped with the aid of one slave, and returned with help. The slave Phillip, apparently the ringleader, was shot and killed while trying to escape, and another, named James, fell

through the ice and drowned while trying to cross the frozen Rappahannock. Other slaves were imprisoned. A white man, Benjamin Bussell, who assisted in quelling the uprising, was wounded and later died.[44]

Chatham's Christmas party ended tragically. The affair constituted a slave uprising, the realization of the white population's greatest fear.

A Tisket, A Tasket, A Red and Yellow Basket

A large brick house on King Street in Falmouth fronts along the Rappahannock River. In 1850, an occupant of the house, Jane Howison Beale, would write in her journal, "I had one pleasant ride around by Falmouth and the sight of those familiar scenes roused up many a dormant memory of the past, for it was there, yes in that brick house on the bank of the river so shaded by trees...."[45]

The handsome brick house was built in 1807 by merchant James Vass of Forres, Scotland, who immigrated to Virginia in the late 1700s. As an industrious entrepreneur, he owned the finest of the three flour mills on the river's bank in Falmouth, the Thistle Mill. His financial success enabled him to build the grand Federal style home. Vass's 1815 personal property tax records indicate he owned eight slaves. That same year, the total slave population taxed as property in Falmouth was 1,296.[46] Five years earlier Stafford County had a population of about 4,200 slaves, 350 free blacks, and 5,400 whites.[47] It is evident that the largest concentration of slaves was in Falmouth.

James Vass's first wife was Susannah Brooke, a member of the prominent Brooke family of Virginia. After Susannah died from a lingering illness, James married Elizabeth Brayne "Betsey" Maury of Fredericksburg in 1816. Her father, Colonel Abraham Maury, had served in the Revolutionary War. Her mother, Mildred W. Thornton, was the daughter of Francis Thornton IV of Fall Hill.[48] Vass family tradition relates that when George Washington visited his Thornton relatives, he would bounce little Betsey on his knee.

Denoting success and wealth of the period, portraits of James and Elizabeth Vass were hung in the grand hallway of their imposing

Falmouth residence. James's portrait depicts him holding a letter of correspondence indicating his status as a successful business man. Elizabeth's portrait depicts her holding a small red and yellow basket. Such a small basket was commonly known in the south as a "key basket," which the lady of the house took with her from room to room during her daily duties. The basket always stayed with her and was never left out of sight. It contained the keys to the cupboards, presses, and chests where fine linens, silverware, valuables, and food were stored. A key basket only appears in southern portraiture and indicates status as "lady of the house." The key basket's purpose was to alleviate the fear of house servants stealing from their master.

Elizabeth Vass with key basket.
Courtesy of Conway House

James Vass died in 1837. By then the family had sold their home in Falmouth and moved across the river to Fredericksburg. Of the eight slaves owned by Vass, we know that Mrs. Vass granted a Deed of Emancipation to a slave named Davenport in 1840, who had been with the family in Falmouth.[49] Another family slave, Adam Green, received his emancipation from Mrs. Vass in 1854. The youngest son of James and Elizabeth Vass was Presbyterian minister Reverend Lachlan C. Vass. During the Civil War, he served as chaplain of the 27th Virginia Infantry, in the famous Stonewall Brigade. His son, Lachlan C. Vass II, and grandson, Lachlan C. Vass III were both missionaries in Leopoldville, Congo, Africa.[50]

Don't Sell Lucy

Andrew Buchanan, a major in the Caroline County militia during the American Revolution, built a stately home on a high hill above Falmouth and the Rappahannock River. The estate was named Clearview.[51] His son William inherited the estate in 1805. On January 19, 1811, William Buchanan, then in Philadelphia, wrote a letter to his attorney with instructions about the disposition of his slaves. Addressed to "Zachariah Vowles Esquire Falmouth Virginia," the letter begins as follows:

> Philadelphia Jany 19th 1811
> Dsir
>
> I hope you will excuse the sudden change which my mind has undergone with respect to the sale of negroes, upon consideration I think it will be much better to defer selling until my return, & hope if this should arrive in time that Lucy may not be sold . . .

Clearview, c.1895.
Courtesy Sillick Collection

The letter continues by addressing financial problems and ends with a request for money from the attorney. Slaves were conveniently treated as property that could be placed in liability. They could be sold or mortgaged as security for the payment of a debt. Some quality or characteristic of Lucy must have made her stand out with regard to her owner's wish that she not be sold. Evidently fortunes did not improve for William Buchannan, and by 1814 Clearview was in the hands of a new owner. The attorney very likely sold the Clearview slaves, including Lucy. Her fate is unknown, as are William Buchanan's reasons for wanting to keep Lucy at Clearview.

SAVED BY THE HORN

Between 1783 and 1816, wheat and flour came to dominate the economy of northeastern and north-central Virginia. Falmouth experienced the height of its commercial prosperity and regional influence in those years. Situated to maximize the Rappahannock's waterpower at the Falls, the town dominated the industrial sector of the Fredericksburg-Falmouth area with its grain mills and merchants' warehouses. In 1791, The Virginia General Assembly authorized the building of a toll bridge across the Rappahannock River at Falmouth. This bridge was built sometime between 1796 and 1807. A Frenchman traveling by carriage through Falmouth described the river scene as, "a bit savage/wild, noisy, rocky, with waves and little islands of greenery romantically placed in the middle of the riverbed."[52]

The bridge bolstered economic development by allowing new consumer access to Falmouth's imported goods. It also granted access to the town by farmers on the opposite side of the river who brought their tobacco, flour, and later cotton to Falmouth's warehouses and mills. Slaves whose labor produced the tobacco, flour, and cotton would have been familiar with the sound of an overseer or driver blowing a horn to summon them to work or "quitting time."[53]

In May 1811, the Trustees of the town of Falmouth created the position of "Town Sergeant," who was responsible for keeping town order. The Trustees also legislated that, "All slaves not belonging to persons residing in town were ordered to depart on Sunday or the usual holidays at 10 o'clock A.M . . . the hours of 10 A.M. and 10 P.M. to be announced by a horn, and if the slaves do not depart at once, they were to be taken by the town sergeant and should be punished by not less than five stripes well laid upon their bare backs and not more than fifteen."[54]

It may be surmised from the ordinance that slaves either from the surrounding countryside or from Fredericksburg across the river were visiting Falmouth on Sunday (Saturday being a work day). Perhaps they were in town to see friends and separated family members as a result of being hired out or sold. Perhaps the new bridge had allowed for a significant increase in visitors to the town, so that the Trustees felt compelled to address the influx of African Americans. Whatever the reason, the white citizens of Falmouth viewed any lingering slaves as a threat from which they had to be saved by the horn.

SEPARATE AND UNEQUAL

Falmouth's Union Church is perched atop "Church Hill." The Union Church descended from an earlier Anglican relic built in the 1700s, a wooden church in the form of a cross that was left to decay after the Revolutionary War, and a second church destroyed by fire. The Union Church was constructed around 1819, and was so named because it was used by four different denominations on a rotating basis. The Episcopalians, Presbyterians, Methodist, and Baptist were each assigned their own Sunday to use the sanctuary.

Union Church in Falmouth c.1870.
Courtesy of Jerry Brent

The Union Church was built of brick and in the Federal style of architecture. As was typical in the South at the time, its architecture also reflects distinct architectural features associated with the attendance of African Americans. A narrow turned stairway at the north end of the narthex leads up to a balcony on the second story. Traditionally in southern churches, such a balcony was the seating assigned to slaves and free blacks.

The church façade contains two separate entrances. The north door was entered by slaves and free-blacks, who would step to the left and climb the narrow stairs to the balcony. The south door was entered by the white congregants, who would proceed into the nave. By design, the stairway in the narthex and the second-story balcony separated African Americans from their white counterparts. Other southern churches with a single front entrance incorporated a side door for this purpose. If a church allowed African Americans to sit in the back of the church nave, they were seated in "Negro pews."

We do know that the Baptist congregation of the Union Church "consisted of white freemen and black slaves. All assembled within the same walls on the Sabbath, but a partition of boards separated the bond from the free. When the Holy Supper was administered, the cup was first carefully served to all of the privileged class, and afterward to their sable brethren . . . the prayers and exhortations of the slaves were graciously suffered to intermingle with those proceeding from the master's lips."[55]

The great African American ex-slave and abolitionist Frederick Douglass wrote:

> I can see no reason, but the most deceitful one, for calling the religion of this land Christianity. I look upon it as the climax of all misnomers, the boldest of all frauds, and the grossest of all libels. . . . The slave auctioneer's bell and the church-going bell chime in with each other, and the bitter cries of the heart-broken slave are drowned in the religious shouts of his pious master. Revivals of religion and revivals in the slave-trade go hand in hand together . . . in union with slaveholders.[56]

During the antebellum period slaves and free-blacks could not own a church. If a building was provided or given as a church to an African American congregation, it had to have white trustees and a white minister.[57] There appears to have been no African American church in Falmouth prior to the Civil War. The Union Church was the only formal house of worship in town. But by the Falmouth community's own design, it compelled African Americans to remain separate and unequal.

A Fable

An old fable tells of a king who wanted to reward the most valuable subject in his kingdom for conducting the most important trade. Tradesmen and craftsmen throughout the land brought samples of their work to present before the king. A tailor of beautiful, finely sewn garments was chosen as the kingdom's most valued subject.

After some time had passed, the tailor's scissors grew dull and he required new needles. He asked the blacksmith to sharpen the scissors and make more needles. Other craftsmen also needed tools made or mended. The carpenter needed his saw sharpened, a new hammer, and more nails. The farmer needed a new hoe and a blade for his scythe. The woodsman needed an axe head. The stonecutter needed a chisel. The gardener needed a spade, and the sheep shearer needed new shears. All of this work the blacksmith refused to do! Soon all work in the kingdom came to an end. The king summoned the blacksmith. Realizing how important the blacksmith was to the wealth of his kingdom, the king changed his mind and honored the blacksmith as the most valuable subject in the land.

In early times blacksmiths were viewed as possessing magical powers. Often the smith worked at night when brilliant sparks could be seen flying from his hand. This was no mystical power but rather the need to work in the dark to watch for "color" in the heated metal. Different temperatures of heat produced different colors. The smith could read the colors and determine the correct time to work the metal, perform a weld, or temper the tool. To temper the hot metal, the smith would extinguish it in water or his secret liquid mixture. Some smiths considered the best quenching liquid to be pure ox blood, which was reserved for special jobs. Cures of disease and sickness were attributed to being dunked in the blacksmith's quenching barrel of magical liquid. In Falmouth, iron rings were worn to cure fits.[58]

Numerous blacksmiths, several of them African American, worked in Falmouth.[59] Abram Howard was a free mulatto who was highly skilled and industrious. He learned his trade in Philadelphia and Baltimore. He made and mended farming implements and household tools, but the more lucrative side of his business was making large scale repairs to milling machinery. In 1823, he established his blacksmith business in Falmouth and strategically leased town Lot 1, which was located near the river and the town's numerous mills.[60] There is little doubt that his skills were much in demand. The milling machines were in constant use and under tremendous stress. Breakdowns were costly to the mill owners; repairs were needed quickly to get the mill back in operation.

A notice in the Fredericksburg *Virginia Herald* on January 27, 1830, described the type and quality of his work. "He is bold to assert that he can execute any work required, in a style superior to any man in this section of the country." The notice further stated that Howard had "now four Forges in constant blast, and hands sufficient for a fifth, (now about to be erected) . . ." No doubt those "hands sufficient" included some or all of Howard's eight slaves. He would own eleven slaves by 1832, far more than most Stafford County citizens at that time.[61]

A Course Man and His Cart

In 1840, The Virginia General Assembly passed a law stating that "A slave condemned to be hung or transported shall be valued by each justice at the cash price for which he would sell at public sale." Whatever value was assigned by the judge "shall be paid to the owner by the Commonwealth."[62] The purpose of this law was to reimburse a slave owner for loosing the value of his property (slave) in the instance of that property being forfeited due the punishment of a committed crime. An example of an attempt to benefit from this law occurred in Stafford County and was witnessed by a young boy from Falmouth named Moncure Daniel Conway.

Conway referred to Stafford County as "The lonely corner of the world where I was born . . ." His family lived in Falmouth in the grand Federal house built by James Vass in 1807. His father was Walker P. Conway, Stafford County Magistrate, the powerful and imposing presiding judge at Stafford County Court. Judge Conway would sometimes take his young son to observe court day. On one occasion, Moncure Conway witnessed the following scene:

> . . . a course man had charged four female slaves with an attempt to poison him. There was no real evidence, and some believed that it was an effort to obtain for the elderly and unmarketable women the payment the county must make if they were executed. When the women were acquitted their owner took them out to his cart, bound them by their wrist to the back of it, ordered the driver to go on, tore down the dresses from their backs, and lashed them with a raw-hide until the cart disappeared on the road. A crowd witnessed the scene, and though there were mutterings none could interfere. The horror made an ineffaceable impression on me . . .[63]

The course man was "Captain" Jack O'Bannon from Falmouth.[64] In the South, the title "Captain" did not necessarily represent a ship's captain or a former army officer. It was sometimes appropriated by men who gained social status as large land holders and owning many slaves. The slow moving cart disappearing out of sight down a lonely road into a lonely corner of the world with its scene of horror behind it was witnessed by a youthful observer, Moncure Conway. The unfortunate women who endured the humiliation and suffering would never know how their pain would help shape the youth's pilgrim journey.

African Princess

Lydia Crain, a young girl in Falmouth during the 1840s, recounted some of her childhood memories:

> I think we were not very early risers in Falmouth, and family prayers made an invariable, solemn service, attended by a large household congregation, white and black. Breakfast was rather late, but I have in my whole life seen no where else such breakfasts as our old African mammy, "Nell," African princess, sent to us. She was the daughter of a native African, who claimed to have been a king in his own country. I am fully persuaded that he must have been a princely personage there, from the traditions of the honor and homage paid him by his fellow-negroes, and of the trust and respect he honestly won from his white superiors, but chiefly from the fact that his daughter was a most royal cook. She and her children and grandchildren formed the household brigade of "servants," for I do not remember hearing them called slaves. Of course, their quarters were a little distance off from "the house," as they always called the white people's quarters.[65]

It is interesting to note that Falmouth can claim among its previous residents an African king and princess. This provides a fascinating window onto the legacy of African culture and status among the enslaved. It speaks to their own social hierarchy, even within the system of slavery.[66]

BEAUTIFUL CLEAR WATER FROM THE SPRING

Lydia Crain, the same young girl in Falmouth who enjoyed mammy Nell's breakfasts, continued her reminiscences.

> We had water from the spring, or springs, in Falmouth; hydrants were unknown, but there was always plenty of it. I can recall its beautiful clearness when it was brought to us in the morning, and I remember the procession of negro women every afternoon coming down the hills with tubs and buckets on their heads. I can see, too, the twilight procession of little negro children, in cold

weather, filing into "the house," each with a stick of wood to mend the fires.[67]

A post Civil War photograph at Clearview, former slaves draw water from a well above Falmouth.
Courtesy National Park Service, Fredericksburg, VA

Long before the coming of the white man, Native Americans drank the beautiful clear water from the springs. In 1608, when Captain John Smith and his band explored the area, which historian John T. Goolrick identifies as the "adjacent shore at Falmouth," Smith reported, ". . . looking at stones, herbs, and springs . . ."[68] Some of these same springs still exist in the hills around Falmouth today. One may still observe, as the author has, the "beautiful clearness" of their water. Since wells were also present in Falmouth, and much nearer the masters' houses, it is interesting to speculate on the importance of the springs to the women required to fetch water. The springs were more out of sight of the master's eye, possibly a safe gathering place where the women could freely converse and share news. Perhaps the spring with its "beautiful clearness" of water represented a brief but refreshing respite from slavery.

Give me a blessing; for thou has given me a south land; give me also springs of water.

_____Joshua 15:19

Sunday Morning Sunshine

Spacious windows in second-floor bedrooms of the Conway House offer a scenic view of the Rappahannock River through the wavy imperfections of the panes of old glass. From this vantage point, one can see the old Colonial seaport long since silted up by the sands of time and sunlight glistening on the river's waters just as serenely as it did when the Conways occupied the house. Moncure Conway recorded this observation:

> The immersion of the colored people was always a picturesque and affecting scene. Dressed in white cotton . . . they moved under the Sunday morning sunshine across the sands opposite our house to the river, and there sang gently and sweetly. There was no noise or shouting. The rite was performed by a white minister. After immersion each was embraced by his or her relatives. There was more singing, and the procession moved slowly away.[69]

Falmouth's African Americans tended to follow the Baptist faith. Baptists had settled in the vicinity of the falls of the Rappahannock River by the beginning of the 18th century. They became a moving force in establishing religious freedom from the Church of England, the established state church. The spiritual independence asserted by the Baptists may have attracted African Americans wishing for their own freedom.

As African American author Anita Wills writes, "The Baptist believed that salvation was not only for an elect few, but for everyone. The fear that this message would get to slaves, caused concern among Anglican officials . . . Baptist refused to post meetings, and get licenses, a requirement for Ministers in Colonial Virginia . . . Baptist churches preaching that all men could be saved was a Revolutionary, and dangerous idea . . ."[70] Through baptism in the Rappahannock depicting the death, burial, and resurrection of Christ, Falmouth slaves were testifying their soul had been set free from sin. But, their corporal forms remained in bondage.

Turn the Pot Upside Down

The shard of a broken clay pot is the first known evidence of African American association with Falmouth. African Americans helped indigenous people improve their pottery techniques, which resulted in a stronger and more desirable pot. With the progression of the Industrial Revolution, the iron pot replaced those made of clay. During the American Revolution, African Americans labored at Hunter's Iron Works to made pots, kettles and the like for George Washington's army (see "Over Time").

It is well known that slaves prepared food for their masters. There was a pot of greens, a pot of salad, a pot of soup, a pot of stew, a pot of cabbage, a pot of roast beef, etc. After cooking collards or turnip greens, the leftover liquid was given to the slaves. This was known as "pot likker."[71] Slaves did the hog killing, the cooking, the washing and soap making, all requiring pots in sizes small to large. This seemingly simple utilitarian object, the pot, also played a role in the human story of slavery. That story is best related by historian Frank White:

> The term "Turn the pot upside down" I understand was used during slavery time. When the slaves wanted to pray or they had got fed up with the master and wanted to let off some steam, they would go into the woods or even into a barn, close the doors, put out a couple of lookouts, turn a pot over their head and then they could "let it all out" as the old saying goes. The pot over their head would muffle or suppress the sound of their shouts, screams, cries or whatever, so that they could express their deepest feelings and emotions without being heard all over the place. They knew that if the master heard them and went to investigate and found out what was going on, they were in deep trouble.[72]

HOLLER

Historian David J. Mays wrote about the punishment received by African Americans for various crimes committed in Virginia:

> The noose, the stake, the burning iron, the knife, and the lash . . . were a part of the life of the time and thought absolutely necessary if the predominant slave-population was to be kept in subjection. For the slaves, punishment was both prompt and severe. The blacks were never allowed time to forget the offense of one of their number before stern justice struck him, and it was inflicted publicly and openly for maximum effect. The branding iron was applied in open court while the victim, pinned down by jailors, screamed with pain as the room filled with the odor of seared flesh; the lashes on the bare back at the whipping-post were indeed "well laid on."[73]

In Falmouth, corporal punishment of slaves was not usually carried out by their owners. The acceptable social custom was for owners to take their slaves to someone appointed to perform that duty. An ex-slave reported that whippings at a slave jail "was done fearfully for 50 cents."[74] From his boyhood experiences Moncure Conway wrote:

> Deeply engraved also on my memory is a small, prison-like building in the center of Falmouth, known as "Captain Pickett's," where negroes were sent to be flogged. The captain was the town constable, and one of his functions was to whip negroes when their owners so ordered . . . A man belonging to a wealthy citizen (Murray Forbes) had to be flogged on some complaint of a neighbor. Mr. Forbes intimated to Captain Pickett his hope that he would be merciful . . . The negro told his master, "Captain Pickett told me to holler and I hollered, but the cowhide fell on the post."[75]

Conway further related that:

> The respectable family-heads of Falmouth were always particularly strict and careful in forbidding their children any play or loitering in the neighborhood of Captain Pickett's . . . About this particular building we lingered and peered with insatiable curiosity, all the more pertinaciously for being so often driven or dragged away. And our curiosity found enough fuel to keep it inflamed; for few hours ever passed without bringing some victim to his door. At this business the captain made his living; and it was by no means dull: he held open accounts with nearly every family in the neighborhood. Around each victim we crowded, and when he or she disappeared and the door was shut, we—the boys—would rush around to all the walls, crevices, and backyards which we knew so well, gaining many a point from which we could see the half-naked cowering slave and the falling lash, and hear, with short-lived awe, the blows and the imploring tones, swelling to cries as the flogging proceeded. But the silent old man of whom I have been writing came at last to prefer no living at all to such a one; for one day a sobbing girl, bearing in her hand an order for forty lashes, was unable to gain admittance; whereupon the neighbors broke down the door, and found that Captain Pickett had hung himself by the side of his own whipping-post.[76]

This c.1920s photograph is believed to be of Captain Pickett's house, the prison was in an unrefined stone structure attached to the rear.
Courtesy LOC

After the Civil War, Conway came to view the Captain himself as a victim of the evil institution of slavery:

> I remember the captain silently walking up and down in front of his grim house, with his iron-grey hair and beard, never smiling, never uttering a word from his compressed lips. When I had left Falmouth, and thought of him as the local figure-head of an evil system, I heard of his suicide. As a matter of fact, the old constable was simply presiding at the last relic of the whipping post . . . Captain Pickett hung himself simply because the shame of being an official negro-whipper became intolerable.[77]

Clearing the Way

Several of the young Conway children of Falmouth walked to a school two miles each way daily, under escort:

> We were accompanied by a mulatto youth, Charles Humstead. Handsome, brilliant, merry, with an inexhaustible store of stories and songs, this colored genius was the most romantic figure of our little world. Along the pathway through the woods his snares and "hare-gums" were set, and rarely failed of their prey. A meadow we had to cross was the haunt of moccasin snakes, and his skill in slaying these dragons guarding our tree of knowledge was wonderful. That indeed was his main function. Advancing ahead of us, stick in hand, treading warily with his bare feet, his eye could not be cheated by the deadly reptile's mimicry of clay, nor did he fail to strike the point on its back that left it helpless. Charles knew all serpent-lore. The tail would not die until sunset, or until it thundered. If rain was needed he hung the snake on a tree . . . I have often remembered . . . our colored comrade in the woods of Virginia.[78]

Charles led children sheltered and protected to school, but could not attend school himself. As a result Conway related, "He found our little town dull." Out of frustration Charles set fire to a dilapidated outhouse, which caused residents to become fearful. Charles was sold and carried away. "He seemed to us all a hero of romance, and such a thing as remembering his color never entered our heads . . . So Charles is now buried, alive or dead, among the cotton plantations."[79]

I see a Humming-bird! I always loved them. Sweet wee thing—I would I were as free to clap my wings and draw sweets from all Flowers! I would not be afraid of poisonous snakes nor Vipers!—not I.

_____Moncure Conway

The Wood-Cellar

"... I taught one of our slaves—Peter Humstead, about twenty—to read. Why he asked to have his lessons in the wood-cellar I did not understand."[80]

The house in which Moncure Daniel Conway grew up overlooks the silvery Rappahannock River. The imposing brick house contains eight fireplaces. A large supply of wood would have been necessary to heat the residence and to support cooking activities not preformed in the outside kitchen during the colder months. Several rooms form the building's basement, one of which was used as the "wood-cellar." While the walls of the other rooms in the basement were given a bright coat of whitewash, the walls of this particular room were intentionally devoid of paint; their natural brick surface created a gloomy and secluded looking interior. A massive brick chimney base juts out from one wall; there was only one entrance and only two basement windows allowed light into this utilitarian room. The rough battered surface of the brick walls provide evidence that for many years firewood had been thrown and stacked against them.

Within this isolated wood-cellar the white family's privileged son, perhaps age nine or ten, taught a slave to read. The slave was Peter Humstead, then about twenty years old. He was a member of the family slaves inherited by Moncure's mother from the Daniel ancestral home Crow's Nest further out in Stafford County. Peter clearly understood slaves were forbidden to learn to read, but his young tutor was not aware why the lessons were to be hidden in the wood-cellar.

Such an Offence

Margaret Eleanor Daniel was born in 1807. She was the granddaughter of the Honorable Thomas Stone of Maryland, a signer of the Declaration of Independence. Margaret E. Daniel's father was Dr. John Moncure Daniel of Crows Nest in Stafford County, Virginia. Margaret herself was a homeopathic doctor who tended many of the African American and poor white residents of Falmouth without compensation.[81]

Margaret E. Daniel married Walker P. Conway in 1829, and in 1838 they moved to Falmouth. The large Federal dwelling they lived in became known as Conway House. Along with performing her many household duties, Margaret was accustomed at a certain time of day to sitting in the formal parlor and reading aloud in French. One day, a baby of one of the slaves had his leg accidentally broken and he was brought to Margaret in the parlor. She set his leg, which healed fully.

The Conways were devout Methodists. A basement room was "fitted up for evening prayer-meetings." Each Sunday in this room Margaret taught "white and black children together" the catechism and had them listen to carefully selected Bible readings. Her son Moncure Conway would write years later, "In some way this equal treatment of slaves got out, and some officious men came with a report that my mother was teaching negroes to read, which was illegal . . . It was prudent to avoid even the suspicion of such an offence . . . so the mixed teaching ceased."[82]

Margaret E. Conway, "taught white
and black children together."
Courtesy of Conway House

The Observer

There was once a peaceful Virginia countryside where the sun glistened on the passing waters of a river and an old social order prevailed, carried over from the days of Colonialism. While flowers burst in bloom, the winds of time swept the clouds along, the tides ebbed and flowed, and to it all moved the stars in their courses. Into this lovely but lonely corner of the world was born a remarkable soul in 1832. To this soul the flowers whispered "Break thy bonds," and the flying clouds said "Be free!" From this quiet place the soul began its journey to learn of the world and bring new ideas into it.

On a beautiful summer's day, two small African American children played, a boy and a girl completely devoid of clothing, completely unaware that their warm brown bodies were observed by a lonely soul hidden among the shade trees along the Rappahannock River. The observer was fascinated by the enchantment of a freedom his world and social order would never permit to his race. He would later write, "Destiny has lavished on my lot everything but freedom."[83]

Moncure Daniel Conway, began a journey that would lead him to become a radical abolitionist.
Author's Collection

Ralph Waldo Emerson, led the Transcendentalist movement of the 19th century. He was Moncure Conway's mentor.
Courtesy LOC

The youthful observer was Moncure Daniel Conway, who had been born to one of the most prestigious families of Virginia. His ancestry included a signer of the Declaration of Independence and the half-sister of Sir Walter Raleigh. He was collaterally related through two lines to George Washington. From his lonely corner of the world Moncure Conway began a journey (referring to himself as a pilgrim in his latter years) to becoming a radical abolitionist. In the early stages of his journey, he wrote a letter to Ralph Waldo Emerson in November 1851. Emerson's reply deeply influenced Conway's journey.

A true soul will disdain to be moved except by what natively commands it, though it should go sad and solitary in search of its master a thousand years.

_____Emerson

BLOOD MONEY

At a private dinner in Warrenton, Virginia, Moncure Conway met US Senator James Murray Mason. He was a grandson of George Mason IV, one of America's illustrious Founding Fathers. Both he and James Madison are considered to be the "Father of the Bill of Rights." Conway wrote about meeting Senator Mason:

> I felt some pride in Virginia as the mother of States and statesmen . . .but Mason was a hard, arrogant man. He was the hero of the "fire-eating" Southerners because he had cracked the whip of "King Cotton" over the North, and brought them to their knees in uttermost abjectness. He had framed the Fugitive Slave Law, and the Northerners had consented to become slave-hounds, to hunt down men and women escaping from bondage. Not many recoveries of slaves were anticipated, but Mason was hailed as the victor.[84]

James Murray Mason, US Senator from Virginia, drafted the Fugitive Slave Law of 1850. Abolitionists referred to it as the "Bloodhound Law."
Courtesy LOC

Moncure Conway and the great American Poet Walt Whitman shared a lifelong literary friendship. Whitman wrote a poem in response to Daniel Webster's speech delivered in Congress in support of the Compromise of 1850, which included the Fugitive Slave Law. This law would have a particular impact on a slave Conway knew from Falmouth, named Anthony Burns. Whitman's poem known as *Blood Money* first appeared in the *New York Daily Tribune*.[85]

Walt Whitman, who is among the most
influential poets in the American canon.
Courtesy LOC

Blood-Money

Guilty of the body and blood of Christ

Of olden time, when it came to pass
That the beautiful God, Jesus, should finish his work on earth,
Then went Judas, and sold the divine youth,
And took pay for his body.

Curs'd was the deed, even before the sweat of the clutching hand grew dry;
And darkness frown'd upon the seller of the like of God,
Where, as though earth lifted her breast to throw him from her, and heaven refused him,
He hung in the air, self-slaughter'd.

The cycles, with their long shadows, have stalk'd silently forward,
Since those ancient days—many a pouch enwrapping meanwhile
Its fee, like that paid for the son of Mary.

And still goes one, saying,
"What will ye give me, and I will deliver this man unto you?"
And they make the covenant, and pay the pieces of silver.

Look forth, Deliverer,
Look forth, first-bourn of the dead,
Over the tree-tops of Paradise;
See thyself in yet-continued bonds,
Toilsome and poor, thou bear'st man's form again,
Thou art reviled, scourged, put into prison,
Hunted from the arrogant equality of the rest;
With staves and swords throng the willing servants of authority,

Again they surround thee, mad with devilish spite;
Toward thee stretch the hands of a multitude, like vultures' talons,
The meanest spit in thy face, they smite thee with their palms;
Bruised, bloody, and pinion'd is thy body,
More sorrowful than death is thy soul.

Witness of anguish, brother of slaves,
Not with thy price closed the price of thine image;
And still Iscariot plies his trade.

Time of Fire

Today, New Year's Day is a holiday enjoyed and well-celebrated by Americans. In the Antebellum period, New Year's Day had a less festive and hopeful association for slaves. New Year's Day was "hiring day," also known to the slave as "heart-break day." With it came the prospect of being separated from one's family and the fear of being rented out to a cruel overseer. Interestingly, Moncure Conway wrote of Falmouth, "Although the slavedealers gathered their harvest in our region . . . It was socially disreputable for a man to sell slaves to them, or indeed to part the members of families on his estate further than by hiring them to neighbors. Hiring-day in Falmouth was not often marked by unhappy scenes . . ."

On the first day of 1853, Conway again witnessed the business of slave hiring. "I feel to-night somewhat sad. I find how little sympathy I have with the existing state of things. As I saw the slave-hiring to-day, I found out how much hatred I had of the institution—and how much contempt for the persons engaged in it. 'You look,' said a friend, 'as if you were not in the world.' I am not." As to put himself in place of the African American slave, Conway continued with, "O my Father, do thou love me in this time of fire."[86]

O Great Father, do thou pity me.
And help me on to Canada where the panting slave is free!

_____a song of freedom by George N. Allen

AUNT NANCY AND BENJAMIN

In 1853, Aunt Nancy, a Conway family slave, confided in Moncure Conway that her husband, Benjamin Williams, had fled to Boston. Sometimes marriages took place between slaves of neighboring plantations and different owners. Such was the case with the slave Williams, who was not owned by the Conway family. Aunt Nancy, knowing Moncure was leaving for the north, asked if he would try to locate her husband so she could secretly communicate with him.

Theodore Parker, a Unitarian minister whose words would later inspire speeches by Dr. Martin Luther King, Jr.
Courtesy Boston Public Library

While in Boston, Conway asked abolitionist Theodore Parker to help him fulfill Aunt Nancy's request since "a Virginian asking the whereabouts of a negro might properly be met with hesitation" in the abolitionist city. Conway related what then occurred:

A few days later he [Parker] went with me through the negro quarters . . . At length we entered into the house of some intelligent coloured people, who saluted Parker with the greatest homage, which he received with pathetic humility. "This," he said, "is a Virginian, but an honourable [*sic*] Virginian, who wishes to find one Benjamin Williams, who was some time ago escaped from his master in Stafford County, Va., and for whom he has a message from his wife, Nancy Williams. I hope you will be able to discover Mr. Williams." After a brief consultation with others of the family, the man went out to bring some neighbors . . . The man returned with several neighbors, and having inquired closely as to the fugitive's appearance, they remembered such a man, who was in Canada. A little later I had the satisfaction of sending his address to a free negro in Falmouth, who conveyed it to aunt Nancy.[87]

Nancy successfully communicated with her husband and eventually joined him. We will visit with Benjamin again in another vignette.

A Trembling Man

In 1853, Moncure Conway visited Henry David Thoreau at his home in Concord, Massachusetts. He recorded a profound experience involving an African American fugitive at the Thoreau residence:

Henry David Thoreau, a famous naturalist best known for his book *Walden* written in 1854. Courtesy LOC

I found the Thoreau's (at their new house near the railroad station) agitated by the arrival of a fugitive from Virginia, who had come to their door at day break. Thoreau took me to a room where his excellent sister, Sophia, was ministering to the fugitive, who recognized me as one he had seen in Virginia. He was alarmed, but his fears passed into delight when, after talking with him about our County [Stafford], I certified his genuineness. I observed the tender and lowly devotion of Thoreau to the African. He now and then drew near to the trembling man, and with a cheerful voice bade him feel at home, and have no fear that any power should again wrong him. That whole day he mounted guard over the fugitive until he was got off to Canada, and I enjoyed my first walk with Thoreau.[88]

Bruised, bloody, and pinion'd is thy body.
                                              _____Walt Whitman

Is a Slave

Anthony Burns was a slave born in Stafford County, who spent a number of his adolescent years in Falmouth working for his master or hired out elsewhere in town.[89] He was baptized and received into the Baptist congregation of the Union Church, which allowed blacks to attend. Two years after his baptism, the white Baptist congregation of Union Church conferred upon Burns "recognition" as a preacher or "exhorter." He was not officially ordained because he was black. "Piety, a gift at exhortation, and a desire for the work of a preacher," were the requisite qualifications.[90]

After being hired out in Richmond, Burns escaped to Boston in 1853. Burns was discovered on May 24, 1854, then twenty years of age, and apprehended under the Fugitive Slave Law of 1850. He became the most famous fugitive slave from Virginia. His trial in May 1854 caused no small stir, including an attempt to rescue Burns. On May 26, members of Boston's ardent abolitionist and anti-slavery factions stormed the jail, but were unable to free the prisoner. The melee resulted in one death and several injuries. Tony Burns and his owner, Captain Charles Francis Suttle, were both known to Moncure Conway, who happened to be in Boston at the time.[91]

The day after the failed attempt to rescue Burns, Conway met Wendell Phillips in the street and both went to an antislavery gathering at Tremont Temple in Boston. Phillips was a prominent Northern abolitionist who refused to wear clothing made from cotton. When he joined the American Anti-Slavery Society, his family tried to have him committed for insanity. Phillips was later indicted for his participation in the attempt to rescue Burns from the Boston jail.

On June 2, 1854, Whitman's poem in response to the Fugitive Slave Law was prophetically fulfilled. "With staves and swords throng the willing servants of authority." As 50,000 spectators stood witness, military force was required to carry out the court order to return Anthony Burns to his Virginia owner.

Anthony Burns, his opposite cheek bore the
scar from an injury incurred while a slave.
Courtesy LOC

Wendell Phillips, who due to his oratorical abilities
was known as "Abolition's Golden Trumpet."
Author's Collection

Wm. Lloyd Garrison.

William Lloyd Garrison, one of the founders of the American Anti-Slavery Society. "I am in earnest—I will not excuse—I will not retreat a single inch—and I will be heard."
Courtesy LOC

Several weeks later, Conway, the great-grandson of a signatory of the Declaration of Independence, attended the annual Fourth of July abolitionist meeting at Framingham, Massachusetts. On the platform William Lloyd Garrison burned a copy of the US Constitution, the Fugitive Slave Law, Commissioner Edward Loring's decision in the Burns case, and Captain Suttle's certified claim to Anthony Burns. Also on the platform were "Sojourner Truth" and Henry David Thoreau. The latter introduced the Virginian, Moncure Conway, who declared that on the subject of slavery, the minds of Southerners were insane.[92] An abolitionist newspaper, *The Liberator*, reported Conway's words:

> It was characteristic of the Southern people to become insane on some subjects, and he believed that they were very nearly insane on the subject of slavery. People of delicacy and tenderness in other respects, who have generally only kind feelings towards other people, as soon as anyone mentioned that subject, no matter if he were their own brother or even their child, they denounced him for it, if he could not feel it in his heart to support that institution... because, in Virginia, they not only had slaves, but every man with a conscience, or even the first throbbings of a conscience, is a slave.[93]

... the most important reform movement in U.S. history—purging the land of slavery.

_____C. Peter Ripley

THE FATHER'S LETTER

In need of a permanent minister, the First Unitarian Church of Washington, D.C., invited Moncure Conway to deliver sermons during the month of September in 1854. The sermon Conway delivered on September 17 admonished the congregation with, "... does not God's whisper sometimes strike the ear, as it came to Cain, 'The poor African, thy brother, where is he?' Alas! How often our reply is in the tone of the first murderer, 'I know not. Am I my brother's keeper? Shall I interfere with slavery?'"[94] The next day, Moncure's father, Walker P. Conway, Stafford County Judge and Magistrate, wrote a letter from Falmouth to his son, who had been associating himself with Unitarians, Transcendentalists, and Abolitionists:

> I cannot refrain from saying I was truly glad you did not find it convenient to come down to-day... I have reason to know that it was fortunate for you that such was the case, and it is my sincere advice to you not to come here until there is reason to believe your opinions have undergone material changes on the subject of slavery.

If you are willing to expose your own person recklessly, I am not willing to subject myself and family to the hazards of such a visit . . . You say in your last [letter] it is strange that you "meet with intolerance nowhere but at home." If you had but a small amount of that best of all senses—common sense—it would not seem at all strange that such should be the fact . . . A single moment's reflection would teach any common-sense person the reasonable propriety of our course. But having exhausted all our rational effort, we hand you over to the mercy of God, through our Lord and Savior Jesus Christ, and pray most earnestly that the ever-blessed Spirit may guide you aright. If you make shipwreck in this life and the next, you must not only wade through the precious blood of Christ and do despite to the Spirit of His grace—but your father's prayers, so long as his life last, will be thrown in the way also.[95]

Walker P. Conway, Stafford County Judge and Magistrate.
Courtesy of Conway House

Wounded in thine own house, Conway wrote, "Say one word against the institution, and see if the hearts that knew your childhood do not freeze to ice, and if the arms once twined about you will not be drawn to strike!"[96] Although his father's words wounded Conway, the young minister was described by a contemporary as someone who ". . . would carry with [him] an earnest regard for home wherever [he] might go." In spite of his father's warnings and intractable position on the institution of slavery, Moncure attempted to visit his "dear old home in Falmouth" the following year.

Who can tell us how to find winter sunbeams without leaving our own homes, and without forgetting griefs which will not be forgotten.

_____Moncure D. Conway

It Was Exile

After the incidents swirling around the fugitive slave Anthony Burns in 1854, Conway returned to Virginia, staying briefly at an uncle's home in Richmond, where he had been invited to preach in that city's Universalist Church. From there he "went up with a light heart to my dear old home in Falmouth." The homecoming was less than idyllic:

> . . . I was twice spoken to by negroes, who whispered that my opposition to slavery and my course about Tony Burns were known among the colored people there, and they hinted expectations that I was contemplating some movement.
>
> But worse was to come. Next morning as I was walking through the main street a number of young men, some of them former schoolmates, hailed me and surrounded me; they told me that my presence in Falmouth could not be tolerated. "Charles Frank Suttle," said one, "says that when he was in Boston you did everything you could against him to prevent his getting back his servant

Tony Burns, and that you are an abolitionist. There is danger to have that kind of man among our servants, and you must leave. We don't want to have any row." By this time a number of the rougher sort had crowded up and there were threats . . . It was exile . . . I was that day banished from my own home and relatives.[97]

Falmouth's Rougher Sort, a photograph
taken in town after the Civil War.
Courtesy Marion Brooks Robinson

Conway left Falmouth and boarded a steamship at Aquia Landing bound for Washington, D.C. He later wrote, "I sat on the deck humiliated and weeping."[98] Moncure Conway freed himself from the dogmas of his culture and became an abolitionist.

An Ex-Slave's Letter

Throughout the North, the Anthony Burns case increased public determination to defy the Fugitive Slave Law. After his "rendition" to Virginia in 1854, no more fugitive slaves were legally returned from New England. Within a year, Burns was freed. He enrolled at Oberlin College in Ohio. On July 18, 1855, the *Oberlin Evangelist* gave an account of Burns' return to slavery and subsequent emancipation:

> Our readers will remember this name, associated with the scenes of his rendition in Boston, something more than a year since. Borne back to the land of hand-cuffs and slave prisons in a national revenue cutter, he lay four months in close confinement, with accommodations too mean and miserable for a beast; he was then put up at auction; stood a long time at the bid of five dollars, until the auctioneer brought forward his Christianity—assured the soul-buyers that Burns was a Baptist preacher, a good Christian man and therefore of reliable veracity and honesty—whereupon he was soon knocked off for $905.00 and driven to North Carolina. Ere long his Boston friends negotiated his ransom for $1200, and finally on paying $1300.00 to his extorting master, they effected a legal purchase and set him free. He comes to Oberlin to prepare himself here, by study, for greater usefulness to his oppressed race.[99]

Upon settling in Ohio, Burns sought to leave the membership of the Union Church in Falmouth. He requested a letter of good standing (as was the custom) from the Baptist congregation in Falmouth, that he might be accepted into the membership of another church. Today, this is known as "transfer by letter." He did not receive a direct reply, but he did eventually learn that the congregation had publicly rebuked him, when he received a copy of the *Front Royal Gazette*.[100] Burns wrote a second, impassioned letter to the church in Falmouth:[101]

> In answer to my request by mail, under date July 13, 1855, for a letter of dismission in fellowship and of

recommendation to another church, I have received a copy of the Front Royal Gazette, dated Nov. 8, 1855, in which I find a communication addressed to myself and signed by John Clark, as pastor of your body, covering your official action upon my request, as follows:—

To all whom it may concern:
Whereas, Anthony Burns, a member of this church, has made application to us, by a letter to our pastor, for a letter of dismission, in fellowship, in order that he may unite with another church of the same faith and order; and whereas, it has been satisfactorily established before us, that the said Anthony Burns absconded from the service of his master, and refused to return voluntarily—thereby disobeying both the laws of God and man, although he subsequently obtained his freedom by purchase, yet we have now to consider him only as a fugitive from labor (as he was before his arrest and restoration to his master), have therefore Resolved, Unanimously, that he be excommunicated from this communion and fellowship of this church. Done by order of the church, in regular church meeting, this twentieth day of October, 1855. Wm. W. West, Clerk.

Thus you have excommunicated me, on the charge of "disobeying both the laws of God and man," "in absconding from the service of my master, and refusing to return voluntarily."

I admit that I left my master (so called), and refused to return; but I deny that in this I disobeyed either the law of God, or any real law of men.

Look at my case, I was stolen and made a slave as soon as I was born. No man had any right to steal me. That manstealer who stole me trampled on my dearest rights. He committed an outrage on the law of God; therefore his man stealing gave him no right in me, and laid me under no obligation to be his slave. God made me a man—not a slave; and gave me the same right to myself that he have the man that stole me to himself. The great wrongs he has done me, in stealing me and making me a slave, in compelling me to work for him many years without wages, and in holding me as merchandize,—these wrongs could never put me under obligation to stay with him, or to return voluntarily, when once escaped.

You charge me that, in escaping, I disobeyed God's law. No, indeed! That law which God wrote on the table of my heart, inspiring the love of freedom, and impelling me to seek it at every hazard, I obeyed, and, by the good hand of my God upon me, I walked out of the house of bondage.

I disobeyed no law of God revealed in the Bible. I read in Paul (Cor. 7:21), "But, if thou mayest be made free, use it rather." I read in Moses (Deut. 23:15), "Thou shalt not deliver unto his master the servant which is escaped from his master unto thee. He shall dwell with thee, even among you in that place which he shall choose in one of thy gates, where it liketh him best; thou shalt not oppress him." This implies my right to flee if I feel oppressed, and debars any man from delivering me again to my professed master.

I said I was stolen. God's word Declares, "He that stealeth a man and selleth him, or if he be found in his hand, he shall surely be put to death." (Ex. 21:16) Why do you not execute God's law on the man who stole me from my mother's arms? How is it that you trample down God's law against the oppressed, and wrest it to condemn me, the innocent and oppressed? Have you forgotten that the New Testament classes "manstealers" with "murderers of fathers" and "murderers of mothers" with manslaver and whoremongers?" (I Tim. 1:9, 10)

The advice you volunteered to send me, along with this sentence of excommunication, exhorts me, when I shall come to preach like Paul, to send every runaway home to his master, as he did Onesimus to Philemon. Yes, indeed I would, if you would let me. I should love to send them back as he did, "NOT NOW AS A SERVANT, but above a servant:—A BROTHER—a brother beloved—both in the flesh and in the Lord;" both a brother man, and a brother-Christian. Such a relationship would be delightful—to be put on a level, in position, with Paul himself. "If thou count me, therefore, a partner, receive him as myself." I would to God that every fugitive had the privilege of returning to such a condition—to the embrace of such a Christianity—"not now as a servant, but above a servant,"—a "partner."—even as Paul himself was to Philemon!

You charge me with disobeying the laws of men. I utterly deny that those things which outrage all right as laws. To be real laws, they must be founded in equity.

You have thrust me out of your church fellowship. So be it. You can do no more. You cannot exclude me from heaven; you cannot hinder my daily fellowship with God.

You have used your liberty of speech freely in exhorting and rebuking me. You are aware, that I too am now where I may think for myself, and can use great freedom of speech, too, if I please. I shall therefore be only returning the favor of your exhortation if I exhort you to study carefully the golden rule, which reads, "All things whatsoever ye would that men should do to you, do ye even so to them; for this is the law and the profits." Would you like to be stolen, and then sold? and then worked without wages? and forbidden to read the Bible? and be torn from your wife and children?

and then, if you were able to make yourself free, and should, as Paul said, "use it rather," would you think it quite right to be cast out of the church for this? If it were done, so wickedly, would you be afraid God would indorse it? Suppose you were to put your soul in my soul's stead; how would you read the law of love?[102]

Elder John Clark, who signed a letter excommunicating Anthony Burns. Personal Property Tax Records of Stafford County show Clark owned eight slaves.
Courtesy Jane Cloe Sthreshley

African American historian Frank White finds Burns' second impassioned letter to the church comparable to Dr. Martin Luther King, Jr.'s, "Letter from a Birmingham Jail."[103] Following his arrest, Dr. King wrote a letter on April 16, 1963, in response to "A Call for Unity," written April 12 by white Alabama clergymen and published in a local newspaper. The clergymen took the position that the Birmingham civil rights demonstration was against the law and Dr. King was an outside agitator.[104]

I assert most unhesitatingly, that the religion of the South is a mere covering for the most horrid crimes—a justifier of the most appalling barbarity, a sanctifier of the most hateful frauds, and a dark shelter under which the darkest, foulest, grossest, and most infernal deeds of slaveholders find the strongest protection.

_____Frederick Douglass

THE UNDERGROUND RAILROAD

Falmouth's history is punctuated with notices of slaves attempting to escape bondage. Some were running away from town, others were intercepted trying to reach Falmouth. A reward notice in 1782 stated, "Ran away last night from Falmouth, a likely Negro wench named Winnie, about twenty-five years of age, with her mulatto child named Nancy . . . Also a likely Mulatto fellow named Jack . . . and a dark Mulatto or Negro lad named Daniel . . ."[105] In 1785, a "Negro Slave . . . was pursued, and taken up at Falmouth, when he was ordered to be committed to Stafford goal [prison]; but on his way had the daring resolution to attack his guard, which he robbed, and made his escape from."[106] In 1789, a "Negro man named Jack" was apprehended in Falmouth, but "again made his escape."[107] In 1799, a "negro woman who calls herself Betty; and a child by the name of Sally" were placed in the King and Queen County prison; prior to their incarceration they had made their escape from a tavern keeper in Falmouth.[108]

No formal date has been assigned to the beginning of the Underground Railroad. Historians continue to debate the issue.[109] It is safe to say it was started by abolitionists and Quakers in the early 19th century. Robert Stanton, former Director of the National Park Service, has written:

> The Underground Railroad story is like nothing else in American history: a secret enterprise that today

is famous, an association many claim but few can document, an illegal activity now regarded as noble, a network that was neither underground nor a railroad, yet a system that operated not with force or high finance but through the committed and often spontaneous acts of courage and kindness of individuals unknown to each other . . . It demonstrates that people can struggle and free themselves from bondage through individual and collective acts of courage. It speaks of the power of freedom and justice. This is an amazing story and a timely one that offers insight into America's need to face our collective history together and recreate our past with each generation.[110]

Was Falmouth a geographically and strategically important stop on the Underground Railroad? Yes, although it did not function in the same way or with the same level of organization as the network in the north, with its safe houses and secret hiding places. Did slaves escaping from Falmouth and the surrounding area use the Underground Railroad once they made their escape out of Virginia? Yes.

To the southeast of Falmouth is a land mass known as the Northern Neck. It lies between the Potomac and Rappahannock Rivers and extends to the Chesapeake Bay. This peninsula included the counties of Stafford, King George, Westmoreland, Richmond, Northumberland, and Lancaster. A twentieth-century description relates, "Prior to the coming of good roads to Virginia and the building of the bridges across the Rappahannock and Potomac Rivers what is known as the Northern Neck, although actually a peninsula, was to those living in the eastern portion almost an island . . ."[111] Geographically, the narrowest convergence of this neck between the two rivers occurs in Stafford County, the northern most county in the Northern Neck, and anyone passing north would naturally pass through Falmouth. Historian and author Oscar H. Darter has written, "Falmouth and Fredericksburg were the conjunction points of roads from Middle Peninsula and Northern Neck in Virginia, being the only doorway to and from the latter area."[112] Just as "all roads lead to Rome," so it would seem with Falmouth.

Reward Poster for Barnaby, Jim, and Billy.
Courtesy of Frank White

In 1856, from a farm known as Travelers' Rest, downriver from Falmouth, three slaves escaped named Barnaby, Jim, and Billy.[113] Their owner offered a reward for his three slaves, but they were never found. Barnaby, Jim, and Billy may have found freedom traveling on what was described at the time as the Underground Railroad.

> ... [the] line has been constructed with admirable skill, as they can testify whose circumstances have compelled them to avail themselves to this mode of transit. Traveling by it cannot strictly be said to be either pleasant or altogether safe; yet the traffic is greatly on the increase. It is exclusively a passenger traffic; the trains are all express, and strange to add, run all one way, namely, from South towards the North: there are no return tickets. The stations are numerous, but by no means conspicuous, and are

selected for convenience more than for show. They lie from ten to fifteen miles apart, having nothing in their external appearance to distinguish them particularly, though they are never or very rarely missed. Once the passenger is fairly on the line, he seldom fails reaching his ultimate destination. Owing to the great danger and the numerous difficulties that attend the running of the train, extreme caution is requisite in regulating its departure, and no small amount of ingenuity and dexterity is brought into play to secure the safety of the passengers. The character of the train varies according to the circumstances and exigencies of the case; but in this respect, comfort is disregarded as a matter of trifling importance, in comparison with the principal object, which is individual security. The Underground Railroad being for the exclusive use of slaves who are running for freedom, its managers are not known in a general way. It is rather a point with them to evade popularity, for detection would bring with it no end of fines and imprisonment. Yet they derive no pecuniary advantage from what is called "the forwarding business." They work, like noble heroes as they are, for suffering and oppressed humanity, and for no other reward than the satisfaction of their conscience. The station-masters belong to almost every class of society, and are dispersed all over the regions through which the underground line passes; for its branches are very numerous, and require extensive and constant supervision . . .[114]

In 1853, Moncure Conway visited the home of Henry David Thoreau in Massachusetts. There he encountered a freedom seeker from Stafford County who was "got off" to Canada. While in Cincinnati, Ohio, Conway stated, "There are several colored families here . . . who came from the same place that I did in Virginia . . ."[115] Benjamin Williams, a Falmouth slave, escaped to Boston and continued to Canada. Conway later learned that Benjamin, aka Collin Williams, "had helped many a slave to escape, and probably knew the principal negroes between Georgetown and Falmouth."[116] Yes, Falmouth was on a "line" of the Underground Railroad. The trail to freedom extended from Falmouth to the 49th Parallel.

A CHOICE

In 1857, Hannah Jones Coalter died. The mistress of Chatham, the Georgian mansion and plantation just below Falmouth, left a will that attempted to manumit her estate's 95 slaves. The provisions of the will gave the slaves a choice of (1) freedom and resettlement in Liberia under auspices of the American Colonization Society; (2) freedom and relocation in the North; (3) freedom and location in Fredericksburg or Stafford or Spotsylvania; or (4) continued bondage. Hannah's half sister, Betty Churchill Jones Lacy, and her husband J. Horace Lacy purchased Chatham from Hannah's estate with the assumption that the 95 slaves went with the property. Finding out they did not, J. Horace Lacy contested the will up through the Virginia Supreme Court. On a 2-1 vote, the court threw out the will on the basis that slaves could not be given a choice.

Hannah Coalter, who attempted to manumit 95 slaves.
Courtesy National Park Service, Fredericksburg, VA

Two separate accounts of this incident were written by Moncure Conway. The first is from his autobiography:

> Our neighbor Mrs. Coalter bequeathed freedom to her numerous slaves. But after the clause of liberation the will said that if her negroes preferred to remain in slavery they might select their masters. The husband of the heir contended that the clause giving the slaves this choice, not legal in Virginia, invalidated the liberating clause. The case reached the Court of Appeals, and a majority of the court sustained the heir's contention; the negroes—to whom Mrs. Coalter, as was proved had long promised freedom—remained in slavery until liberated by the war.[117]

A more detailed version appears in Conway's *Testimonies Concerning Slavery*:

> Adjoining my father's estate, on the Stafford side of the Rappahannock, was a fine mansion and estate, known as Chatham. It had belonged to a distinguished judge (Coalter), and at his death fell into the hands of his widow. There were nearly one hundred slaves connected with the estate, who had always been treated kindly. Mrs. Coalter lived with her daughters entirely alone on this estate, her mansion being a mile from any other; she employed no white overseer, and had no white resident on the estate, the management of which was entrusted absolutely to one of her slaves. Under this man the lands yielded finely, and the family wealth continued. Mrs. Coalter further secured the devotion of her slaves by assuring them frequently that at her death they should all be free . . . But one of her relatives, a lawyer, who was called in to give the will a legal form, persuaded her to alter the clause giving the slaves their freedom, and make it read that they should have their freedom if they should so choose, and if not, that they should select for themselves owners from among her

blood-relatives. The old lady, in her simplicity, had her will so written, and soon after died. No soon had this occurred, than one Lacy, who had become by marriage her next heir, entered court with a claim, that since the laws recognize slaves as chattels, they did not and could not be allowed to have the power of legal choice as to their condition. The inferior courts decided in favor of Lacy. It was carried through the Supreme Court of Virginia, which confirmed the decision of the lower courts . . . so the State of Virginia deliberately joined with Lacy in robbing ninety-five human beings of their liberty.[118]

James Horace Lacy, who robbed 95
human beings of their liberty.
Courtesy National Park Service, Fredericksburg, VA

During the late Antebellum Period, Virginia had the largest number of slaves in North America, nearly half a million, and nearly 55,000 slave holders.[119] Between the two farms of Chatham in Stafford

County and Ellwood on the eastern edge of Orange County, J. Horace Lacy and his wife would own 240 slaves before the Civil War.[120] Lacy will appear again in further vignettes as a major in the Confederate army.

A Kiss

Miss Anna Dunbar of Falmouth was a great-granddaughter of Lady Spotswood, wife of a Royal Governor of the Virginia Colony. Her home stood on the hill behind Conway House and was known as Dunbar House.[121]

> The kind maiden lady who lived in that house with only her black retainers [servants] around her never, it was said, went above the ground floor. In her lovely old parlor the ivy vines, which had grown through the walls, twined themselves under the ceiling above the family portraits, and she had put up brass hooks to sustain their stems. On the first landing of the stairway was an ancient looking harp that had belonged to her sister—dead long years before—and over its frame and around its strings an ivy vine had twined also at its own graceful will. There it stood where its former owner had placed it, its music dead, too, never touched, never passed by the surviving sister.[122]

In 1858, while in Cincinnati, Moncure Conway married the lovely Miss Ellen Davis Dana of that city. As with any young bridegroom, Conway wished to present his new bride to his parents and family in spite of his former banishment. John d'Entremont, Conway's biographer, writes:

> Now, after a three-year separation, Moncure wanted to see his parents again. He had a wife now. He wanted her to know something about his home, and he wanted his parents to know something about her. Surely she would be welcome in Falmouth.

The very silence surrounding this visit says something about the disaster's dimensions. No word of it is spoken in family correspondence until seventeen years later (and then only sparingly), and Conway omits it from his memoirs. There is a small wonder in this, for it opened wounds which never healed. Ellen was the most wounded, at least on the surface. Undoubtedly family and neighbors were nervous about Ellen before they saw her. They knew she was a lifelong Unitarian, a Yankee, an abolitionist. That Mildred Conway liked her (she had been a bridesmaid at her brother's wedding) helped little, for Mildred's own allegiances were suspect. When Ellen arrived, the neighbors were alert for offensive or scandalous behavior. They were not disappointed.

Ellen Dana Conway: a Unitarian, a
Yankee, and an abolitionist.
Courtesy Archives and Special Collections, Dickinson
College, Carlisle, PA

Who said what to whom is unfortunately lost, but more than one witness recalled a pivotal episode. Early in their visit Moncure and Ellen went with some neighbors and the slave Dunmore Gwinn to the farm of Anna Dunbar, a widow who had previously owned Gwinn and had been friendly to Moncure in his youth. Dunbar owned four slaves: a man, a woman (Gwinn's sister), and two girls, ages four and one. The older child, whom Gwinn introduced as his niece Evelyn, was sitting on the farmhouse steps as the party arrived. Ellen, delighted by the little girl, spontaneously embraced and kissed her. That was the event which, Conway recalled, "upset the Constitution of the United States" and, Gwinn remembered, "set the magazine on fire."

It was not really so terrible—after the Civil War, Anna Dunbar could admit she had done such things herself. But for a Godless Yankee abolitionist to impose on their hospitality and then run around publicly kissing slaves seemed to many Falmouth citizens a deliberate and unforgivable insult. Word of the transgression spread rapidly. Ellen, at the very least, was made to feel unwanted. Probably, at this point Ellen let some people know just how little she wanted them. Inevitably Moncure was forced to defend both his wife and himself. During one tense scene he drove his uncle Valentine Conway into a rage by telling him he would be ruined if he continued to support slavery. Mercifully for everyone the trip was cut short . . . For the next seventeen years Moncure's only contact with Virginia was the continuing correspondence of his mother. Ellen went away with a vision of Virginia as the most "loathsome place on earth."[123]

Conway's biographer continues by providing insight on the incident: "Perhaps Ellen's action bothered people so much because she punctured their preconception of the hypocritical Yankee who claimed to love blacks but could not bear to touch them, a stereotype embodied six years earlier by Miss Ophelia in *Uncle Tom's Cabin*. Ellen was a more honest and consistent abolitionist than Ophelia, and thus, perhaps, less easy for slave owners to tolerate."[124]

Moncure Conway would later lead the little Evelyn on a "Train Ride to Freedom" to Yellow Springs, Ohio. Her descendents still living there, who give Evelyn's name as Evaline, have maintained through five generations of oral history that Eveline's father was a prominent white man from Falmouth.[125]

Evaline Gwinn, as a young woman in Ohio. She was the little girl who received the kiss from Ellen Conway.
Courtesy of Jean McKee

Ellen Conway served as a nurse early during the Civil War. While living in England after the war with her husband, Ellen supported the struggle of women's rights in Great Britain and in America with her American friends Susan B. Anthony and Elizabeth Cady Stanton.[126]

In Britain, she befriended the celebrated feminist Annie Besant who lovingly composed the tribute "A leaf on a Grave" upon Ellen's death on Christmas Day, 1897.[127]

> *. . . whispering not "farewell," but au revoir.*
>
> _____Annie Besant

An Ancient and a Modern Compromise

On December 20, 1860, South Carolina seceded from the Union and was followed within two months by the states of Mississippi, Florida, Alabama, Louisiana, and Texas. The Union was breaking apart and civil war seemed imminent between north and south. The Confederate States of America was formed on February 9, 1861. On March 24, the Reverend Moncure Daniel Conway delivered a discourse in the First Congregational Unitarian Church in Cincinnati, Ohio. Conway's use of Biblical scripture and the Devil's temptation of Jesus created a powerful metaphor of the nation, as seen in excerpts from "An Ancient and a Modern Compromise."

> We hear much, now-a-days, of compromises. We are called on, in the name of patriotism, to remember that the Constitution of our country was a compromise. Unfortunately it was; and to-day we reap the harvest of such seed . . . that those who begin with the compromise of Principal have given themselves to the toils of a glittering, bright-eyed, golden-scaled serpent, which must inevitably crush them at last. See, before you, Americans! The consequences of a compromise proposed and accepted, in the weakness, dissolution and earth where into the nation is plunged from the graceful eddies and whirls of compromise!
>
> Now let us turn into the past, and consider an instance and lesson of another kind; an instance of a compromise

proposed and rejected, and the consequences of the same.

Here is the compromise proposed:—
"The Devil taketh him into an exceeding high mountain, and showeth him all the kingdoms of the world and the glory of them, and saith unto him, all these things will I give thee, if thou wilt fall down and worship me!"

And here is the compromise rejected:—
"Then said Jesus, 'Get thee behind me, Satan.'"

And finally, here are the consequences:—
"Then the Devil leaveth him, and behold angels came and ministered unto him."

My friends, it is only in crystals that one sees plainly any mingled substance which is inferior. You cannot see a speck of dirt in the heart of a pebble, but you can see it clearly in the heart of a pure crystal. It is so with the evil at the heart of this country. The wrongs which for ages lay unobserved in the stony heart of absolutism and ignorance, preserved now in the centre of a Republic, discolor all the rays shining through it.

America is to-day in the wilderness of temptation, and beside us is the tempter. Up into the mountain the tempter leads us—the exceeding high mountain of our national greatness and pride. From that apex, ready to crumble under our feet, how keenly the kingdoms of this world and their glories strike the senses! On one side, the kingdom of political unity; on another, the kingdom of cotton; near by, the realms of trade; and there, the kingdom of ecclesiastical power. The tempter never slumbers so long as God is awake. "What is it," he whispers, "that divides your nation? . . . It is your hatred of African Slavery. It is your love of freedom. Only give over these; only consent to the fetter on the limbs of the black man; and see all these kingdoms are yours, with all their glories! See, the nation is one again: the coffer is full . . . wounds are healed so soon as Northern and Southern Christians consent to kneel around a common alter, there to eat the broken body and drink the shed blood of the African race. All these shall be yours," says the tempter, "if only ye will turn from the shrine of Liberty, and worship Slavery; and you may call your idol patriotism, union, concession, compromise, fraternal feeling, peace, or any other fine name you please."[128]

The compact which exist between the North and the South is a covenant with death and an agreement with hell.

_____William Lloyd Garrison

PART III

THE CIVIL WAR

After a 34-hour bombardment, Fort Sumter in Charleston Harbor, South Carolina, surrendered to the Confederates. The Federal fortress was evacuated the next day, on Sunday, April 14, 1861. The following Sunday, April 21 the Reverend Moncure Conway admonished in his sermon, "Watchmen, what of the night? The eye that sleeps not alone sees how soon all 'still small voices' may be drowned amid the strong wind and earthquake and fire of civil war . . ."[129]

To the Union army, Falmouth offered a geographic midpoint of its operations in Virginia.[130] It was accessible by land, river, and train. Placing troops here was strategically useful for the defense of Washington, offense against Richmond, and addressing any threats from the Shenandoah Valley. One year after Fort Sumter, the war came to Falmouth in April 1862.

That spring, the Union army descended upon the village, causing most of the white population in the area to flee and opening a gateway to freedom for local slaves. For nearly five months, thousands of African Americans entered this gateway like Exodus of old. After the battles of Second Manassas and Antietam, Falmouth beheld the "watch-fires of a hundred circling camps" when the Union army returned in the fall of 1862, determined on ". . . trampling out the vintage where the grapes of wrath are stored."[131]

In December, the Union army fought the disastrous battle at Fredericksburg and immediately after returned to its Falmouth camps for the winter. Disease was pervasive. By the spring of 1863, "Acres of land were covered with dead horses and mules, scattered about in convenient groups. Their bloating, decaying, festering bodies filled the air with an intolerable stench, and afforded a disgusting feast to the thousands of buzzards which gorged themselves until unable to fly or walk."[132]

After the battle of Chancellorsville in May 1863, the Union army moved away from Falmouth to pursue the Confederate army to the west and north. With the army gone, the great 1862 and 1863 exodus of self-emancipating slaves came to an end. But the war had taken a new turn. African Americans were joining the Union ranks and fighting and dying as soldiers for the liberty of their brothers and sisters. In the spring of 1864, General Ulysses S. Grant began a new campaign against Robert E. Lee's Confederate army, and new battles were fought upriver from Falmouth as Grant moved inexorably toward Richmond. Ultimately, battles and disease produced 30,000 graves in the area. In southern soil lay the future poets of New England, and the South would pay for its madness.

A Prophet

As the peaceful Virginia countryside was toiled over by a people held in bondage, the dark and foreboding winds of war blew the breath of freedom across the South. The first great battle of the Civil War was Bull Run, also known as Manassas and later as First Manassas. The battle was fought on July 21, 1861, just forty-odd miles north of Falmouth. Moncure Conway wrote of the slaves in Falmouth, ". . . they have told me that there was never a moment when the hope of freedom was not before them; that good or bad treatment made no difference with them when freedom was in the question . . . They told me that after the battle of Bull Run the masters went into their kitchens and told them the war was over and the South victorious, and that many negroes were absolutely sick with grief . . ."[133]

Conway also relates a vivid account of an African American slave called "the prophet Bill" who could neither read nor write.

> When the South was preparing for war, this negro came to some of the chief white men and said, "If there were twelve men in the South who believed in God as I believe in Him, there would be no bloodshed. God is just. His time has come." The prophet's master resolved to sell him away farther South where the war would not reach and liberate him. Bill discovered this intention and ran away to a forest ninety miles distant. One night he lay down in the woods, and fell, as he says into a trance: it was at the close of that first terrible battle of Manassas where the army of the North was repulsed by the South with heavy loss. The hopes of the negroes grew faint, but Bill had a vision in which he saw Satan in the form of a huge elephant, a hundred feet high, with sharp spears sticking out all over him; and he saw Christ descend from Heaven and bind a chain around this elephant so that the monster could not move. He arose from the ground and went about among the negroes telling them of this vision, and they had no difficulty in identifying the elephant as the devil of Slavery, and the descending Christ as host of Freedom. The negro

prophet and the negroes generally seem never to have wavered again in their faith that the year of liberation had come. They remained quiet and orderly, and toiled on for their masters with patience.[134]

The truth is these poor people had in them what their owners had not—a deep faith in the rectitude of this universe.

_____Moncure Conway

THOUGH IT COST MY LIFE

As a witness to the struggle of African Americans to gain their freedom, Moncure Conway relates how his own journey led him to a "call on the President." The following is his account of his profound encounter with President Lincoln:

> Having to visit Washington in January, 1862, I had the happiness of finding myself once more in cordial relations with my old friends. The antislavery feeling in Congress, in the absence of Southern members, and in the city had grown strong enough to institute a course of lectures by prominent men from all parts of the country on the national crisis. The lectures were given in the theater of the Smithsonian Institution. My own lecture was given on January 17, and was attended by Secretary Chase and other leading statesmen. The title of my lecture, "The Golden Hour," was derived from an old journal which contained this pretended advertisement: "*Lost,*—Yesterday, somewhere between sunrise and sunset, a Golden Hour, set with sixty diamond minutes."

> *The Golden Hour of the nation was that in which for the first time in its history the murderous madness of slavery had unsealed the constitutional war power to extricate forever that root of all our evils* [italics original].

Senator Sumner suggested that I should call on the President. I had misgivings because of my public animadversions in Cincinnati on his removal of Fremont, but Sumner prepared the way for a call by Channing and myself, the hour of 8 A.M. being fixed by the President. When we arrived at the White House a woman with a little child was waiting in the anteroom. She now and then wept, but said nothing. The President saw her first, and she came out radiant. We conjectured that some prisoner was that day released. The President received us graciously. Mr. Channing having begun by expressing his belief that the opportunity of the nation to rid itself of slavery had arrived, Mr. Lincoln asked how he thought they might avail themselves of it. Channing suggested emancipation with compensation for the slaves. The President said he had for years been in favor of that plan. When the President turned to me, I asked whether we might not look to him as the coming Deliverer of the Nation from its one great evil. What would not that man achieve for mankind who should free America from slavery? He said, "Perhaps we may be better able to do something in that direction after a while than we are now." I said, "Mr. President, do you believe the masses of the American people would hail you as their deliverer if, at the end of this war, the Union should be surviving and slavery still in it?" "Yes, if they were to see that slavery was on the downhill." I ventured to say, "Our fathers compromised with slavery because they thought it on the downhill; hence war today." The President said, "I think the country grows in this direction daily, and I am not without hope that something of the desire of you and your friends may be accomplished. Perhaps it may be in the way suggested by a thirsty soul in Maine who found he could only get liquor from a druggist; as his robust appearance forbade the plea of sickness, he called for soda, and whispered, 'Could n't you put a drop o' the creeter intu it unbeknownst to yourself?'" Turning to me the President said, "In working in the antislavery movement you may naturally come in contact with a good many people who agree with you, and possibly may overestimate the number in the country who hold such views. But the position in which I am placed brings me into some knowledge of opinions in all parts of the country and of different kinds of people; and it appears to me that the great masses of this country care comparatively little about the negro, and are anxious only for military successes." We had, I think, risen to leave and had thanked him for his friendly reception when he said, "We shall need all the antislavery feeling in the country, and more; you can go home and try to bring the people to your views; and you may say anything you like about me, if that will help. Don't spare me!" This was said with a laugh. Then he said very gravely, "When the hour comes for dealing with slavery I trust I will be willing to do my duty though it cost my life."[135]

President Abraham Lincoln.
Courtesy LOC

In July 1862, Conway published a book entitled *The Golden Hour*, with a specific chapter addressed to "The President of the United States." In the book, Conway challenged and admonished Lincoln to carry out the emancipation of slavery. Six months later, Lincoln issued the Emancipation Proclamation, which declared, "all persons held as slaves within any State or designated part of a State, the people whereof shall then be in rebellion against the United States, shall be then, thenceforward, and forever free."[136] This move garnered the President great enmity among Southerners and Confederate sympathizers. His prophetic words to Conway were realized on April 15, 1865, when Lincoln died from an assassin's bullet.

. . . Might we not look to you as the coming Deliverer of the Nation from its one great evil?

_____Moncure Conway

Orderly and Obedient

As the winds of war blew southerly toward Falmouth and the home of Walker P. Conway, his wife Margaret left Conway House and Falmouth and went to live with their daughter Mildred in Easton, Pennsylvania. Their exiled abolitionist son, Moncure, was living in Cincinnati. The Conway's two other sons had joined the ranks of the Confederate Army. In late March of 1862, Mrs. W.P. Conway received a letter from her husband who had stayed behind in Falmouth.

> Frances and her two youngest children went with Mr and the Miss Eustaces and is very much pleased . . . Nancy and Alfred still occupy their room in our kitchen . . . Alfred and James Prior cultivate my gardens.—Nancy and Eliza wash for me . . . James Parker works in Fred'g . . . My servants give me no trouble. They show every disposition to do what they can;—are orderly and obedient . . .[137]

Walker P. Conway wrote again during the first of April, just before the Union army descended on Falmouth, "The Northerners will see that these Negroes, instead of going to them, will remain loyally at our side through this ordeal."[138]

OUR FIRST FALLEN

A Union officer provided a description of the Virginia countryside about Falmouth in the fateful spring of 1862. To his eye, it was ". . . a picturesque, well-wooded, scantily-settled country—a silent, sleepy region, but little vexed with Yankee enterprise or modern agricultural improvements, its roads—romantic forest-paths instead of wide, well-worn prosaic turnpikes—arched with foliage and vocal with the music of birds."[139]

With the first light of dawn, on April 17, 1862, the Union army's "iron hoof of war" moved against Falmouth.[140] A few miles above the town, the first casualty was a boyish-faced 22-year-old cavalry officer named Lt. James Nelson Decker. From Orange County, New York, the lieutenant was described as "impetuous and venturesome." Lt. Decker "fell at the head of his men, having reached the center of the rebel camp."[141] Discovering enemy pickets in the road ahead, Lt. Decker led a charge against his foe, and encountered an officer of the 9th Virginia Cavalry whom he slashed at with his saber, but missed. The Confederate officer wheeled his horse around, drew his pistol, and shot Decker through the heart.

Lt. James Nelson Decker, the first fallen in
the Union advance on Falmouth.
Author's Collection

Given the description of the Virginia countryside about Falmouth, it is not unlikely that Lt. Decker departed life in what must have seemed a lonely corner of the world. A comrade wrote, "After riding two miles we heard picket shouts, and Lieut. Decker's voice came ringing back to us to urge us still faster onward, and then pressing his spurs to his horse he disappeared in advance with the platoon. Two minutes later, as we turned a corner in the road, we saw his bleeding corps . . ."[142]

The Captain of Company D, 2nd NY Cavalry wrote a letter to Lt. Decker's mother, a widow, informing her of her son's death. She responded in a letter to the Captain, "Had I another son to fill his place, and assist in preserving our glorious Union, I would give him to you with a mother's blessing."[143] The fellow officers of the 2nd NY Cavalry, also known as the Harris Light Cavalry, offered their heartfelt tribute, "Our first fallen! Our bravest. He shall ever be remembered in the roll-call of the brave-hearted and the true."[144] Lt. Decker was the first to fall while riding in the vanguard of freedom. It would arrive in Falmouth with the next morning's dew.

FREEDOM'S PRICE

Above Falmouth, a small Confederate force hastily erected a barricade of fence rails in the road. In the early morning hours of April 18, 1862, the Confederates ambushed the Union cavalrymen who were leading the advance on the town. A number of Federal soldiers were killed or wounded during the ensuing skirmish. In the morning, the Union's elite Second Regiment of Sharpshooters, clad in green uniforms, and the 14th Brooklyn Chasseurs, known as the "red legged devils," were the first infantry units to enter Falmouth. Wyman S. White, First Sergeant of Company F, 2nd US Sharpshooters Regiment, had hurriedly passed by the earlier scene of the previous night's action on his way into Falmouth. White's diary entry follows:

> . . . we marched past the barricade and place of the charge and I shall never forget the shock and the feelings of the sight of the dead and wounded men as they lay there in the dust of the road in their own life's blood. One of the wounded lay there with his bowels protruding from a saber wound, still alive and conscious. These were terrible scenes for me and they were sickening, I pulled my cap down over my eyes for I had seen enough and it seemed that the sights like this would be almost unendurable to soldiers in battle.[145]

Another soldier, Charles Teasdale of Company E, 14th Brooklyn Chasseurs NY State Militia, followed the Sharpshooters into town. He also recorded the scene of the ambush in his diary:

> . . . we saw the bloody evidences of the struggle which took place at 1 o'clock this morning when we were aroused by the firing . . . One poor fellow in almost the last agonies of death. I shall never forget his look of unutterable anguish. He was sitting in a dry ditch

with his back to the bank which skirts the road on the east side where I suppose he had been put until the ambulance could come up. He had all his clothing undone and he had his bowels torn open some said by a glance shot. His entrails were all exposed. The roads are dusty and the dust raised by the troops, horses and artillery had lodged on the entrails of the poor fellow as he lay there. I am inclined to the thought that it was a saber stroke that gave the poor fellow such a ghastly wound and his death.[146]

The "poor fellow" and his comrades who fell outside of Falmouth were a price exacted for the freedom clouds gathering upon the town's doorsteps. The waters of the Rappahannock River were about to stir like those of old Jordon.

Tell ye your children of it, and let your children tell their children, and their children another generation.

_____Joel 1:3

JUDGMENT DAY

On the morning of April 18, 1862, the vanguard of the Union army entered Falmouth with a force of two cavalry regiments, a regiment of US Sharpshooters, a regiment of Chasseurs, and a battery of US Regular Artillery. Their objective was to save the bridges over the Rappahannock River leading into Fredericksburg. Confederate forces had already prepared the bridges with pitch, tar, and straw, however, and they set the bridges ablaze as they retreated to the other side of the river. A slave in Fredericksburg, John Washington, along with other African Americans in the city, climbed the rooftops and gazed upon the glistening bayonets of the Union troops as they descended upon Falmouth from Ficklen's Hill.[147]

A Civil War soldier's sketch of Fredericksburg
showing the burnt bridge over the Rappahannock
River and just a small portion of Falmouth.
Courtesy of Earl Robinson

From this same hill on the western edge of Falmouth, Battery B, 4th US Artillery, began firing at Confederate targets across the river. Slaves from Falmouth who witnessed the sight related the scene to a correspondent of the *New York Tribune*. "I have just had a long interview with some twenty of these negroes, who yesterday, arrived here from Falmouth, Va. They say that when McDowell's army first came there, while the white women and children ran screaming to the woods, the colored people stood still; that when they saw the bridges on fire, and saw the 'streams of lighting' (shells) leaping across the Rappahannock, they were sure that Judgment Day had come."[148]

Slaves who had escaped from Falmouth later described the scene to Moncure Conway who recorded their accounts of the Union troops' first arrival in the village.[149] ". . . the Negroes gathered together in their kitchens and cabins, praying and singing their accustomed hymns; and wherever the soldiers entered, they found most of the houses empty, but in the Negro-quarters they found groups of Negroes on their knees."[150]

Bless You Honey

As the Union army approached Falmouth, many of the town's white citizens fled, as did their neighbors from the City of Fredericksburg. Slave owners, while concerned for their own safety, also feared the loss of their property. Their slaves might flee to the Union lines or be taken away by the Yankee invaders. One way slave owners tried to mitigate the potential flight of their slaves was to insinuate that the advancing host was to be feared above all else. Slaves from Falmouth later related this experience to Moncure Conway, who recorded that, "These negroes certify that before the advent of our army they were told that the soldiers were their worst enemies—that they would be maltreated and sent to some foreign land. This was told them by the best citizens, and created a real fear which mingled with their hope of liberty."[151]

In his memoir, slave John Washington recalled that his master had said, ". . . if the Yankees were to catch me they would send me to Cuba or cut my hands off or otherwise maltreat me."[152] Among the first Federal troops entering Falmouth were the 2nd US Sharpshooters. One member, First Sergeant Wyman S. White, Co. F, recorded the following in his diary:

> After the rebels had all disappeared, the whole command marched down into Falmouth Village with bands playing and flags flying. We were greeted by the colored people who came running in from all directions to see the Yanks and to get near and hear the music. This was strange for they had been told that the "Yanks" were something terrible and that they had horns like an ox. One old colored woman told that her master told her that the Yanks would harness the colored people to their artillery and make them work like mules and horses. "But bless you honey, you Yanks are the bess o people," the old lady added.[153]

THE CROSSING

While freedom arrived in Falmouth with the Union army, slavery remained on the opposite side of Jordon. On the Fredericksburg side of the Rappahannock River, 23-year-old John Washington hurried with other slaves to the river's edge to "get right opposite the 'Union Camp' and listen to the great number of 'Bands' then playing . . ." Union soldiers in a small boat on the river called out, "Do any of you want to come over?" John Washington quickly said yes. The soldiers rowed over to the bank, where Washington and two other slaves climbed aboard, and then ferried the three men to freedom on the Falmouth shore.[154]

On April 18, 1862, John Washington was the first known of more than 10,000 African Americans to gain freedom by entering the Union lines at Falmouth during the spring and summer of 1862.[155] Later in life, he wrote of his experience, "A Most Memorable night that was to me the Soldiers assured me that I was now a free man . . . Before morning I had began to feel like I had truly escaped from the hands of the Slave Masters and with the help of God, I never would be a Slave no more . . . I began now to feel that life had a new joy awaiting me."[156]

John Washington's autobiographical memoir entitled "Memorys of the Past" is one of the few written accounts by an ex-slave documenting the experience of being a slave and then finding his way to freedom. Washington was able to lead his family members to the safety of Washington, D.C. (Congress had passed a law emancipating the Federal City on April 16, 1862), where he lived for most of his adult life. He died at his son's home in Cohasset, Massachusetts, in 1918, at 80 years of age. John Washington was considered the "most notable Cohasset resident."[157]

John Washington c.1875. He gained freedom by crossing the Rappahannock River at Falmouth. Courtesy National Park Service, Fredericksburg, VA

As Good Abolitionist as Any of You

The abolitionist Moncure Conway relates this account of "my dear old home," Conway House, when the Union troops first arrived in Falmouth on the morning of April 18, 1862:

> It had been long since tidings concerning my relatives in Virginia had reached me. A small parcel containing an old china cup and saucer and silver spoon had been sent me from Washington at the request of a Union soldier who had saved them from the wreck of things in Conway House, Falmouth. These relics are connected with a curious incident. When the Union army under General McDowell entered Falmouth they found the village deserted by the whites. My father was in Fredericksburg, and my two brothers far away in the

Confederate ranks. The house was left empty and locked up, the house servants remaining in their abode in the back yard. Yet as the Union soldiers were filing past a shot was fired from a window of Conway House, or from a corner of its yard, and a soldier was wounded. It was never known who fired the shot; our negroes assured me that the house was locked and watched. The Union soldiers, alarmed and enraged, battered down the doors, and, finding no one, began vengeance on the furniture. It happened, however, that in my mother's bedroom was hung a portrait of myself, and this caught the eye of a youth who had known me in Washington. He cried to his furious comrades to stop. The servants were called in, and were much relieved when they found that it was to speak of my portrait. Old Eliza cried, "Its mars' Monc the preacher, as good abolitionist as any of you!"

It was some consolation to me that, though long regarded as the black sheep of the family, my portrait saved Conway House from destruction, for that was contemplated. The house was of brick, and the largest in Falmouth; it was made a hospital, and the seriously wounded soldier was its first inmate. My father heard of the incident with distress, and under a flag of truce crossed the Rappahannock to express to the Federal commander his horror at the deed and give proof that all the members of his family were distant from the spot. He was believed and granted his request to visit the wounded soldier. With a good deal of emotion he approached the young man, expressed his horror of the crime, and his distress at seeing him suffering. He exclaimed, said my father, in telling me this story, "Oh, I glory in it!" My father would have been glad to make some kind of practical redress, but it was impossible, and he left his house with feelings of admiration for the sufferer.[158]

Portrait of Moncure Daniel Conway. The portrait, and Eliza's emphatic statement confirming its identity, saved Conway House from destruction. Courtesy of Conway House

A sound of battle is in the land, and of great destruction.

_____ Jeremiah 50:22

THEY TOOK THE NURSE GIRL

In 1862, the United States Army included two elite regiments of US Sharpshooters. One of those regiments was sent to fight in the theater of war known as The Peninsula Campaign against Richmond.[159] The other regiment was sent to Falmouth. The sharpshooters carried special rifles as opposed to the standard single-shot muzzle loading weapons.[160] Their uniforms and gear were issued or adapted to allow the men to blend into their surroundings in the field. They wore green coats instead of the typical Union blue, sky blue trousers, brown leather leggings, and carried a Tiffany calfskin covered backpack, all for camouflage. In some cases, their uniforms incorporated black buttons instead of the shiny brass general issue. Some members used a black ostrich plume to adorn their green cap when the war first carried an air of romance.

First Sergeant Wyman S. White of the 2nd US Sharpshooters recorded the unit's arrival in Falmouth in his diary on April 18, 1862:

> We marched into the village and were quartered in a private house known as the Ford [Forbes] house . . . When they found that Union Troops were surely coming, they made a hasty retreat from their home. They took only the most necessary and valuable property and a limited amount at that. The furniture in the house was hardly disturbed, the piano was left and even the china closet and larder was hardly disturbed. Their colored servants were nearly all left in the huts in the garden in the rear of the house. The kitchen was a log building in the rear and unattached to the house . . . One of the servants left was the cook. Besides that there were three other servants left and it was said that they took the nurse girl along.[161]

Murray and Sallie Forbes, along with a daughter, Kate, fled across the Rappahannock River to Sallie Forbes' ancestral home, the Thornton's of Fall Hill. Murray Forbes was elderly and infirm and normally was attended to by a nurse girl. Sallie Forbes wrote a letter in which she described events relating to those of the same day as those recorded by First Sergeant White:

> Oh what an interruption to all our happy intercourse and tranquility, this lovely season everything seeming to be at peace but Man, I write from Fall Hill . . . Our bridges being burned I had previously come on this side of the water and our house occupied by Federal Soldiers, on Good Friday every Servant we had left us and have never heard from them except that they were waiting on the soldiers, Our Carriage driver telling us the night before that he would never leave his old master (using his own expression) until his hands were cold in death . . . Dave thought he would go over in a

boat and see what had become of his Old mammy . . . when before he could reach our home a company of 8 men arrested him . . . . I fear he will be kept under arrest sometime longer, he is allowed however to walk about the town accompanied by 6 men with their horrid bayonets . . .[162]

The "men with their horrid bayonets" were Company F of the 2nd US Sharpshooters, which had been given the duty of provost guard for the town of Falmouth. Company F, including First Sergeant White, were soldiers from New Hampshire. The headquarters of the Provost Marshal was established in a house across the road from the Forbes House. Dave was David Sterling Forbes, a son who had left Falmouth prior to its occupation, but was arrested when he returned and was suspect of having "Southern feelings." A man of 27 in 1862, his allegiances would certainly have been in question. Later he was released with no word of what became of his "Old mammy." Ascertaining the well-being of an old mammy was sometimes used as a metaphor or code for Southern spy activity. If Sallie Forbes was correct and, ". . . every Servant had left us . . . ," one must wonder who took the nurse girl. She, too, may have emancipated herself and begun a new life.[163]

A rare photograph of United States Sharpshooters.
Members of Company F, 2nd USSS in Falmouth
on provost guard duty in April or May, 1862.
Courtesy of David Rider

Elizah Followed by a "B"

In John Washington's account of his self emancipation on April 18, 1862, he records being well-acquainted in Falmouth and spending his first night of freedom sleeping on a wooden bench in the house of Mrs. Butler, a free black. John Washington wrote in his "Memorys of the Past" that Mrs. Butler gave up a room in her house for three or four soldiers and himself to sleep in while, "A good fire was kept burning all night in an old fashioned fire-place."[164]

The Falmouth Land Tax of 1865 records that Elizah Butler was the owner of Lot 67. It was unusual for a black person to own land in the South in the 1860s. Elizah is listed in the 1860 census as a "wash woman." The building on Lot 67 was valued at $100 and the land valued at $50. Lot 67 was on the northern fringe of town where the land was less desirable due to its hilly topography. Apparently it was an area where a number of free blacks lived. On the tax record, Elizah Butler's name was followed by a "B," indicating that she was black.[165] The practice of labeling black landowners would continue even after the war ended in 1865.

April Wind

The Federal soldiers who died in the advance on Falmouth were buried in the Falmouth cemetery behind the Union Church. The following scene took place on April 19, 1862, graphically recorded by ex-slave John Washington:

> The soldiers had a sad duty to perform . . . The funeral was one of the most solemn and impressive I had ever witnessed in my life before. Their company (cavalry) was dismounted and drawn up in lines, around the seven new graves which had been dug side-by-side. The old Family Burying Ground wherein these new made graves had been dug contained the bones [of] some of the oldest and most wealthy of the Early Settlers of Falmouth. On some of the tombstones could be dimly traced the birthplaces of some in England, Scotland,

and Wales as well as Ireland. And amidst grand old tombs and vaults, surrounded by noble cedars through which the April wind seemed to moan low dirges, there they was now about to deposit the remains of (what the rebels was pleased to term) the low born "Yankee." Side-by-side they rested those seven coffins on the edge of these seven new made graves. While the chaplain's fervent prayer was wafted to the skies and after a hymn (Windham) had been sung those seven coffins was lowered to their final resting place. And amidst the sound of the earth falling into those new made graves, the "Band" of Harris Light Cavalry broke forth in dear old "Pleyal's Hymn" and when those graves were finished there was scarcely a dry eye present. And with heavy hearts their company left that little burying ground some swearing to avenge their deaths.[166]

Soldiers were buried at Union Church much like this sketch entitled "Soldiers' Graveyard, In The Camp Near Falmouth, Va."
Courtesy LOC

The seven soldiers buried that day were:[167]

Lt. James Nelson Decker, Company D, 2nd NY Cavalry, 22 years old, killed at 7:00 PM on April 17, 1862.

Pvt. Patrick Devlin, Company M, 1st PA Cavalry, killed April 18, 1862.

Pvt. John Heslin, Company L, 2nd NY Cavalry, 20 years old, killed at 11:30 PM on April 17, 1862.

Pvt. Josiah Kiff, Company H, 2nd NY Cavalry, 21 years old from Indiana, died of wounds on April 18, 1862.

Pvt. John Murphy, Company G, 2nd NY Cavalry, 23 years old, died of wounds on April 18, 1862.

Pvt. Thomas Norton, Company M, 1st PA Cavalry, died of wounds on April 18, 1862.

Pvt. George Weller, Company H, 2nd NY Cavalry, 26 years old from Indiana, killed April 18, 1862.

Earth that all too soon hath bound him, gently wrap his clay.

_____John Reuben Thompson

THE CAMP

Upon occupying Falmouth in the spring of 1862, the Union army went into bivouac. The numerous camps about Falmouth were a Mecca for slaves seeking freedom. A soldier from New York recorded the reaction of area slaves to the Union army's initial artillery fire to the Fredericksburg side across the river:

> The account given by the numerous contrabands seeking refuge in camp, of the panic occasioned by our sudden appearance, was most ludicrous. "Lord! Didn't dem fellows go," said one, "when you all come up here on de hill, and dem shells went *swish-swish* right through de place! Yah, yah, massa thought de devil coming—sure—massa! Didn't stop nothing 'tall. Dey just throw down de pack and run right smart, Yah, yah, thought de devil was after 'em!"[168]

The ex-slave John Washington wrote of the Union soldiers who invited him to cross the river to freedom:

> They insisted upon my going up to their camp on the Hill, and continued to ask all kind of questions about the "Rebs." I was conducted all over their camp and shown Every thing that could interest me most kind attention was shown me by a Corporal in Company H 21st New York State Volunteers. He shared his meals and his bed with me and seemed to pity me with all his manly heart. His name was "Charles Ladd," But our acquaintance was of short duration a few weeks thereafter the army advanced and had several skirmishes and I never seen him again.[169]

On April 25, only one week after Falmouth was occupied, another soldier from a New York regiment wrote, "Contrabands are coming in in droves every day . . ."[170] William Ray, a Wisconsin soldier described the conversation among the ex-slaves, "And some more Negros come in. They tell some funny stories about how they fooled their masters and run away. They all appear to be quite smart negros."[171] The ex-slave John Washington continued with his impression of the camps at Falmouth, "Day after day the slaves came into camp and every where that the 'Stars and Stripes' waved they seemed to know freedom had dawned to the slave."[172]

Safe Within the Lines.
Courtesy LOC

Captain Rufus Robinson Dawes of the 6th Wisconsin Volunteers poignantly summed up the situation taking place within the camps about Falmouth and on Stafford Heights:

> Our camps are now flooded with negroes, with packs on their backs, and bound for freedom. No system of abolition could sweep away the system [of slavery] more effectively than does the advance of our army. Behind us the slaves, if they choose, are free . . . So far the slave holders have vainly called upon our military authorities, for assistance in returning fugitives. Thus, the great question of liberty is working its own solution. The right must, and surely will, triumph in the end. Let us thank God, and take courage.[173]

Come into my tent, beneath the welcome shade of a stately pine . . .

_____New York soldier "Camp opposite Fredericksburg"

HOE CAKES AND OTHER LUXURIES

After the initial Union advance on Falmouth, additional Federal troops marched toward the village singing Dixie; the flow of Union regiments continued for several days.[174] One regiment was the 20th New York State Militia, known as the Ulster Guards. Lt. John Vernou Bouvier was a member of Company E.[175] He was the great-grandfather of Jacqueline Lee Bouvier, the wife of President John F. Kennedy. Another soldier from the Ulster Guards recorded his observation:

> Falmouth was an insignificant village, lying along the river's bank, at the foot of Stafford Heights, in Stafford County, and, with few exceptions, its buildings were in that state of dilapidation common to old southern towns. Painting, repairing, or any attempt to keep houses or grounds in neatness and order, seemed never to have been thought of. "Time's erosive fingers' have left their indelible marks . . ."[176]

Lt. John Vernou Bouvier is seated at top left. The photograph was taken after his appointment on the staff of Brigadier General Marsena R. Patrick.
Courtesy Steward R. Osborne Collection

On the evening of April 23, 1862, the Second Wisconsin Infantry "entered the town of Falmouth. . . . The inhabitants—principally females—gazed at us listlessly. As we passed by, the 'colored folk' turned out en masse, answering good naturedly the numerous questions asked, and laughing heartily at the inquiries we made of things in general."[177] No doubt soldiers hungry from the march inquired about the availability of food.

Very quickly after the Yankees' arrival, African Americans in Falmouth saw in the army an economic opportunity. They sprang to life as enterprising entrepreneurs. During the army's stay, they collected fresh food and baked hoe cakes (fried unleavened cornmeal cakes), all of which they sold to soldiers eager to supplement their palate of standard army rations.

A soldier in the 21st New York Militia remarked, "We marched along through the antiquated place [Falmouth], whose age could hardly give it an air of respectability, so apparent was the corresponding social ruin or stagnation . . . On the day after our arrival, the negroes came flocking to the guard line, with baskets of eggs, hoe-cakes, and other luxuries, and proved themselves sharp bargainers, doing a lively business . . ."[178]

Washington Street in Falmouth, where an African American boy carries a basket of goods to sell.
Courtesy National Park Service, Fredericksburg, VA

BLACK DISPATCHES

The abolitionist Moncure Conway observed at the beginning of the Civil War, "At Washington our generals were warned to prevent slaves from entering the Federal lines . . . Three days before the disaster to the Union army at Bull Run a special military order was issued for the exclusion of negroes, and there is little doubt that the rout was owning to General McDowell's ignorance of the Confederate positions, concerning which any negro could have informed him."[179]

The army and its commanders learned the lesson. When the Union army first arrived at Falmouth, it sought information from African Americans coming into its lines. Some African Americans were eager to help; they volunteered to serve as guides and even as spies for the Union army. On April 20, 1862, a Confederate cavalry commander operating downriver from Falmouth sent this communiqué, "There are so many negroes to inform against me that I shall have to move with the utmost precaution."[180]

Noted African American abolitionist Frederick Douglass wrote, "The true history of this war will show that the loyal army found no friends at the South so faithful, active, and daring in their efforts to sustain the government as the Negroes—Negroes have repeatedly threaded their way through the lines of the rebels exposing themselves to bullets to convey important information to the loyal army of the Potomac."[181]

Frederick Douglass, a leader of the abolitionist movement. In 1845, he authored *Narrative of the Life of Frederick Douglass, an American Slave.*
Courtesy LOC

African American agents had actually infiltrated Falmouth a little more than one month prior to its occupation. They were employed by Brigadier General Daniel Sickles, who reported his African American scouts went as far as Fredericksburg. One of those scouts, Jim, was "a very intelligent and reliable man."[182] Reporting on activities in Fredericksburg no doubt involved seeking out African Americans in Falmouth who could offer information on the Confederates across the river.

Another "intelligent contraband" was Alfred Peyton. "It was he who, at Catlett's Station, informed General McDowell of the state of affairs at Fredericksburg. The general telegraphed this information to Washington as having been obtained from an 'intelligent contraband,' and the words became immortal. He was guide for our column . . ."[183]

Modern intelligence experts have documented the contribution of African Americans to the Union war effort. A 1998 article written for the Central Intelligence Agency's (CIA) journal *Studies in Intelligence* states succinctly, "This source of information represented the single most prolific and productive category of intelligence obtained and acted on by Union forces throughout the Civil War."[184] The article continues:

> Information gathered resulted from frontline tactical debriefings of slaves—either runaways or those having just come under Union control. Black Americans also contributed, however, to tactical and strategic Union intelligence through behind-the-lines missions and agent-in-place operations . . . The value of the information that could be obtained, both passively and actively, by black Americans behind Confederate lines was clearly understood by most Union generals early in the war . . . After the war, however, the intelligence contributions of Black Americans became obscure. While racial prejudice probably played a part in this, as it did regarding the military contributions of black American Union military units, several other factors added to this lack of recognition. Historically, most successful spies do not want their identities made public. Even individuals who may have provided one-time pieces of useful intelligence usually prefer anonymity. This was particularly true in the emotional period after the Civil War, when many of these black Americans lived near people still loyal to the South.[185]

The Reliable Contraband.
Courtesy LOC

The term "Black Dispatches" was commonly used for intelligence gathered on Confederate forces and provided by African Americans.

The chief source of information to the enemy is through our Negroes.

———————General Robert E. Lee

JEFF DAVIS AND HIS COACHMAN

The President of the Confederate States of America, Jefferson Davis, visited Fredericksburg on March 22, 1862. Though mentioned only scantily in the historical record, John Hennessy, Chief Historian of the Fredericksburg and Spotsylvania National Military Park, has noted the significance of Davis's brief visit:

> Davis arrived from Gordonsville at midnight on the 21st and proceeded to the home of J. Temple Doswell . . . There he met with Generals Theophilis Holmes, the

nominal Confederate commander in Fredericksburg, and Joseph Johnson.

Davis did not linger long at Doswell's house. He, Doswell, and his generals soon crossed the Rappahannock River and "were absent some hours examining the country." There are few details on their ride—we know only that they returned through Falmouth, and likely across the Falmouth bridge. As they trotted through the village, the President commented to Doswell, "Your town of Fredericksburg is right in the wrong place." Indeed, the result of the day's junket was momentous for the town: Fredericksburg could not be defended on the north bank of the river; ergo, if the Union armies advanced toward the town, Confederate forces would yield the place. And so it would be.[186]

William Andrew Jackson was a Richmond slave who had been hired out by his owner in the latter part of August 1861 as coachman for Jefferson Davis. This was a prestigious position and one which could convey privilege and security for the servant and his family, especially during the time of great uncertainties. Jackson, however, "had from his earliest days longed to gain his freedom."[187]

It is not known if Jackson accompanied the Confederate President as he traveled by train to Fredericksburg. Davis rode on horseback with his generals through Stafford and Falmouth and not by carriage or presidential coach. However, Jackson's unique position at the Confederate White House enabled him to learn that both Falmouth and Fredericksburg soon would be occupied by the Union army. Jackson did not wait long and knew when to make for freedom. He made his escape from Richmond on April 27. On May 3, he arrived in Fredericksburg, and, as an escaped servant of the Confederate President, created quite a sensation. Union troops had occupied the city only the previous day.

After being questioned by Brigadier General Rufus King, Jackson was passed to the Stafford side of the river and to Major General Irvin McDowell at his headquarters at Chatham. During the "examination and cross-examination" by McDowell, Jackson provided detailed information about the Confederate defenses around Richmond. The Union commander at Falmouth now had information directly from the White House of the Confederacy. This prompted McDowell to send a report to Secretary of War Edwin M. Stanton, who arranged for Jackson to obtain a free pass for New York.[188]

For more than a week, northern papers carried the story of the escape of Jeff Davis's coachman. On May 8, a New York paper, the *Oswego Commercial Times*, reported that Jackson could read and write, and "talk as well as a member of Congress." His notoriety attracted the attention of northern abolitionists, who enlisted him to speak on the anti-slavery lecture circuit. By June, he was lecturing in Brooklyn, and engagements in the northern cities of Hartford, Connecticut, and Fairhaven, Massachusetts, soon followed.

William Andrew Jackson, the escaped coachman of Jefferson Davis. From a sketch that appeared in *Harpers Weekly* on June 7, 1862.
Courtesy LOC

The self-emancipated coachman was willing to "stand up for the Constitution and the Union as it ought to be." He joined a black regiment being raised by Governor William Sprague in Providence, Rhode Island. Jackson did not get the chance to serve, however. On September 20, 1862, President Lincoln rejected the regiment's request to join the United States army. The government's official policy to accept black regiments would not begin until 1863. One can imagine what Jackson's fate would have been if he had returned south and was captured.[189]

Jackson next traveled from Boston to New York, where he boarded the steamship, *City of New York*, bound for Great Britain. On November 5, 1862, he arrived in Liverpool. Two days later he was at the London home of George Thompson, presenting him with a letter of introduction from William Lloyd Garrison. Thompson, a former Member of Parliament and co-founder of the London Emancipation Society, was perhaps the most important British abolitionist to support the Unionist side in the American Civil War.

On November 28, 1862, Jackson appeared in the *Liberator*, ". . . from mere chattel in Richmond to a recognized freeman in London. Making his appearance there as 'a swift witness' against slavery and the rebellion, we have no doubt he will do good service at this crisis." On the First of January 1863, the *Anti-Slavery Advocate* reported, "He [Jackson] asked for the sympathy of Englishmen on behalf of his brethren in bondage, and of those who were fighting for their freedom." The *Sheffield Daily Telegram* wrote on January 9, "ANTI-SLAVERY LECTURE—Last evening Mr. Jackson, a coloured man, who is described as an ex-coachman and slave of Jeff Davis, delivered an address on slavery in the Temperance Hall . . .his wife and children being slaves in America at the present time."

Alan Rice, Reader in American Cultural Studies at the University of Central Lancashire, Preston, United Kingdom, has written about the abolition movement in Great Britain on behalf of America and its relevance with Lancashire cotton mill workers:

> The period of the American Civil War (1861-65) and the subsequent shortage of cotton produced was a tremendously difficult time for the economy of Lancashire and for its workers. Times were so hard that the period came to be known as the "cotton famine."

> There were many escaped former enslaved African Americans who toured Lancashire and the rest of Britain to condemn the southern slaving states of America . . . Probably the most famous of these touring former slaves was William Andrew Jackson. He escaped from slavery as the coachman of southern leader Jefferson Davis. He was a great speaker and used his speaking skills to rouse people into supporting the anti-slavery northern states of America. He was widely praised by Lancashire workers.[190]

Due to such efforts as Jackson's, the Confederate States of America never gained the much-coveted foreign recognition as a legitimate government. By August 11, 1865, Jackson had returned to the United States. On that date the *Liberator* reported that Jackson had spoken to a Massachusetts audience on the subject of "negro suffrage." The paper attested that Jackson, ". . . looking back on his slave life, he felt that his existence did not commence till 1862, though he was thirty years old."[191] For a brief moment in history, the escaped coachman for the President of the Confederacy passed through Falmouth and into freedom.

THE BEATING

In a letter dated May 5, 1862, an incident was described in a report by Major H.E. Davis, Jr., at the time he was the Union Provost Marshal of Falmouth:

> . . . an interesting case arose in this village [Falmouth], connected with the peculiar institution of the inhabitants which I report that if erroneous action has been taken to receive instruction as to what course to pu[r]sue in similar cases.
>
> Mr. Green resident of this place while engaged in correcting his female slave with great brutality was stopped by some officers who happened to be passing;

he made a complaint of this so called interference to the officer acting in my absence. He told Mr. Green that these gentlemen acted perfectly right, and declined giving him any redress. The woman is now under the care of one of our Surgeons & suffering severely from the beating she received.[192]

A prominent citizen and merchant of Falmouth was Captain Duff Green, who died in 1854. Of his six sons, which was the "Mr. Green . . . engaged in correcting his female slave" is not known. One of the sons was named Duff McDuff Green, also known as Duff Green, Duff Green, Jr., and nicknamed "Long Duff Green." Two sons, Charles Jones and James Lane Green, each married one of two sisters in a family from New York. The latter Green, a known ardent Confederate, paraded his Yankee wife around town when the Union soldiers were in residence.[193] Although serving in the Confederate army, some of the sons appeared in Falmouth at various times, either on business or having been arrested and released on suspicion of being Confederates. In 1863, John M. Whittemore, the father-in-law of Charles and James, conspired with Duff Green to get the Green's cotton out of Falmouth and shipped to New York.[194]

One wonders if the "female slave" was returned to her owner, or if she found safety and freedom under the auspices of the Union authorities. If she was returned to Mr. Green, he would certainly have wanted to get her out of Falmouth and put her to good use. An interesting notice appeared one year later, May 14, 1863, in the *Daily Dispatch*, Richmond, Virginia:

> Fifty Dollars Reward—Run away from the subscriber, at Danville, Va, on the 2 ult, servant woman Annie, about 20 years old medium height, color black. Said woman was temporarily hired to Mr. James M. Walker, of this place, and went off in company with a negro man, each riding mules. She came from Prince William county, near Brentsville, Va. and may be making her way to that county. The woman is the property of Duff Green, of Falmouth, Va. I will pay the above reward for

her arrest and delivery to me, or if secured in jail, so that I can get her.

W. Henry White
Agent for Duff Green
Danville Va, May 5, 1863

Before the Civil War, another son, Alexander Morson Green, left Falmouth and lived in another part of Stafford County with his cook, Nancy Ross, who was an African American. She bore him two children born into slavery. Alexander Morson served in Company A, 9th Virginia Cavalry. We will visit this family again in the vignette "Born in Virginia."

A Good Laugh

When the Union Army first entered Falmouth, the abolitionist Moncure Conway was in exile from his home and native state of Virginia. He was living in Cincinnati, Ohio, and was minister of the First Congregational Unitarian Church of that city.[195] On May 14, 1862, he wrote a letter to his sister, Mildred, who was living in Easton, Pennsylvania:

> . . . the visible presence of God's angel down there [Falmouth] jamming open the prison doors of those poor blacks. How little thought I that the great saving hand was so near them, when, choking, I bade them farewell forever. We have only to pray that the nation's heart may become regenerated, and that by ceasing from its defiant insult to God and outrages to man, it may be a new creature in Christ. Then it will be united.
>
> Did you see that delightful letter from Frd'g. [Fredericksburg] in the Tribune of 12th. It speaks of Mrs. Lacy's going over to see her grounds and finding everything in good order "except the mysterious

disappearance of fifteen to twenty negroes." I laughed till I cried at the picture it brought up.[196]

Mrs. Betty Lacy was the wife of J. Horace Lacy, an officer in the Confederate Army. The Lacy home, Chatham, had been the old Fitzhugh home and the scene of a slave uprising in 1805. Mrs. Lacy had vacated the property, as many whites did upon the arrival of the Union Army in April 1862, and was staying on the Fredericksburg side of the river. Evidently, she thought she would find all her "negroes" loyal and working the estate upon her return.

Mrs. J. Horace Lacy, Mistress of Chatham.
Courtesy National Park Service, Fredericksburg, VA

No doubt Conway found this story very amusing, as he knew the history of the Lacy family and its slaves. When J. Horace Lacy purchased Chatham, he successfully had the former owner's will overturned in court; the 95 slaves she had wished to manumit upon her death remained enslaved to Chatham's new owner (for that story, see the earlier vignette "A Choice"). Conway tells us that Lacy, "sold almost all the youngest of the ninety-five slaves so wronged to the far South, through sheer fear of living on his farm with them after his crime."[197]

One of Lacy's slaves set free during the war was Andrew Weaver who later claimed "I was a slave of Major Horace Lacy." In the spring of 1862, Weaver hired himself out to an officer in the 1st New Jersey Cavalry. He traveled to Washington, D.C., and at age 19 enlisted in the 23rd United States Colored Troops on July 8, 1864. Within a month of enlisting, Weaver was wounded at the Battle of the Crater in Petersburg, Virginia. After the war, he lived in Alexandria, Virginia. Weaver died on May 20, 1915, in Washington, D.C., and is buried in Arlington National Cemetery.[198] Almost nothing is known about the fate of the other Chatham slaves.

JUBILO

By late May 1862, the Union army had rebuilt or constructed no less than four bridges over the Rappahannock River between Fredericksburg and the Falmouth side of the river.[199] Not only did these bridges simplify the army's movements into Fredericksburg and the counties south of the Rappahannock, they also swung wide the "gateway to freedom" for slaves in those areas to make their way north.[200] To the thousands in exodus it was a jubilee.

The joy, excitement, and zeal of the newly-freed slaves were witnessed throughout the Union lines. A Union soldier recorded, "The wild, fervid religious dances, with their accompanying chants, sometimes beginning with Genesis and giving a complete synopsis of the leading points of Bible history from Adam to Peter . . . lasted for hours . . ."[201]

Captain George F. Noyes of the 76th New York Infantry observed, "Their joy seemed to overflow their whole being, and bubbled up in wild exclamation and grotesque grimace."[202] Noyes also described a religious practice amid the Union lines that may have been inspired by the Biblical account of the fall of the ancient city Jericho.[203] Old Uncle Berryman, related the officer, "was the patriarch of the flock, and led their somewhat peculiar worship. Standing in the center, the vociferous and perspiring worshipers moved swiftly around him, singing, as they revolved, hymns..."[204]

The song *Year of Jubilee*, also known as *Kingdom Coming*, was introduced by Christy's Minstrels in Chicago in April 1862. It was published the next month and quickly spread across the north at the same time that Falmouth was occupied by Union troops that spring. As white audiences throughout the north were entertained by *Year of Jubilee*, the camps about Falmouth became safe havens from slave catchers, overseers, masters, and the de-humanizing institution of slavery. Through song, dance, and ritual, African Americans arriving in Falmouth expressed their "jubilo."[205]

> The massa run, ha,ha!
> The darkey stay, ho, ho!
> It must be now the kingdom coming,
> And the year of jubilo.

... proclaim liberty throughout all the land unto all the inhabitants thereof: it shall be a jubilee unto you.
Leviticus 25:10

Cooks and Hostlers

Escaping slaves entering the Union lines, called "contraband," often found employment as cooks and hostlers for army officers (a hostler would groom and care for the officer's horse).[206] Although acting in a servile capacity, for the first time in their lives these African Americans were paid for their labor. Numerous Civil War photographs depict Union officers at "mess" being waited on by an African American. One photograph identified as taken in Falmouth shows a "group of soldiers in front of a tent. A black man pours from a bottle into soldier's cup. Black man identified as Duke."[207]

Duke, waiting on Union officers in Falmouth.
Courtesy LOC

A Union soldier at Falmouth, John Harrison Mills, Company D, 21st NYSM, recorded that African Americans generally employed as cooks could "throw a lively meal . . . He also ran various errands, filled the canteens at the spring, made foraging expeditions after the indispensable corn-meal for the inevitable hoe-cake, stole eggs and milk, and committed various other troublesome sins . . ." for the soldiers.[208] A sketch by Civil War artist Edwin Forbes depicts an African American leading an army mule behind him. He is identified as "Dick" who looks rather forlorn "on return to camp." The time of the sketch suggest Dick was one of many freed slaves who were employed by the Union army encamped about Falmouth.[209]

Dick, on return to camp at Falmouth.
Courtesy LOC

The observant and prolific Captain George F. Noyes wrote about an African American boy within the Union lines:

> Our quarter-master, a wag in his way, had discovered somewhere a bright-eyed boy whom he made his servant, initiating him by the following affirmation: "You, Pompey, solemnly declare that you will support the Constitution of the United States, look out for my horse, and black boots to the best of your knowledge and belief; so help you, General M'Dowell." The boy was naturally much impressed with the ceremony,

kissed a copy of the "Army Regulations," and faithfully kept his pledge.[210]

On a more serious note, Noyes expressed his own opinion of the African Americans in camp:

> We had quite a number of these newly-freed men about our head-quarters, in the employ of the government as teamsters, blacksmiths, etc. A patient, docile race, eminently trustworthy, with mental faculties quite undeveloped, it always seemed wonderful to me that they succeeded so well in their new experiment of freedom. It may take a generation to develop their best qualities of self-support; but even now they very readily fell into the performance of their respective duties. I have witnessed their exultation when, for the first time in their lives, they received honest pay for their honest labor, and am satisfied that this is impulse sufficient with them, as with us, to induce their best efforts. I have seen them painfully spelling out their letters—great six-foot men even, struggling over the difficulties of a child's primer, and am convinced of their capacity and desire for education. I have employed them personally and for the government, and feel that they are honest and faithful, anxious to be instructed what to do, quick in learning, and energetic in doing it.[211]

THE BIRTHDAY PARTY

A northern newspaper declared, "This Lacy is known to be a violent secessionist, who has thrown his influence to the uttermost . . . a rebel of the straitest [sic] sect . . ."[212] On June 10, 1862, Major Lacy was captured on his birthday while visiting Greenwood, a family home of his wife's relations. His wife Betty related, "My mother insisted that he should stay and eat his birthday dinner with us, a pleasure for which he had to pay dearly . . ."[213] *The Washington National Republican* carried an account of the incident:

An important arrest was made near this city [Fredericksburg] yesterday evening, in the person of Major Lacy, formerly a volunteer aid to Gen. Ruggles, of the Confederate army. The rebel officer was taken at his farm, a short distance from the city, while on a visit for the purpose of removing a part of his family and servants further south. It seems that he labored under the mistaken idea that this city had been entirely evacuated by our forces, and that no danger stood in the way of open communication with the place.

He was arrested and brought to this city by a detachment of cavalry, and is now in confinement here. When the cavalry approached his house, he was sitting on the balcony with his family, but upon discovering his pursuers, endeavored to escape by a back door. The house was quickly surrounded by the guard, and search made. His family endeavored to mislead the soldiers by retaining their positions on the portico, and feigning merriment over what they endeavored to represent as a good joke, saying that Lacy had been gone several hours, and was near Richmond by that time. Captain ----------, however, was not to be so easily deceived, and continued the search. At length the horse of Captain ---------- suddenly came upon the rebel officer, who was secreted in the high grass near the house. Upon being discovered, he pointed a pistol at the captain, who, at the same moment, aimed at Lacy, demanding his surrender, which he soon acceded to. A sudden plunge of the captain's horse at this moment caused the discharge of his pistol, and narrowly escaped shooting Lacy. The ball cut off a portion of one of his fingers.

Lacy has taken a very active part in the rebellion in various ways. He is a man of no little notoriety, which commenced with his defrauding about one hundred slaves, belonging to his wife's aunt, Mrs. Coulter, out of their freedom, by breaking the will of Mrs. C., which provided for their freedom at her death if they should choose it. By dint of legal strategy, Lacy managed to get possession of this choice lot of flesh and blood, and has since fattened on his ill-gotten gain, and is now regarded as wealthy. Among other property, he owns the house [Chatham] and grounds opposite the city, which General McDowell recently occupied as his headquarters.[214]

Major Lacy was brought under guard to Chatham. Moncure Conway wrote that some 20 self-liberated slaves from Chatham were among those who witnessed Lacy's ignoble return to his estate, "in the trappings of a major, a prisoner to his former home, then the head-quarters of General McDowell. This Lacy, the man most marked by all the slaves of that region, passed through a large crowd of those who had lately been owned by himself and his neighbors, his hands tied, his head hung down; and yet not one jeering word or imprecation was flung at him by those he had wronged."[215]

After Lacy was taken to Chatham, he was held as a prisoner of war for two months at Fort Delaware near New Castle, Delaware, until exchanged. Lacy survived the war and held on to Chatham until unable to pay the property taxes. In 1872, Chatham was sold. Lacy was remembered "as a formidable old fellow, always dressed in black, given to lounging in front of a downtown [Fredericksburg] store."[216] As Lacy lounged in the shade of a storefront, he probably glanced at one of his fingers and remembered his ill-fated birthday party. He perhaps remembered that he once occupied a place among Virginia's gentry and still considered himself in that respect. On one occasion, someone from out of town asked, "Who is that man, and what does he do?" The answer was, "That's Major Lacy, and he don't do nothin'. He's a gentleman!"[217]

It Didn't Belong Here

Numerous stories about the Union occupation of Stafford County and Falmouth have been handed down through the years as oral history. One such story concerns a house in which the family's portraits hung in the formal hallway. Among these portraits hung one of a female slave whom the family dearly loved and highly regarded. A Union soldier slashed all the portraits with his sword. Another soldier asked why he had slashed the portrait of a slave? His answer, "It didn't belong here."[218]

INDEPENDENCE DAY

Moncure Conway wrote, "Who can misread or doubt the prophecies written broadly over all the mountains, prairies, savannahs, lakes, and rivers of America? What heart can have a misgiving that the superb grandeurs and resources of that continent have been prepared for a race of slaves and slave-drivers? . . ."[219]

During the spring and summer of 1862, the pleasant landscape of Falmouth's green walled hills accommodated the arrival of additional Union troops. The Union army camps spread over Stafford Heights and the rolling farm lands opposite Fredericksburg. On June 18, 1862, Fredericksburg's pro-Union newspaper, *The Christian Banner*, reported that an average of 200 fleeing slaves a day entered the Union lines.

Despite general disappointment over the battle cry of "On to Richmond," and that their counterparts in McClellan's army on the Peninsula had not been able to capture the Confederate citadel, McDowell's army at Falmouth observed the Fourth of July, 1862, as a special day of ceremony and frolic. A soldier wrote at the end of the day, ". . . the spirits of earth and air who, as the poets tell us, flit on invisible wings about these groves and hillsides, must have heard sentiments uttered on this occasion . . . and these contraband of war [ex-slaves] . . . To them it was Independence Day indeed."[220]

. . . to the poor Negro the banner of the Union, which hitherto has seemed to symbolize the stripes on his back, shall float up to be what it was meant by the fathers to signify,—the morning-stars and streaks of a new dawn for Humanity.

_____Moncure Conway

Canaan's Freedom Wagons

As self-emancipating slaves streamed into the Union lines at Falmouth and continued north through the army's extensive camps, soldiers and "special artists" working for newspapers sketched the travelers. A common depiction was slaves escaping by wagon. In these scenes, the wagon is usually crammed with women and small children, belongings piled high, men walking alongside the vehicle, and older children trailing behind. An article in *The Christian Banner* describes a particularly spectacular scene:

> We continue to chronicle the unceasing stampede of Contrabands, in order that our readers may learn some of the delicious fruits of the lemon, secession. They continue to come rolling in from every Southern point of the compass. A contraband from Essex county came in town on Tuesday last, bringing his wife and children, and traveling in elegant style. He came in a fine buggy, drawn by a splendid horse, the whole party well dressed, and had plenty of money. They provided, and brought along with them a large supply of comforts of life. The man reports that his master had gone to Richmond with a quantity of "cattle, chickens" &c. &c. and that he expected to return on Saturday the 12., inst, after which time he was going to take said contrabands to Richmond, or somewhere down South. The master left these loyal subjects in charge of his possessions until his return. No sooner, however, had he gotten fairly on his way to Richmond, than this pair of trusty, loyal contrabands took all they wished, and all that they could bring, and left master's affairs at home to take care of themselves as best they could. Really, it reminds us somehow of the old Jews when about to make their exodus from Egypt, they borrowed all they could from the Egyptians, before they left for the promised land of Canaan, never intending to return a single article to the owners, and the negroes take all they can conveniently, without the least idea of ever returning to their masters

a single cart, ox, horse, wagon, buggy, or anything else. Within the last few days several hundred have crossed over to the North side of the Rappahannock river on their way to parts unknown.[221]

Freedom Wagons, on their way to parts unknown.
Courtesy LOC

THE FUGITIVE SLAVE OF THE BOSTON RIOTS

In 1860, Reverend Anthony Burns became the pastor of Zion Baptist Church in St. Catharines, Ontario, Canada. Sometime between 1844 and 1853, the church was built by slaves who had escaped from the United States. It had 300 members at the time Burns became pastor. It was one of only two black churches in St. Catharines. The other church was the British Methodist Episcopal Church built in 1855. St. Catharines was the destination to which Harriett Tubman delivered her freedom seekers between 1852 and 1858. Henry Banks, a fugitive slave originally from Stafford County, had escaped from Spotsylvania County to St. Catharines. He stated, "I do not think it was intended for any man to be a slave. I never thought so, from a little boy."[222] The colony of fugitives in St. Catharines, known as the "City of Refuge," numbered from around 800 to estimates of 1,200.

Reverend R.A. Ball of the British Methodist Church provides a description of Burns. "He is a fine-looking man, tall and broad-shouldered, but with a slight stoop, indicating a weak chest . . . He was a fine speaker and was considered to be well educated. He was unmarried and very popular with both the white people and the people of his own race."[223] Ball noted that Burns bore the marks of slavery with scars upon the cheek and a disfigured hand as the result of a work-related accident.

On July 27, 1862, Anthony Burns died in St. Catharines of tuberculosis. He was 28 years old. Maltreatment during his four-month confinement in Lumpkin's infamous slave jail, in Richmond, Virginia, in 1854 weakened his general health and left him susceptible to disease. The two story brick jail was located within a complex known as "the devil's half acre," just three blocks from the state capital. Lumpkin's "sat amid a swampy cluster of tobacco warehouses, gallows, and African American cemeteries . . . the city's most notorious slave jail was down a hill some eight feet below the rest of Lumpkin's complex—the lowest of the low."[224]

While confined in jail, Burns was "wearing my chains Night and Day."[225] Through a trap door, Burns was isolated in an empty room and fettered with his hands behind his back, unable to undress himself when necessary. Poorly fed once a day and given water only "every two days, he became seriously ill and weak."[226] Robert Lumpkin purposely placed Burns in solitary confinement from the other slaves so he could not communicate to them any ideas of freedom.

The day after Burns' death, Reverend Hiram Wilson, a Congregational minister and graduate of Oberlin College, wrote to Reverend Lenard A. Grimes, an African American minister of the Twelfth Baptist Church in Boston. Reverend Wilson had spent 28 years living in Canada, helping escaped slaves to adjust to life in the Canadian wilderness. Grimes was an ex-slave from Virginia whose church was often known as "the fugitive slave church." It was through his efforts in 1855 that funds were raised to purchase Burns' freedom. Wilson's letter, excerpted here, was published in the Boston *Liberator*.

> Dear brother—Having just returned from the burial of the Rev. Anthony Burns, I feel it to be my duty to write you promptly respecting the termination of his earthly pilgrimage.
>
> I am the more inclined to address you as a brotherly act, inasmuch as you took a deep interest in him in Boston, some years ago, raising the means of his ransom, and putting yourself in serious jeopardy to obtain his freedom, going down personally into the dark and horrible prison-house of slavery in the South to accomplish so noble a purpose.
>
> Anthony Burns is no more! His immortal spirit took its flight to the spirit-land at 3 o'clock yesterday (Sabbath) morning, after a decline of some four months, of consumption . . . His illness was brought on, perhaps, by over-exertion and exposure, last winter and early spring, in trying to clear the Zion (Baptist) Church here of debt, of which he had been pastor for a year or more. Success attended his efforts; he not only cleared it of debt, but succeeded in making some important repairs, improvements, &c; and when everything seemed to be going on prosperously, his health failed, and he was laid aside. It was a great trial to him, as he told me, to be laid aside from his active and useful labors. He retained

a very affectionate remembrance of his friends in the East who had taken so much interest in him, and often spoke of them . . . During his protracted illness, a deep and tender sympathy was felt towards him by many of the colored people, and a considerable number of the white population. The members of his church were strongly attached to him . . . The concourse around his peaceful grave were mostly colored—the adults of whom, like himself, had fled from bondage; and yet there was quite a number of white people of various churches and different nationalities. While there consigning his mortal remains to the silent dust, I thought of the awful excitement a few years ago in Boston, attended upon his arrest, and rendition to the hands of bloody men, who are now in open rebellion against the government, and against God and humanity. I seemed to have a sort of panoramic vision of the pro-slavery treachery—the arrest, the court proceedings, the mass meetings, the vast array of marshals and of the military, and the countless throngs of people blocking up the streets of Boston—his dark and awful doom as a victim of the Fugitive Slave Law, and the hellish exultations of the Slave Power on the one hand—while lamentations spread all over the coasts of New England, and rolled back to the Rocky Mountains. I thought of that iniquitous system as having culminated to the awful crisis now hanging over the American people. The name of Anthony Burns fills an important place in the history of events which led to the great conflict now pending between the marshaled host of freedom and the fiendish friends and minions of slavery, and will be pronounced with honor when the fetter shall have fallen from the limbs of millions of his suffering brethren.[227]

On his grave marker, under the name, "Rev. Anthony Burns," appears, "The Fugitive Slave of the Boston Riots." His grave is located in Victoria Lawn Cemetery in St. Catharines.[228] The Zion Baptist Church building was razed in 1958. A signboard bearing the name

"Anthony Burns" hung outside of the church until 1951. Today, few in number, the congregation operates out of a house on Raymond Street in downtown St. Catharines. An organization known as the Cemetery Gardening Angels has planted and maintains a beautiful array of flowers around the grave of Anthony Burns.[229]

The flowers bursting into bloom whispered "Break thy bonds," and the flying cloud said "Be free!" The strain was taken up by the winds, I heard it in the ebb and flow of the tide, and to it moved the stars in their courses.

_____Moncure Conway

A Small Candy-Shop and Sixty Dollars

Dunmore and Eliza Gwinn, husband and wife, were the "house servants" of the Conway family in Falmouth. They lived in a cabin in back of "the house." Conway House was an elegant Federal style home designed to separate the movement and uses of its owners and their servants. The main rooms on the first and second floors of Conway House contained a servant bell pull system. At a central station there was an assemblage of graduating brass bells. Each bell had its own distinctive tone. By using the "bell pull" in a certain room, the corresponding bell would ring. The bell was not heard in the room, but rather at the servant's station. So, a servant had to recognize each bell tone in order to know where they were summoned.

Conway House, where servants responded
to the ringing of a bell.
Author's Collection

By July 1862, the Gwinns answered bells no longer. The Union army occupied Falmouth, and the resourceful Dunmore and Eliza left Conway House and town. They successfully "set up a small candy-shop in Georgetown [District of Columbia], taking in washing, and saved sixty dollars."[230] Several of their older sons went into the employment of Union officers in Georgetown.[231]

Dunmore and Eliza Gwinn in Washington, D.C.
Courtesy Antiochiana, Antioch College,
Yellow Springs, OH

THE TRAIN RIDE TO FREEDOM

Dunmore and Eliza Gwinn were not the only ones seeking freedom in the District of Columbia. In mid-July 1862, a group of 60 to 70 slaves left Falmouth for a certain cabin among a line of "negro cabins" in Georgetown. The cabin belonged to an ex-slave who years before had escaped to freedom from Falmouth and now helped others to do the same. Arriving in the midst of a terrific thunder storm, the freedom seekers huddled within the walls of their safe haven when an unexpected knock came at the door. "Who is it?" was called out, answered by "A friend," a Quaker sign used on the Underground Railroad. The friend was Moncure Conway, recently arrived from Ohio.[232]

Conway had traveled back east to locate his father's slaves. He hoped to find them by seeking out the cabin of "an old mulatto whom I had known in boyhood and who now resided in the farthest suburbs of Georgetown. He had helped many a slave to escape, and probably knew the principal negroes between Georgetown and Falmouth . . . The house was that of Collin Williams, fugitive 'Benjamin' I had tried to find in Boston nine years before at the request of his wife, who had joined him in Georgetown."[233] The Georgetown cabin was a station on the Underground Railroad and Collin Williams was a conductor. Conway described the band of freedom seekers he found inside the cabin:

> They had never known a white face which was not that of a master. They had never been beyond the little neighborhood in which they were born—had never seen cities, railways, steamers;—these, with the whole Northland, were as much a vision to them as the eternal fields arrayed in living green for which they had so long sighed and sung. The terrible storm, the natural misgiving as to the step they had taken, the fearful doubt as to the destiny which awaited them and their children,—all combined to make them sit together and weep in silence.[234]

Conway had a plan. He would take them to Yellow Springs, Ohio, for resettlement. Yellow Springs was home to the free-thinking Antioch College and was a community that would be accepting of a "colony" of former slaves. Scott Sanders, archivist of Antioch College, wrote that Moncure Conway "had long admired the work of his friend Horace Mann, a staunch anti-slavery man who had been president of Antioch College for its first six years, until his death in 1859. Surely, Conway felt, Mann's powerful influence remained behind to create a community where the colonist could thrive . . ."[235]

With the addition of his father's two house servants, Dunmore and Eliza Gwinn, who had previously arrived in Georgetown, Conway took the Falmouth band of freedom seekers to Baltimore, Maryland. The Emancipation Proclamation had not yet been issued and Baltimore was a city seething with southern sympathizers. The year before, Baltimore citizens had rioted against Federal troops traveling through the city. The mob attacked a Massachusetts regiment; 17 people were killed and more than 30 were wounded.[236]

Conway and his band of freedom seekers had to traverse the streets of pro-slavery Baltimore in order to board a train to carry them west. Moving from one end of the city to the other with a large group of African Americans created no small stir. Despite an angry mob which had formed at the Baltimore & Ohio Railroad station, Conway was able to board the freedom seekers on a passenger car.

Handbill for B&O RR and Little Miami
RR which led to Yellow Springs.
Courtesy LOC

The freedom seekers received a Heaven sent window of opportunity and were fortunate to leave when they did. Previously, the rail line between Baltimore and western Virginia (now West Virginia) had proved difficult for Federal forces to keep secure from Confederate raiders. The line was secure in late July 1862, however, when the train with the Falmouth slaves departed. Soon afterward, rail service from Baltimore to the west would again be disrupted by the Army of Northern Virginia's movement into western Maryland.[237] When Conway said, "I came here to gather my people together," he was indeed a Moses leading the former slaves to the Promised Land.[238] The "train ride to freedom" was headed for the free state of Ohio, where a small settlement named Yellow Springs was located in the southwest rolling hills between Dayton and Columbus.

When I Can Read My Title Clear

On the "train ride to freedom," Moncure Conway noted that his charges, "would neither talk nor sleep . . . every station at which the train paused was a possible danger." Later, however, ". . . when the name of a certain wooding-up station was called out, I observed that every eye danced, every tongue was loosed, and after some singing they all dropped off to sleep. It was not until next day that I learned that the station which had wrought such a transformation was the dividing line between the slave and the free States. How they knew it I cannot divine; it was a small place, but there the shadow of slavery ended."[239]

Upon arriving in Yellow Springs, the Conway "people" left the train station and were first sheltered in a large barn owned by Moses Grinnell. The "Conway Colony" was established. They built houses of wood on the edge of a glen north of the village, along the Little Miami River. Dunmore Gwinn and Eliza, known as "Aunt Lizy," had a good house with pigs and poultry and five well kept acres said to be on the left side of the road on the hill slope overlooking the end of the "Water Cure." One of the Colony's first achievements was the founding of the First Anti-Slavery Baptist Church of Yellow Springs in May 1863. In November that same year, "The Colored Sabbath School of Yellow Springs" was organized. Church history relates, "The Sunday School served as a training ground for many of its former slave members who learned to read and write there."[240]

In 1907, the *Yellow Springs News* gave a quaint description of former Conway house servants, Dunmore and Eliza Gwinn. "Here they lived and died, typical relics of the southern slaves who had belonged to 'quality.'"[241] Grandmother Baber, daughter of little Evaline Gwinn in the earlier vignette "A Kiss," would have the children sit at her feet and tell them about the "train ride to freedom" from Virginia.[242] Descendants of the Falmouth slaves still live in Yellow Springs and areas of Ohio today. With pride they embrace their ancestry and revere those who stepped out of the shade of old Virginia.

Dunmore and Eliza Gwinn in Yellow Springs.
In this post Civil War photograph the status of
"house servants" is still portrayed by the white
handkerchiefs and Dunmore's butler coat with tails.
Courtesy Antiochiana, Antioch College,
Yellow Springs, OH

"When I Can Read My Title Clear" was an old African American Methodist hymn favored by the slaves at Conway House in Falmouth.[243] When Moncure Conway first found the freedom seekers in a Georgetown cabin they were singing a hymn from within. They again sang a hymn after leaving a "certain wooding-up station" where the fleeting shadows of slavery ended.

>When I can read my title clear,
>To mansions in the skies,
>I'll bid farewell to every fear,
>And wipe my weeping eyes.
>
>Should earth against my soul engage,
>And fiery darts be hurled,
>Then I can smile at Satan's rage,
>And face a frowning world.
>
>Let cares, like a wild deluge, come,
>And storms of sorrow fall;
>May I but safely reach my home,
>My God, my heaven, my all.
>
>There shall I bathe my weary soul,
>In seas of heavenly rest;
>And not a wave of trouble roll,
>Across my peaceful breast.

They were tossed about by destiny, but still able to raise their song in the night.

———————Moncure Conway

An Old Hoe

One Conway family slave does not appear to have made the trip to Yellow Springs, Ohio. James Prior did not seek emancipation, but choose to remain behind in Falmouth. Perhaps because he was elderly, and despite the uncertainties associated with the war in mid-1862, Prior stayed. Records indicate he survived the war. On March 6, 1867, Captain Hector Sears made an entry in the list of "Prominent Whites and Freedmen in Stafford County" he was compiling for the Virginia Freedmen's Bureau. Of twelve names listed, six were identified as "Colored," including James Prior, who was noted as living in Falmouth.[244] The 1871 tax records for Falmouth show he occupied an unspecified lot owned by Walker P. Conway. No record thereafter or information about his final years was found.

In 1862, before the Union occupation, Walker P. Conway wrote that "Alfred and James Prior cultivate my gardens" (vegetable gardens supplying the household). Alfred Gwinn was eight years old at the time. So, seemingly the gardens were worked by a young boy and an old man.[245]

Moncure Conway returned to his family home in Falmouth ten years after the Civil War. In 1875, he looked upon dilapidated property, including the, ". . . once beautiful gardens and terraces running to weeds." After 140 years, a much rusted old hoe was discovered and pulled from the ground behind Conway House. The hoe dates to the mid-19th century and was handmade by a blacksmith.[246] Perhaps it was Alfred's before he left for Yellow Springs. James would have needed to keep his hoe. One can imagine young Alfred laying his hoe aside for the last time as he departed for freedom. Today his descendants are living in Springfield, Ohio.

Alfred Gwinn, son of Dunmore and Eliza, went on the Train Ride to Freedom at age eight. Courtesy of Jean McKee

THE DOCTOR'S COACH DRIVER

The slave Richard Herod belonged to Dr. Lawrence B. Rose, who was said to be descended form a very wealthy and old aristocratic family.[247] Dr. Rose's house on Willow Street in Falmouth was up the hill and around the corner from Conway House. Herod was the doctor's coach driver. He was married to a Conway slave named Nancy Butler Gwinn, daughter of the Conway house servants, Dunmore and Eliza Gwinn. Nancy did the washing and kitchen work at Conway House. Couples often lived separately when owned by different masters. Visits were permitted on Sunday, or when arrangements allowed. When the Conway slaves left Falmouth in mid-July of 1862 to seek freedom in the north, Herod joined his wife and their daughter, Elizabeth. Dr. Rose may have been away at the time, as he was an acting surgeon in the Confederate Army.[248]

Once in Ohio, Richard Herod helped to organize The First Anti Slavery Baptist Church of Yellow Springs and was one of the church's four original trustees. On February 15, 1865, he volunteered as a private in Company M, 5th US Colored Heavy Artillery. Richard served until February 14, 1866.[249] He returned to Yellow Springs and became an ordained minister in the church he helped to found. He also worked at the town's hotel. In 1907, Richard was described as in feeble health, deeply religious, and truly pious.[250]

TOGETHER THEY WENT TO WAR

The youngest son of Walker P. and Margaret E. Conway was Peter Vivian Daniel Conway. He was named after a great uncle, Peter Vivian Daniel, an associate justice of the Supreme Court of the United States (1842-1860). Justice Daniel sided with the majority in both the 1847 decision that affirmed the constitutionality of the Fugitive Slave Act of 1793 and in the Dred Scott Decision in 1857, which ruled, in part, that African Americans could never become US citizens.[251]

Born in 1842, young Peter went by the name "PVD." He possessed a winsome personality and was well liked. PVD enlisted in the Fredericksburg Artillery, recovered from a severe leg wound received on the third day at Gettysburg, rejoined his unit, and served in the Army of Northern Virginia until the surrender at Appomattox Court House.[252] The antithesis of his brother Moncure, the family black sheep for his abolitionist views and actions, "dear Peter" was Walker Conway's pride and hero. Historian John d'Entremont describes how Walker P. Conway felt about PVD, "No father could ask for a finer son. He knew his place. He did his duty."[253]

PVD Conway, the antithesis of his brother Moncure.
Author's Collection

Peter Gwinn was a son of the Conway's house servants Dunmore and Eliza Gwinn. Peter accompanied PVD as a body servant during the Civil War and the two may have been companions in childhood. A Conway cousin related years later that the Conway children "played with the black children every day." Together they grew up and together they went to war.

After the war, Peter Gwinn settled in Washington, D.C. He went by the name Peter McGwinn, and was employed as a "photographer printer."[254] PVD stayed briefly in Baltimore after the war, but came back to Fredericksburg and joined his father's banking business. He was president of Conway, Gordon & Garnett National Bank. PVD wore his leg wound from the war as a badge of honor. Peter Gwinn and PVD corresponded, apparently keeping up a lifelong friendship.[255] Peter Gwinn died in 1911. Three years later, PVD's bank failed. He moved to San Diego, where he died in 1924.

Return to Slavery and a Return to Freedom

Not all slaves found their pathway to freedom easily. For freedom seekers who passed through the Union lines at Falmouth, their northward trek often led them to Aquia Landing. This was the terminus of the Richmond, Fredericksburg, and Potomac Railroad. From Aquia Landing, most travelers continued by steamer up the Potomac River to Washington, D.C. As historian and author Edmund J. Raus, Jr. writes, "Others took advantage of the opportunity to emigrate to Haiti. On July 11, 1862, a bark outfitted by James Redpath, general agent of the Haitian Bureau of Emigration, anchored off the wharf at Aquia Landing, and within ten days the ship set sail with 450 new black colonists."[256] Edmund J. Raus, Jr. provides a further account:

> . . . a soldier in the 26th New York met a group of blacks returning disappointed to Falmouth. The trip north had been full of dangers. The railroads would not carry them beyond Washington without a bond, and there was always the fear, particularly for those entering Maryland, of being arrested as fugitives and sold back into slavery. Also, they had met hostility from the black residents of Washington, who complained that the new arrivals ("country darkies") were generally driving down wages. For blacks stranded in Falmouth there remained few options . . . some chose to return to slavery.[257]

Moncure Conway described James Parker as, "The most intelligent of our negroes . . . a handsome mulatto, who had been my father's valet." Walker P. Conway took temporary residency in Fredericksburg after the Union army arrived in Falmouth. He moved on to Richmond when Fredericksburg also fell, leaving his valet behind. Parker "penetrated into the Confederate lines, at risk of re-enslavement, to find my father and continue in his service, but was told he must return to freedom."[258] James Parker was among those led by Moncure Conway to freedom in Yellow Springs, Ohio, in July of 1862. Conway later wrote, ". . . there was a single one who hesitated some time before he left—a man who had for many years been his master's personal attendant and companion, and was much attached to him."[259]

Alice Parker, a Conway slave who was a favorite of Moncure's sister, Mildred. Alice went on the Train Ride to Freedom and afterwards to Easton, PA, where Mildred was living with her husband, Professor Francis Andrew March of Lafayette College.
Author's Collection

THE BLACK SCOUT OF THE RAPPAHANNOCK

During the summer of 1862, the battle cry "On to Richmond" faded away for the Union troops encamped about Falmouth. Instead of using the area as a spring board for another advance on the Confederate capital, a nervous President Lincoln wanted to maintain a force midway between Washington and Richmond. Traveling by the roads of the day, Falmouth was approximately fifty-five miles south of Washington and sixty-three miles north of Richmond.[260]

During that summer of disappointment, a Union cavalryman from Indiana wrote, "Another sultry day—and like most days in Camp—uninteresting Spent it in my tent reading . . ." [261] In Union occupied Fredericksburg across the river from Falmouth, "the men were enjoying a comfortable afternoon, lying in the shade of the trees, writing letters to friends at home, sleeping, amusing themselves as they would." A camp scene of the 2nd New York Cavalry was described, "The once gay and dashing Colonel lay lazily in his tent, permitting a cigar to burn itself slowly away between his lips , . . . while behind his chair stood two contraband attendants with fans."[262]

Earlier that spring the first infantry brigade to enter Falmouth was commanded by Brigadier General Christopher C. Augur. The brigade was composed of militia and volunteer regiments from the state of New York. One of the officers on General Augur's staff "employed a local black to scour the countryside encouraging other slaves to escape."[263] The identity of the "local black" is unknown, but could have been a contraband named Dabney.

That summer, Captain George F. Noyes, reflecting on the army's activities in the area, provided a fascinating account of the scout Dabney:

> Quite a large body of troops were now assembled, and occasional expeditions of cavalry were sent out to disturb the quiet of the enemy, burn the railroad bridges, and thus interrupt his communications, sometimes having a brush with the enemy's cavalry and bringing in some prisoners. Their usual guide was a native-born Virginian, in whom we all became much interested. He seemed to me a sort of Daniel Webster in ebony—a strong, clear-headed man, who had reached a true conception of the real issue in this war, and devoted himself, body and soul, on the right side. Knowing all the roads and by-ways in this section, and brave as a lion, he led our boys with all the cool

courage needed in a scout, established a comprehensive system of espionage among the people of his own color, and thus brought in much valuable information. The rebels did him the honor to offer fifteen hundred dollars reward for his head, and well they might, for he was worth to the Union cause any two of the best of us. As he sallied forth with military cap, blue coat adorned with the button of old Massachusetts—its ense petit placidam sub libertate quietem singularly appropriate to his situation—with his revolver in his breast, and a good horse under him, he was naturally looked up to with admiring eyes by his brother contrabands. "He sets great store on himself. He's a jet black nigger; got no white blood in his veins." This latter physiological peculiarity, as it grows more and more infrequent at the South, is gradually becoming quite a badge of colored aristocracy; and no one could see Dabney without being convinced of the pure blood of the black scout of the Rappahannock.[264]

"Button of old Massachusetts" from a State Militia uniform.
Courtesy of Plez Bagby

Dabney wore a Massachusetts "blue coat." During the Civil War, the buttons on Massachusetts state uniforms were embossed with the motif of a bent arm bearing a raised sword as if ready to deliver a blow. The Massachusetts state motto, *ense petit placidam sub libertate quietem*, means "By the sword we seek peace, but peace only under liberty."[265] From Noyes' account, it seems that the symbolism suited Dabney well.

And in thy majesty ride prosperously because of truth and meekness and righteousness; and thy right hand shall teach thee terrible things.

_____Psalms 45:4

THE UNSUNG HERO OF THE ABOVEGROUND RAILROAD

In the preceding vignette, we learned that one of the officers on General Augur's staff employed a local black to scour the countryside encouraging other slaves to escape. The elusive Dabney, alias Black Scout of the Rappahannock, may have been the "local black." Colonel Edward Brush Fowler of the 14th Brooklyn, NY State Militia, provides the identity of the officer:

> Major George B. Halstead [Halsted], assistant adjutant general on General Augur's staff, a thorough lover of the enslaved race and an earnest worker for their emancipation, employed a native black man, who would each day scour the country to bring in "contrabands," and the major would keep them at night in a barn near headquarters and send them each morning, by train and boat, to Washington and freedom.[266]

Major Halsted hailed from New Jersey and belonged to an old and distinguished family of that state. His ancestry included a colonel and a general who fought in the Revolutionary War. Like Moncure Conway, he was a descendant of a Signer of the Declaration of Independence. When the Civil War began, Halsted emulated the example of his ancestors and was one of the earliest volunteers to leave civil life to serve his country. He was quite possibly the first individual with the US Army engaged not only in actively seeking out the enslaved, but also in organizing their passage to freedom. At this stage of the war, the Union army had no policy for freeing slaves. Freedom seekers were allowed to enter the lines only as contraband of war under the Confiscation Act of 1861.[267] Seeking out slaves for the deliberate purpose of emancipating them was a bold step and a courageous undertaking, accomplished without official sanction of either the military or the government.[268]

Major George B. Halsted, "a thorough lover of the enslaved race and an earnest worker for their emancipation."
New Jersey State Archives, Department of State

Consistent with his beliefs, Halsted hired Dabney out of his own pocket. The "native black man" was indeed a leader and someone the slaves felt to be trustworthy. He carried out his mission well, bringing in those willing to cross Jordon and begin a new life in freedom. Halsted's efficient operation—using a barn to move slaves in at night and out in the morning—appears to have successfully channeled hundreds of slaves, if not more, to freedom. Halsted's position as a staff officer may have allowed him to secure the use of the Military Railroad, overcome army bureaucracy, and obtain the proper passes for the freedom seekers.[269] Thousands would eventually take the same route Halsted orchestrated via rail and steamship north. Major Halsted rightfully deserves encomiums as the unsung hero of Falmouth's aboveground railroad to freedom.[270]

The night is far spent, the day is at hand . . .

_____Romans 13:12

ZION

During the spring and summer of 1862, the occupation of Falmouth by the Union army opened a "gateway to freedom" for slaves from the surrounding countryside and Fredericksburg. The army offered opportunity for employment or a new life of freedom further north. The following incident represents how the opportunities provided by the army's presence influenced the life of a boy named Zion during that fateful spring under the Stars and Stripes. Captain George F. Noyes provided this account in May, 1862:

> A little imp carved out of ebony had somehow joined our staff within the last day or two. He rejoiced in the name of "Zion," and acted as boot-black-in-chief with the rank of contraband. Grotesque in appearance, wonderfully endowed with dirt and rags, his bright, cheerful face and funny ways interested us. The major resolved to extricate him from his coating of mud, cloth him, and educate him as waiter; so they proceeded together . . . for the necessary apparel.

The major took Zion into a clothing store in occupied Fredericksburg:

> Entering the shop the major said, "Now, Zion, take off your coat, Wkaf—Wkaf—for, Massa Major?" said the boy, imploringly, at the same time backing toward the door and making evident preparations for flight. It took some time to persuade him that he was to have a new jacket and not the usual whipping; but finally he consented to disrobe. Buttons there were none; the various rags were tied on somehow, and had to be cut off with a knife. In the evening, what with copious lavations and his new suit, Zion seemed a different creature. We began to think of him as a permanent fixture; but that night he left us new cloths and all, forever.[271]

Like so many others, Zion probably followed the trail to freedom from Falmouth, through Stafford County to Aquia Landing, and boarded a steamer to Washington, D.C.[272] There he would disappear into the anonymous pages of history. Let us believe Zion lived a good life, not as a slave, but this time all dressed up in freedom.

O Zion, . . . get thee up into the high mountain . . .

_____Isaiah 40:9

TEN THOUSAND TO THE LAND OF FREEDOM

The Land of Freedom and the Promised Land were synonymous to those dehumanized by the institution of slavery. In 1834, Great Britain banned slavery in all of its colonies. Canada instantly became the Promised Land to slaves in the United States, both because slavery was outlawed there, and also because the US Fugitive Slave Laws of 1793 and 1850 were unenforceable in that country. For decades before the Civil War, slaves took to the Underground Railroad in attempts to gain permanent freedom in Canada. On April 16, 1862, President Lincoln signed the Compensated Emancipation Act. This law prohibited slavery within the District of Columbia. The District became the new "Promised Land" for freedom seekers. For slaves in Falmouth and the region, their land of freedom was near at hand.

For nearly five months after the Union army occupied Falmouth in April 1862, the army used the Richmond, Fredericksburg, and Potomac Railroad line abandoned by the Confederate forces. The line ran between Fredericksburg and Aquia Landing, where Aquia Creek meets the Potomac River. From the terminus at Aquia Landing, the journey to Washington, D.C. continued upriver by ship, usually steamers. Major George B. Halsted first utilized the line to pass contrabands to freedom. Former slave John Washington recorded, "Hundreds of colored people obtained passes and free transportation to Washington and the North. And made their Escape to the Free States." [273] An old "Negro spiritual" may have been heard at the wharfs of Aquia Landing sung to the tune of "Give Me that Old Time Religion."[274]

> Tis the old ship of Zion,
> Tis the old ship of Zion,
> Tis the old ship of Zion,
>   Get on board,
>   Get on board.
>
> It has landed many a thousand,
> It has landed many a thousand,
> It has landed many a thousand,
>   Get on board,
>   Get on board.

As the hot and humid Virginia summer lingered into August of 1862, the bulk of the Union Army of the Potomac under the command of Major General George B. McClellan was encamped below Richmond. It occupied a well fortified position at Harrison's Landing on the James River. General Lee decided to pull his army from Richmond and begin an offensive campaign into northern Virginia. He hoped this move would relieve the Confederate capital by drawing Union forces away to protect Washington, D.C.

Lee also intended to meet a new threat imposed by Major General John Pope, Lincoln's new general with a new army. Assembled from scattered forces in the Shenandoah Valley and troops ordered to leave Falmouth, Pope's army was designated the Army of Virginia.[275] The new general boasted, "I have come to you from the West, where we have always seen the backs of our enemies . . . I hear constantly of . . . lines of retreat and bases of supply. Let us look before us and not behind."[276] Following defeat in Culpeper County at Cedar Mountain on August 9, 1862, the Army of Virginia fell back on its supply lines toward Washington, leaving Aquia Landing vulnerable. Nineteen days later, Pope suffered another defeat at the Battle of Second Manassas. Confederate forces now controlled the interior of the state.

A swelling of Jordon's tide was about to take place. On August 29, the rumor of a Confederate advance on Fredericksburg caused more than 1,000 African Americans to flee to the Falmouth side of the Rappahannock River.[277] One Union soldier entered in his diary for September 2nd that the number leaving on that single day alone was 3,000.[278] The remaining Union troops occupying Falmouth and Fredericksburg began to withdraw in those early days of September 1862. The gateway to freedom was closing as slaves rushed to get to Aquia Landing before it snapped shut.[279] In a report dated September 17th, W.W. Wright, the Engineer and Superintendent of the US Military Railroad, made this observation:

> During the last two days the contrabands fairly swarmed about the Fredericksburg and Falmouth stations, and there was a continuous black line of men, women, and children moving north along the road, carrying all their worldly goods on their heads. Every train running to Aquia was crowded with them. They all seemed to have perfect confidence that if they could only get within our lines they would be taken care of somehow. I think it safe to estimate the number of contrabands that have passed by this route since we took possession of the road at 10,000.[280]

. . . to the land of Freedom, led by the fiery and cloudy pillar of War; but they have been followed by a host whose cry has been heard, and whose broken chain denotes the liberation of a nation which bore about its own neck the other end of that chain.

_____Moncure Conway

A Great Battle

Sumner's Corps of Union Troops entering
Falmouth in November, 1862.
Author's Collection

After fighting two great battles, Second Manassas in August and Antietam in September 1862, the Union army returned to Falmouth and Stafford Heights opposite the City of Fredericksburg in November.[281] Following the Battle of Antietam, President Lincoln issued the Emancipation Proclamation, which was to take effect on January 1, 1863. Lincoln and the Republicans hoped a crushing victory over Lee's army before the New Year would bolster the Lincoln administration's credibility and ensure speedy implementation of the President's new edict. That hope ended in December. The Union army fought the battle of Fredericksburg and was decimated by the advantageously situated and well led Confederate Army of Northern Virginia.

This disastrous defeat for the Union took place across the river from Stafford Heights, just downstream from Falmouth. The poet Walt Whitman visited the hospitals in search of his brother, First Lt. George Washington Whitman, Company D, 51st New York Infantry, who was among the many wounded on the battlefield. Whitman wrote his first important poem of the Civil War based on his visit.[282] The scene he describes took place on the Stafford side of the Rappahannock River among the numerous hospital tents in the rear of Chatham Manor:

A Sight in Camp in the Daybreak Gray

A sight in camp in the daybreak gray and dim,
As from my tent I emerge so early sleepless,
As slow I walk in the cool fresh air the path near by the hospital tent,
Three forms I see on stretchers lying, brought out there untended lying,
Over each the blanket spread, ample brownish woolen blanket,
Gray and heavy blanket, folding, covering all.

Curious I halt and silent stand,
Then with light fingers I from the face of the nearest first just lift the blanket;
Who are you elderly man so gaunt and grim, with well-gray'd hair, and flesh all sunken about the eyes?
Who are you my dear comrade?

Then to the second I step—and who are you my child and darling?
Who are you sweet boy with cheeks yet blooming?

Then to the third—a face nor child nor old, very calm, as of beautiful yellow-white ivory;
Young man I think I know you—I think this face is the face of the Christ himself,
Dead and divine and brother of all, and here again he lies.

WATCH NIGHT

The First African Baptist Church of Boston was organized in 1805. It is the oldest extant African American church in the United

States. In January 1832, William Lloyd Garrison organized the New England Anti-Slavery Society at the church. Thirty years later, William Lloyd Garrison, Jr., his sister Fanny Garrison, and Moncure Conway attended the Watch Night Service at the First African Baptist Church on New Year's Eve, 1862. They were among a small party of white guests among the African Americans gathered to anticipate the legal enactment of the Emancipation Proclamation. "Watch Night" was the name given for the evening hours leading up to the stroke of midnight and the start of a New Year. It has its basis in Judeo-Christian scripture, Lamentations 2:19: "Arise, cry out in the night; in the beginning of the watches pour out thine heart like water before the face of the Lord." Conway recorded the sermon delivered by the minister:

> Brethren and sisters, the President of the United States has promised that, if the Confederates do not lay down their arms, he will free all their slaves tomorrow. They have not laid down their arms. Tomorrow will be the day of liberty to the oppressed. But we all know that evil powers are around the President. While we sit here they are trying to make him break his word. But we have come this Watch Night to watch and see that he does not break his word. Brethren, the bad influence near the President tonight is stronger than Copperheads. The old serpent is abroad tonight, with all his emissaries, in great power. His wrath is great, because he knows his hour is near. He will be in this church this evening. As midnight comes on we shall hear his rage. But, brethren and sisters, don't be alarmed. Our prayers will prevail. His head will be bruised. His back will be broken. He will go raging back to hell, and God Almighty's New Year will make the United States a true land of freedom.

Conway relates that these words caused a profound sensation and that the congregation frequently erupted in cries of "Glory" and tears of joy. His account continues:

But the excitement that followed was indescribable. A few minutes before midnight the congregation were requested to kneel, which we all did, and prayer succeeded prayer with increasing fervor and amid shouts of rapture. Presently a loud prolonged hiss was heard. There were cries, "He is here! He's here!" Then came a volley of hisses; they proceeded from every part of the house,—hisses so entirely like those of huge serpents that the strongest nerves were shaken; above them rose the preacher's prayer, gradually becoming a wild incantation. Finally the strokes of midnight sounded, and immediately the hisses diminished and gradually died away as if outside the building. Then the New Year of jubilee that was to bring freedom to millions of slaves was ushered in by the chorus of all present singing a hymn of victory. The hymn was the old Methodist "Year of Jubilee," which I had so many years heard sung in Virginia by the negroes when their night was without any star save that burning in their faith.[283]

> Blow ye the trumpet, blow
> The gladly solemn sound:
> Let all the nations know,
> To earth's remotest bound,
> The year of jubilee is come!

How We Got Over

The tradition of the "Watch Night" service in African American churches is the subject of an article written by Charyn D. Sutton. Sutton was an African American community activist from Philadelphia. In her article written in December 2000, she explains the historical significance of the service:

> Many of you who live or grew up in Black communities in the United States have probably heard of "Watch

Night Services," the gathering of the faithful in church on New Year's Eve. The service usually begins anywhere from 7 p.m. to 10 p.m. and ends at midnight with the entrance of the New Year. Some folks come to church first, before going out to celebrate. For others, church is the only New Year's Eve event. Like many others, I always assumed that Watch Night was a fairly standard Christian religious service—made a bit more Afro centric because that's what happens when elements of Christianity become linked with the Black Church. Still, it seemed that predominately White Christian churches did not include Watch Night services on their calendars, but focused instead on Christmas Eve programs. In fact, there were instances where clergy in mainline denominations wondered aloud about the propriety of linking services with a secular holiday like New Year's Eve.

However, there is a reason for the importance of New Year's Eve services in African American congregations. The Watch Night Services in Black communities that we celebrate today can be traced back to gatherings on December 31, 1862, also known as "Freedom's Eve." On that night, Blacks came together in churches and private homes all across the nation, anxiously awaiting news that the Emancipation Proclamation actually had become law. Then, at the stroke of midnight, it was January 1, 1863, and all slaves in the Confederate States were declared legally free. When the news was received, there were prayers, shouts and songs of joy as people fell to their knees and thanked God. Black folks have gathered in churches annually on New Year's Eve ever since, praising God for bringing us safely through another year . . . many of us were never taught the African American history of Watch Night, but tradition still brings us together at this time every year to celebrate "how we got over."[284]

As 1863 began, Joseph B. Ficklen, a prominent citizen of Falmouth, who owned 27 slaves, worried about his financial ruin resulting from having to pay his slaves for the first time. He also faced the problem of his slaves deciding if they were staying to work for wages or leaving altogether.[285] Lieutenant George Breck of the 1st New York Light Artillery, then posted in Stafford County, sent a letter to a Rochester, New York, newspaper. His account bears witness to the effect the Emancipation Proclamation had on the previously enslaved:

> ... the "poor slave," passengers for Freedom—swarming northward in response, we suppose, to the emancipation edict ... The slaves, just before and since the first of January, have been leaving their "Ole Massa's" in this section of the Old Dominion, taking with them all their personal effects, and, as observed, a sufficient number of mules, carts, &c., for transportation of their families and household chattels.[286]

The traditional spiritual "Oh Freedom" is believed to have been conceived by freed slaves and sung by them after the Emancipation Proclamation.[287] The edict released more slaves from servitude in Virginia than in any other state. "Oh Freedom" is still known in Stafford County. It is conceivable the air about Falmouth was filled with the spiritual's resounding choruses.

Oh Oh Freedom!
Oh Oh Freedom,
Oh Freedom over me and Before I'll be a Slave,
I'll be buried in my grave,
and go home to my Lord and be Free.

THE FAITHFUL SERVANT

In the Union Church Cemetery in Falmouth lies a small stone marker over the grave of a slave named Osborne Merricks. The epitaph reads as follows:

IN MEMORY OF
OSBORNE MERRICKS.
Servant of
Murray Forbes
Aged 85 years.

"Well done thou good and faithful
servant thou hast been faithful over
(remaining inscription buried below ground)

Merricks' owner, Murray Forbes, was a successful Falmouth resident. In 1850, he "was a 65-year-old Stafford merchant with $38,000 in real estate and 13 slaves. Forbes had once been director of the port of Falmouth, as well as a businessman and land owner . . . The slave Osborne was the coachman for the Forbes family. A daguerreotype photograph of him still exists showing him posed with a top hat and a carriage whip."[288]

Osborne Merricks, coachman and faithful servant.
Photograph by Berry Fitzgerald from the original,
courtesy of Ruth Coder Fitzgerald

As noted in an earlier vignette, when the then elderly Forbes and his family left Falmouth as the Union army approached the town in April 1862, his wife Sallie Forbes wrote that, "Our Carriage driver telling us the night before that he would never leave his old master (using his own expression) until his hands were cold in death." Sallie Forbes was referring to old "Uncle" Osborne Merricks. He must have reconsidered the thought of his hands turning cold in death without experiencing freedom once during his life. Uncle Osborne remained in Falmouth within the Union lines after the Forbes family fled. His freedom was short lived. By January 1863, a Union soldier recorded reading the epitaph on his gravestone.[289]

Isaac "Ike" Taylor was a school teacher in Illinois before the Civil War. He and his brother, Henry, enlisted together in the 1st Minnesota Infantry. In 1863, the regiment was encamped just below the Union Church in Falmouth. Taylor was granted permission to visit the old cemetery. While reading the various inscriptions on tombstones, he recorded in his diary several he found of interest. His entry for January 9, 1863, was "cloudy in morning" followed by the epitaph of Osborne Merricks. Taylor recorded the complete verse from Mathew 25:21, which was visible at the time. "Well done, thou good and faithful servant: thou hast been faithful over a few things, I will make thee ruler over many things: enter thou into the joy of thy lord." Standing before the grave of a "faithful servant" must have been odd for someone like Taylor whose life was far removed from experiences of the "peculiar institution." After living most his life as a slave, Uncle Osborne experienced freedom only briefly. "Ike" Taylor left Falmouth with the 1st Minnesota Infantry in June 1863. He would soon join Uncle Osborne in death and enter into "the joy of thy Lord," from a quiet town in Pennsylvania called Gettysburg.[290]

REBEL NEGRO PICKETS AND THE TEAMSTERS' DUEL

At the beginning of 1863, weeks after its disastrous defeat in the Battle of Fredericksburg, the Union army settled in for an unusually harsh winter with low morale, desertions, sickness, and boredom, in its camps around Falmouth. Captain Rufus Robinson Dawes of the 6th

Wisconsin Infantry termed the winter the Union army's "Valley Forge." Meanwhile, the victorious Confederate Army of Northern Virginia encamped at Fredericksburg kept an active watch on the Union camps. In *Harpers Weekly*, January 10, 1863, a sketch appeared accompanied by an article entitled "Rebel Negro Pickets."

> So much has been said about the wickedness of using the negroes on our side in the present war, that we have thought it worth while to reproduce on this page a sketch sent us from Fredericksburg by our artist, Mr. Theodore R. Davis, which is a faithful representation of what was seen by one of our officers through his field-glass, while on outpost duty . . . As the picture shows, it represents two full-blooded negroes, fully armed, and serving as pickets in the rebel army.

Rebel Negro Pickets.
Courtesy LOC

While no fighting took place that January, correspondents with the army continued to send stories and pictures of life in camp to their publishers. On January 17, *Harpers Weekly* published the "Teamsters' Duel," depicting an incident within the Union camps about Falmouth:

> ... a sketch by Mr. Waud ... is one of the humorous scenes in which our camps abound. When a quarrel arises between two colored teamsters a challenge passes, and the combatants lash each other with their long whips until one of them confesses that he can endure no more ... The other is pronounced the victor, and very frequently admonishes his vanquished foe of the necessity of better behavior in future, amidst the roars and laughter of the white spectators.

The Teamsters' Duel.
Courtesy LOC

A Brave Act

The Union lines were not always a safe haven for African Americans, even those in the service of Union officers. Sometime after Christmas of 1862, Major General Oliver Otis Howard had, "near Falmouth, sent two contrabands (ex-slaves not officially freed) into town on horseback on an errand. On their way back, the two servants encountered some troops of the 'Irish brigade' walking back from picket duty. When the Union soldiers ordered them to dismount, one of the blacks fled. When the other man held his ground and refused to dismount, he was shot, and later died at a field hospital."[291]

Union Pickets along the Rappahannock
River opposite Fredericksburg.
Courtesy LOC

A slightly different account of this story was published in the *New York Sun* on November 28, 1906. W.L.D. O'Grady, a former member of the 88th New York Infantry, Irish Brigade, had been a witness to the incident in Falmouth. His letter, entitled "Gen. Howard's Colored Groom," was published in the *Sun*:

General O.O. Howard doubtless remembers the death of his colored groom in the main street of Falmouth, Va., on the morning of December 26, 1862. Details of five skeleton regiments were returning from their miserable Christmas picket when in the narrow gorge excavated by artillery and wagons till the "sidewalks" were from four to eight feet higher than the roadway they encountered a "chesty" negro, mounted and leading another horse. There was a scramble of the infantry up the slippery banks to avoid injury, and some harsh language, when the negro imprudently told the "d___d white trash to get out of the way." He fell dead.

I was there (a private then), saw the flash, saw the negro fall, but I did not know who killed him until July 3, 1888, at our dedication reunion at Gettysburg. The man was dead then, and I have forgotten his name. I do not believe six men knew who it was at the time.[292]

Yet another account, possibly related but certainly similar, is found in the diary of Ike Taylor (seen in the vignette "The Faithful Servant"). In mid-January 1863, Taylor sardonically records, "A contraband dies in our regimental hospital from effect of gun-shot wound inflicted by a 'brave' Union soldier. The negro refused to get off from his masters horse and deliver it over to a stranger. That soldier has immortalized himself in that brave act."[293]

Saluted by Death and Kissed by Immortality

As the bitter month of January 1863 came to an end, Major General Ambrose E. Burnside, commanding the Army of the Potomac, ordered a tactical flanking movement up the Rappahannock River above Falmouth. Burnside's plan was for the Union army to cross the river at a fording place west of Fredericksburg and then turn east to outflank the Confederate army in Fredericksburg on its left rear. The ill-fated movement, doomed from the beginning, was abandoned when the army became bogged down by the severe winter weather and treacherous Virginia mud. The "Mud March" served only to further exhaust and demoralize the Union troops, who spent days struggling to return to their former camps at Falmouth.

On January 25, a young officer posted at Stafford Court House wrote his sister Effie, "They say the Rebels put out a large placard opposite Falmouth, saying: 'Burnside stuck in the mud.' 'Shan't we come across & help you with your pontoons?' The letters were large enough to be easily read from our side." The letter was signed "Your loving brother, Rob." Robert Gould Shaw later became Colonel of the 54th Massachusetts and led his US Colored Troops to glory in an assault against Fort Wagner, near Charleston, South Carolina.[294]

. . . everything softened and made unreal by distance, poor little Robert Shaw erected into a great symbol of deeper things than he ever realized himself.

_____William James in *Blue-Eyed Child of Fortune*

A CLOTHES-LINE TELEGRAPH

In early 1863, Dabney Walker and his wife Lucy Ann entered the Union lines around Falmouth. They had been slaves on a farm in Spotsylvania County. Whether Dabney Walker and Dabney, "The Black Scout of the Rappahannock," were the same person is unknown.[295] What does seem clear is that the Walkers became one of Major General Joseph Hooker's most useful sources of information about the Army of Northern Virginia.

In 1863, rumors circulated about a "clothesline telegraph" between Falmouth and Fredericksburg. Historian Edwin C. Fishel writes, "A spy had been placed in Fredericksburg, from where she (there is evidence that she was a Negro woman) was to communicate across to Falmouth by means of a simple 'clothesline code.'" According to Fishel's account, John C. Babcock, who was assigned to Hooker's Bureau of Military Information, described the process to Hooker's Chief of Staff, Major General Daniel Butterfield: "A clothesline with one piece denotes that the forces in the vicinity of Fredericksburg are on the move. An empty line denotes that they have all gone away. Two pieces shows that they are in force as they have been since the fight, three pieces that they are being reinforced. One piece has been displayed all day yesterday and today, till 4 P.M. when observer came away."[296]

The clothesline telegraph operator in Fredericksburg was allegedly a "Negro woman." That woman was Lucy Ann Walker. Her method for communicating information is described in further detail in another account:

> In the early part of 1863, when the Union army was encamped at Falmouth, and picketing the banks of the Rappahannock, the utmost tact and ingenuity were displayed, by the scouts and vedettes, in gaining knowledge of contemplated movements on either side; and here, as at various other times, the shrewdness of the African camp attendants was very remarkable.
>
> One circumstance in particular shows how quick the race are in learning the art of communicating in signals. There came into the Union lines a negro from a farm on the other side of the river, known by the name of Dabney, who was found to possess a remarkably clear knowledge of the topography of the whole region; and he was employed as a cook and body servant at headquarters. When he first saw our system of army telegraphs, the idea interested him intensely, and he begged the operators to explain the signs to him. They did so, and found that he could understand and remember the meaning of the various movements as well as any of his brethren of paler hue.
>
> Not long after, his wife, who had come with him, expressed a great anxiety to be allowed to go over to the other side as servant to a "Secesh woman," whom General Hooker was reluctant about sending over to her friends. The request was granted. Dabney's wife went across the Rappahannock, and in a few days was

installed as laundress at the headquarters of a prominent rebel General. Dabney, her husband, on the north bank, was soon found to be wonderfully well informed as to all the rebel plans. Within an hour of the time that a movement of any kind was projected, or even discussed among the rebel generals, Hooker knew all about it. He knew which corps was moving, or about to move, in what direction, how long they had been on the march, and in what force; and all this knowledge came through Dabney, and his reports all turned out to be true.

Yet Dabney was never absent, and never talked with the scouts, and seemed to be always taken up with his duties as cook and groom about headquarters. How he obtained his information remained for some time a puzzle to the Union officers. At length, upon much solicitation, he unfolded his marvelous secret to one of our officers. Taking him to a point where a clear view could be obtained of Fredericksburg, he pointed out a little cabin in the suburbs near the river bank, and asked him if he saw that clothes-line with clothes hanging on it to dry. "Well," said he, "that clothes-line tells me in half an hour just what goes on at Lee's headquarters. You see my wife over there; she washes for the officers, and cooks, and waits around, and as soon as she hears about any movement or anything going on, she comes down and moves the clothes on that line so I can understand it in a minute. That there gray shirt is Longstreet; and when she takes it off, it means he's gone down about Richmond. That white shirt means Hill; and when she moves it up to the west end of the line, Hill's corps has moved up the stream. That red one is Stonewall. He's on the right now, and if he moves, she will move that red shirt."

One morning Dabney came in and reported a movement over there. "But," says he, "it don't amount to anything. They're just making believe." An officer went out to look at the clothes-line telegraph with his field-glass. There had been quite a shifting over there among the army flannels. "But how do you know but there is something in it?"

"Do you see those two blankets pinned together at the bottom?" said Dabney. "Yes, but what of it?" said the officer. "Why, that's her way of making a fish-trap; and when she pins the clothes together that way, it means that Lee is only trying to draw us into his fish-trap." As long as the two armies lay watching each other on the opposite banks of the stream, Dabney, with his clothes-line telegraph, continued to be one of the promptest and most reliable of General Hooker's scouts.[297]

Lucy Ann Walker put her life in jeopardy to provide vital intelligence to the Army of the Potomac. When the two armies moved away from Fredericksburg and Falmouth in June 1863, she evidently was able to rejoin her husband. They both lived in Washington, D.C., after the war.[298]

A Mule Driver or Dabney.
Courtesy LOC

Artist Edwin Forbes drew a sketch entitled "A mule driver" at Kelly's Ford, Virginia, on November 23, 1863. In an 1890 volume of Forbes' sketches, text was added that identifies Dabney as the sketch's subject.[299] Whether the sketch truly represents the intrepid Dabney, or whether Forbes simply applied Dabney's name to the sketch to lend interest to the reader and improve book sales, is impossible to know.

THE BLIGHT

The cruelty of slavery and a society based upon it debased not only African Americans, but also those among the white population not fortunate enough to fall within the aristocracy. Poor whites remained tethered to a socially oppressed class order. Throughout the antebellum period, public education was denied to those below Southern gentry. A northern newspaper declared, "Never will Virginia's White children be generally schooled until her Black ones shall cease to be sold."[300] In 1861, 85,000 poor white adults in Virginia could not read or write.[301]

During the war, soldiers from northern states continued to note the lack of general education in Virginia. With most of the affluent residents of Falmouth having fled elsewhere, Lieutenant Josiah Marshall Favill, adjutant of the 57th New York Infantry, wrote of those who remained in the village in late 1862: "As for the rest of the inhabitants, they are what are called poor whites, and are very poor indeed, both mentally and physically, mostly women and children with a few decrepit old men."[302]

In February 1863, Private William Ray of Company F, 7th Wisconsin Volunteers, was stationed as a "safeguard" at a house near the picket line assigned his unit. The picket line and house were beyond the village of Falmouth, further out in Stafford County. In his diary, Ray recorded his impressions about the family he found at the house:

> Supper over, we chat with the Family awhile. They consist of the two old folks and their two grown up Girls or young ladies, more properly speaking and they all were so ignorant that one person raised in the North would know more than them all. Oh but they were worse than any Negro that had been in the North 6 months. I never had an Idea before how Ignorant a person could be. But I see where the Blight of Slavery has been. There is Ignorance to the worst degree. The poor white is Below the negro if anything.[303]

The chaplain of a Pennsylvania regiment recorded his similar observations:

> . . . the negroes of Virginia are superior to the poor whites of the same state. The negro is much more the active, hopeful, and earnest: the white man is ignorant to a proverb, listless and indifferent to all present interest, and unconcerned about his future. But the negro has a much more lively, cheerful nature, and a shrewd aptitude for acquiring useful arts which throws the whites into the shade . . . They speak of the

wrongs they have suffered with a calmness and spirit of forgiveness which, if borne by white men, would place on their heads the crown of martyrdom . . . Something of that universal impulse felt by the human mind in all lands, found its way into every slave cabin . . .[304]

The human mind, inspired by the heart, shapes in the future an ideal that survives the decay of dogmas.

_____Moncure Conway

The Madness

As a witness of the cruel institution of slavery, the abolitionist Moncure Conway described a virtual state of madness among the slave-holding whites who became themselves slaves to the institution. "That institution seems actually to have been so worshiped as at length to have been invested with the awful power of creating a generation of human beings in its own image and likeness; one which, at its faintest wish, is willing to sacrifice to its idol all that is human or generous."[305] On May 22, 1856, Charles Sumner, Senator from Massachusetts, was beaten into unconsciousness in the Senate by the Representative from South Carolina. Sumner was a member of the Unitarian Church in Washington, D.C., and while he was convalescing in bed, was often visited by his minister, Reverend Moncure Conway.[306] That same year, Conway was sent packing from his pulpit due to his anti-slavery sermons.[307] A lady residing in Stafford County wrote, "Moncure Conway has been dismissed from his church in Washington for preaching Abolition. Even the Unitarians have good taste enough to be disgusted with him."[308]

The year 1862 witnessed a mass exodus of thousands of self-emancipating slaves. Not surprisingly, slave owners and other whites became upset about this turn of fortune. A correspondent for the *New York Times* reported "From Fredericksburg" on September 7, 1862, that "It is not a very grievous spectacle to witness the madness and dismay manifested by the Secessionists, as they look on and see this army of their 'most trusted and faithful servants' going off."

Captain Noyes, whose unit had spent the spring of 1862 at Falmouth and returned for the Battle of Fredericksburg, expressed his insightful, even prescient, perspective on the South's slave-holding society and its inherent influences on individuals:

> Somehow I had never been able to get up a feeling of hatred against the Southerner, even after the attack on Sumter—pitying him rather as the worst victim of an accursed system which surrounds his cradle, and is the companion of his childhood, whose divine origin and sanctions are impressed upon him from the pulpit, and taught him at the school, entering unquestioned into all the ramifications of his social life. His present suicidal madness had seemed to me only a part of the disease. It was not, then, with any desire for revenge, but solely to restrain him from blindly involving North and South in one common ruin, we had come hither; and it was thus impossible for me to look upon these citizens of Fredericksburg as my enemies, but rather as my countrymen, to come back by-and-by, when their insanity was over, to the old fraternal relationship, perhaps forever disenthralled from that system which was the cause of their present madness.[309]

Comfortable Quarters

In January 1862, in acknowledgment of outstanding service, the 20th Massachusetts Volunteer Infantry was assigned to provost guard duty in the village of Falmouth. Between December 11 and 13, 1862, the regiment had sustained more than sixty percent casualties. Under fire, it had led the pontoon crossing of the Rappahannock River, helped push the Confederate sharpshooters from the river to allow the engineers to construct the bridge, and charged against the stone wall at the foot of Marye's Heights during the Battle of Fredericksburg. In the Twentieth's sector of battle lay more than 7,000 dead and wounded comrades.

The ensanguined field of battle was described as "... anything calculated to leave a stronger or more lasting impression upon the mind than what met the eye of every beholder during the last moments of the battle ... its color of crimson and of red." The survivors of the Twentieth "... saw the blood-red sun pausing above the hills and wished it gone—saw the dusk come on and thought it slow in coming—saw the hills lifting higher in the evening gloom and looking down upon them with a more savage frown—saw the red earth epaulements turn to dusky brown and loose the sharpness of their outlines—saw the day fade into night and all the stars come out—felt the air grow cold and the earth freeze...."[310]

Performing as provost guard meant the men could spend the cold winter with comfortable quarters in the vacant homes in the village, a more desirable situation than occupying little huts they would have to build on some bleak hillside. Josiah Fitch Murphy, Orderly Sergeant, Company I, was wounded on December 11. Once recovered, he rejoined his regiment in March 1863. He wrote, "I finally returned to my regiment which was located at Falmouth Va. just above the city of Fredericksburg on the opposite side of the river [Rappahannock] only a short distance from were [sic] we camped when we went into battle. I found our regiment occupying negro or slave quarters with nice wooden bunks to sleep in doing picket duty on the river front."[311]

The 20th Massachusetts used the Conway House for its winter quarters. Orderly Sergeant Murphy's reference to "negro or slave quarters" likely refers to the kitchens and cabins nearby and behind Conway House, including the cabin of the house servants Dunmore and Eliza Gwinn. The cabins were vacant; the Conway slaves had found more comfortable quarters in the free state of Ohio.

THE DIVINE IDEA

The somewhat indefinable phrase "Divine Idea," the "Idea," or "Fair Ideal America" derived from the American intellectual Transcendentalist movement, which flourished in the second quarter of the 19th century. The ideology implies our Founding Fathers' concept that all men are created equal, which was fundamental to our nation's independence.[312] The Transcendentalists ascribed "Divine" attributes to "all men are created equal." No man was to hold property in another man. Sadly, the institution of slavery was left intact by the First Constitutional Convention and the abolitionist view of "the right of every man to himself" plunged the Nation into a great divide.

Julia Ward Howe, author of the *Battle Hymn of the Republic*.
Courtesy LOC

In December of 1862, the Battle of Fredericksburg resulted in a horrific sacrifice of life by the Union army. Julia Ward Howe visited the Falmouth area in the spring of 1863. From Chatham Manor, she looked across the Rappahannock River on the scene of the late great battle:

> Farewell, brisling heights! Farewell, sad Fredericksburg! Farewell, river of sorrows; farewell, soldiers death-determined, upon whose mournful sacrifice we must shut unwilling eyes. Would it were all at end! The dead wept and buried, the living justified before God. For the deep and terrible secret of the divine idea still lies buried in the burning bosom of the contest.

Suspected by the few, shunned by the many, it has not as yet leapt to light in the sight of all. This direful tragedy, in whose third dreary act we are, hangs all upon a great thought. To interpret this, through waste and woe, is the first moral obligation of the situation . . . This terrible development of moral causes and effects will enchain the wonder of the world until the crisis of poetical justice which must end it shall have won the acquiescence of mankind, carrying its irresistible lesson into the mind of the critics, into the heart of the multitude.[313]

In the beauty of the lilies Christ was born across the sea,
With a glory in His bosom that transfigures you and me;
As he died to make men holy, let us die to make men free,
While God is marching on

_____Julia Ward Howe

The God of Battles

In late April and early May of 1863, the Union army at Falmouth moved west in echelon as it embarked on its spring campaign. The result was the Battle of Chancellorsville. On the evening of May 2, after nearly routing the Union army, Confederate Lieutenant General Thomas Jonathan "Stonewall" Jackson personally reconnoitered the battlefield. Accompanying Jackson on this ill-fated reconnaissance was Captain James Fitzgerald Forbes of Falmouth. Both officers were wounded by troops of the 18th North Carolina Infantry who mistakenly thought they were firing on Yankee cavalry in the gathering darkness. Jackson was hit twice in the left arm and once in his right hand.[314] Captain Forbes' horse was killed and he was shot through the body. Forbes was the son of Murray and Sallie Forbes, who fled Falmouth the preceding year (in the vignette "They took the Nurse Girl").

Captain Forbes was taken to a nearby house where a member of Jackson's staff placed a mattress on the floor in order to make him as comfortable as possible. Although lying mortally wounded, Forbes ordered that a wounded Federal officer be moved from the hard floor to the mattress and placed alongside him. There, both men died.[315]

Captain Forbes died on May 4, six days before Jackson, who succumbed to a deadly complication, pneumonia, at Guinea Station in Caroline County.[316] Neither Jackson nor Forbes—one known to the world, the other only to Falmouth—would live to see the Confederacy defeated, their way of life changed forever. Instead, both men were linked together in a single fateful moment, one of the greatest turning points in American military history. It is quite possible had the mighty Jackson not been mortally wounded, the Confederacy would have won the war and slavery left intact.

Dr. Hunter McGuire, the attending surgeon to General Jackson, wrote an account of the last words of "this stern worshiper of the God of Battles."[317] "A few moments before he died he cried out in his delirium, 'Order A.P. Hill to prepare for action! Pass the infantry to the front rapidly! Tell Major Hawks'—then stopped, leaving the sentence unfinished. Presently a smile of ineffable sweetness spread itself over his pale face, and he said quietly, and with an expression, as if of relief, 'Let us cross over the river, and rest under the shade of the trees.'"[318]

A WAIL FROM THE HOUSE OF BONDAGE

On May 22, 1863, the United Stated War Department's General Orders No. 143 established the Bureau of Colored Troops. The Bureau recruited African Americans and organized regiments to fight for the Union. These regiments were designated United States Colored Troops. Two of the Lacy slaves, a coach driver from Falmouth, a slave from Spotsylvania, and another from Orange County to the southwest, have been identified as USCT members.[319] Others probably enlisted while in Washington or Georgetown after leaving Stafford County. By the end of the war, over 180,000 African Americans served in the ranks of the USCT. The African American soldiers were commanded by white officers. One of them, Captain George E. Sutherland, shared his recollections:

> The songs of any soldier's camp, especially in the evening hour are that part of war that no historian

has portrayed. When the boys gathered together, and sung out upon the night air their hopes and loves and sadness in a common song; when they told in music the heart's deepest thoughts of home and mother and heaven; when they sung, "We shall meet, but we shall miss him," "Tramp, tramp, tramp, the boys are marching," "We are coming, Father Abraham," and many others which each soldier recalls, there was knit a bond of sympathy for each other, and fixed a devotion to duty and country that only the next fierce battle fully revealed. But the song of the negro, like his religion, was a moan. It was a wail from the house of bondage, and contained the weird and suppressed sadness of long and cruel servitude.

You stand a little distance from a camp fire. The night is still. Presently you hear one deep, rich voice: *"I know moon rise, I know star rise,"* and then two or three, *"Lay dis body down."* Then the single voice again: *I walk in the moon light, I walk in the star light,* and the refrain is taken up by half a dozen, *"To lay dis body down."*

The single voice goes on: *"I'll walk in the grave yard, I'll walk troo'de grave yard,"* and then you are lifted as by a Creation chorus, for now there are fifty voices, and with such wonderful, deep, rich, melody as only the negro can produce, they join in together:

"To lay dis body down."
"I go to de judgment in de ebening of day,
When I lay dis body down.
And my soul and your soul will meet in the day
When I lay dis body down."

While listening to this wild imagery, poured forth in sad cadence, one could but feel—"Woe to those by whom the whole life of a race has been so shadowed and dejected that its constant song is of an oppression broken only by death, the grave and the judgment." It was a blessed mercy that nearly every slave could sing, and in this way, through years of bondage, give relief to his accumulating and pent up sorrow.[320]

The 3rd USCT Regimental Flag inscribed, "Rather Die Freemen, Than Live To Be Slaves."
Courtesy LOC

. . . as my strength was then, even so is my strength now, for war, both to go out, and to come in.

_____Joshua 14:11

WRITING ON THE WALL

An event of epic proportion took place in American history as the mass migration of a people formally held in bondage moved through

Falmouth and Stafford County while making their way to freedom. The movement of literally thousands of these freedom seekers left little if any physical evidence behind to mark their journey. With the exception of a single written account by ex-slave John Washington, not a trace remained to memorialize their former status or passing.

In contrast, the vast number of Union soldiers who made possible the "gateway to freedom" left a sizable record of physical evidence to attest to their presence. Numerous accounts of Falmouth during the war exist in reports, period newspapers, and soldiers' letters sent home. Camp debris now seen as relics and artifacts have been sought after and collected by individuals, historians, and museums. Some of Falmouth's buildings bear tangible witness to the war. Union soldiers left their names and graffiti carved into brick and scratched in plaster walls.

After the war, Falmouth residents purposely removed graffiti and other vestiges related to the Union occupation.[321] The hand of time also did its work to sweep away evidence of the army's presence in the town. At least four personal testimonials to the presence of Union soldiers survived in Falmouth, however. When looking at the ghastly causality figures the Union army sustained, one can surmise the staggering sacrifice in human life and suffering laid upon the altar of freedom. By fate, these seemingly insignificant examples of graffiti remind us of the army that made that sacrifice. The stories of three of these men remind us that not all the casualties of war occur on the battlefield.

Edwin H. Eames left his mark on a window frame in the attic of Conway House: "Edwin H. Eames Bloody F 20th Mass. V." Eames was in Company F of the previously mentioned 20th Massachusetts Volunteer Infantry. Originally from Maine, he was the tenth child in a family of eleven children. He enlisted at 17 years of age as a drummer boy. Eames participated in all the major battles of the war in which the Army of the Potomac fought. The 20th Massachusetts suffered one of the highest casualty rates among Union regiments during the war. Eames returned home to Maine and never married. He died in 1881 "from wounds received in battle."[322]

Daniel Shanahan, also of Company F, penned a letter in April 1863, but it was never mailed. It was found under a floorboard of the attic in Conway House in 2003. Shanahan was wounded at the Second Battle of Reams Station, near Petersburg on August 25, 1864. He was taken prisoner and confined at Libby and Belle Isle in Richmond and at Salisbury, North Carolina. He survived the war, but suffered dizzy spells from a fractured skull wound. Unable to hold a job in Boston or elsewhere after the war, Shanahan eventually ended up in Minnesota and lived as a trader among the Indians (possibly Objibwe) in Crow Wing County. He was denied a pension for his wound, the result of a government mix up with another soldier from Minnesota. Shanahan succumbed in 1884 from the chronic "lung fever" he contracted while in a southern prison. He left behind two destitute children by a wife described as a "notoriously characterless squaw." On the children's behalf, a concerned party wrote the US Pension Office and related their dire condition. The children were denied assistance by the US Government, which at the time held the view that a marriage to a Native American was not a legal union.[323]

Inside the Union Church, in the balcony to which African Americans were restricted during services, another soldier etched his identity in the plaster: "7 M Edward Wise Co I." Prior to the Battle of Fredericksburg, the men of the 7th Michigan Volunteer Infantry heroically volunteered to row across the Rappahannock River and clear the shore of Confederate sharpshooters who were preventing, most effectively, the Union army's engineers from building the pontoon bridges required for the army to pass over the river and launch an attack on the Confederate army. This was what we would call a suicide mission today, and for that reason the 7th Michigan became known as the "Forlorn Hope." Wise survived the crossing and the war, and returned to Michigan. He worked as a railroad engineer and in the paper mills. Wise hired himself out as a hand to work on a farm in the hopes that the change would improve his health. He hung himself in a barn in 1887. The *Monroe Democrat* attributed his death to sunstroke sustained during the war, which was said to have affected his mind. The newspaper noted, "He complained a great deal of his head."[324]

Writing on the wall, Edward Wise
graffiti inside Union Church.
Photograph by the author

A wall of the Duff Green Warehouse bears the inscription "J. COLLINS Co I, 5th MICH CAV." The brick warehouse belonged to the Green family of Falmouth.[325] Five of six sons are known to have served in the Confederate army.[326] Although James Collins was an insignificant actor on a larger stage, his mark represents the indelible hand of the liberator writing on the wall of slavery (see "The Beating"). The Fifth Michigan Cavalry was part of the Michigan Brigade known as the "Wolverines" and commanded by Brigadier General George Armstrong Custer. Collins was in Falmouth for about a week in August 1863, with the Fifth acting as scouts and pickets. After leaving Falmouth, James Collins was later captured on July 9, 1864, at Morton's Ford along the Rapidan River in Orange County. He was sent to the infamous Andersonville Prison where he died and was buried.[327]

In May 1864, two large scale battles took place west of Falmouth. The Battle of the Wilderness and the Battle of Spotsylvania Court House brought another round of mass casualties. More than 26,000 wounded inundated Fredericksburg and Falmouth. As the war progressed, more men would die and many more wounded would suffer to the south as the two opposing armies converged on Richmond and Petersburg.

Therefore this crisis is the most solemn hour that Eternity has dialed on Time; and ages past and coming meet here, and stand unveiled and expectant.

———————Moncure Conway

TESTIMONIES CONCERNING SLAVERY

Historian John d'Entremont, in his biography of Moncure Conway, gives us the following description of the abolitionist: "Moncure Conway was the most thoroughgoing white male radical produced by the antebellum South, and the threat his values of equality and individual autonomy posed to the Southern social system was as real and as fundamental as a threat could be. It is for this reason that Conway stands as one of the most important and illuminating antebellum Southern deviants, and as a major figure in American history."[328] Despite being banished from Falmouth, Conway nevertheless became an emissary to Great Britain for the abolitionist cause in America. From Boston in 1863, the famous Northern abolitionist William Lloyd Garrison wrote:

> Mr. Conway is on an anti-slavery mission to England, and cannot fail at this time to make something of a sensation when the particulars of his remarkable case are known. He is a native Virginian, the son of a large slaveholder whose slaves the son has safely conveyed to a free State since the rebellion broke out, (the father adhering to the cause of the Southern Confederacy,) and related to some of the most prominent families in the Ancient Dominion. His abolitionism is of the strongest quality, and his zeal and enthusiasm, as well as his moral intrepidity, of the true heroic stamp. No such witness against slavery and the rebellion has yet appeared in England.[329]

In 1863 and 1864, while living in England, Moncure Conway's efforts included convincing the British not to recognize the Confederacy as a legitimate government. Many of Britain's political and social figures sympathized with the South. From his lectures and speeches, Conway published a 145-page book, called *Testimonies Concerning Slavery*. Stafford County historian and author Albert Z. Conner wrote about this son of Falmouth and his belief in a "New South."

> At the end of *Testimonies*, Conway turned to the social outcomes he was projecting for the warring South, the "Negro race," and America. This was the most remarkable and insightful work he wrote during the war, and perhaps during his life and long career. Conway first forecast that, once the South's searing hatred had turned to mere animosities, the country would see the emergence of what would later be termed a "New South"—a place of greater industrial and economic potentials, public education, and legal and, conceivably, eventual social justice. He remarkably predicted that "the aristocracy of slavemongers shall be plucked up by the roots" because the planter class had been or would be broken and dispersed by the war. He then attempted to predict for his British audiences the resulting future directions of America itself. Conway expressed these directions in core values and terms of the French Revolution of "Liberty, Equality and Fraternity,"—keeping in mind that the 1789 French *Declaration of the Rights of Man and of the Citizen* had been liberally and openly lifted from George Mason's (IV) Virginia Declaration of Rights and its derivative U.S. Declaration of Independence. Here Conway put his own, brilliantly particular stamp on the underlying political theories of America in expressing these three as a *progression or sequence* rather than as co-equal branches of democracy. He related that Liberty, the preoccupation of his anti-Federalist ancestors and contemporaries in the Confederate States, was the heart's goal of every person, whether Northerner or Southerner, male or female, black or white. The Civil War in which, to Conway's mind, the abolitionists rather

than the Southerner anti-Federalists were deemed the true revolutionaries, was truly a war for Equality, which he defined as "the right of each to do and be his best, under God, without human hindrance." The highest order of this progression, according to Conway, would be a (future) drive toward the "full glory" of "Human Fraternity," apparently meaning full respect for each person by society.[330]

. . . when wars shall cease—when, after the wind and the fire, shall come the still small voice that shall lead Liberty and Equality to their full glory in Human Fraternity.

_____Moncure Conway

THEN I LAID MY BURDEN DOWN

On May 15, 1864, the American Freedmen's Inquiry Commission submitted its "Final Report" to the Secretary of War, in which was stated, "No race of men appears better to have obeyed the injunction not to return evil for evil, or to have acted more strictly in the spirit of the text: 'Vengeance is mine! I will repay, saith the Lord.'"[331]

A former slave from Northern Virginia, in which Falmouth is included, gave this testimony to a Union officer:

> I knew that a day of revenge would come for all this, but I did not expect it to fall on us in the way of war between North and South . . . my soul was moved, and I cried, "O Lord! why has this curse come on Virginia?" And it appeared to me as plain as I ever heard human speech, a voice spoke to me and said, "O man! knowest thou the land most highly favored of heaven, and where, because God was good, men became desperately wicked, and inflicted the greatest wrongs?" And the voice said, "Virginia." Again I heard, "Knowest thou, O man! the land where human beings were bred as cattle for the market, and where every year thousands

of them were sent forth to a fate which they dreaded more than death?" The answer came, "Virginia." Again the voice said, "Knowest thou the land where, in the midst of the greatest blessings, there has been the deepest misery; where most faces were washed in tears, and most hearts torn with anguish; and where the constant wail of distress, inflicted by man on his fellow, was going up into the ears of God?" And the voice said, "Virginia." Again the voice said, "God is just." Then I laid my burden down. And as often as I have mourned since, I have been silenced by that voice, "God is just."[332]

> *He is coming like the glory of the morning on the wave,*
> *He is Wisdom to the mighty, He is Succor to the brave,*
> *So the world shall be His footstool, and the soul of Time His slave,*
> *Our God is marching on.*
>
> ──────── Battle Hymn of the Republic

WITH MALICE TOWARD NONE

On March 4, 1865, Abraham Lincoln delivered his Second Inaugural Address just fifty-five miles to the north of the war torn village of Falmouth. That place had played an important role in the "gateway to freedom" and the self-emancipation of thousands of former slaves. The last two paragraphs of the Address relate to the great question of slavery then facing the nation:

Fellow-Countrymen:

One-eighth of the whole population were colored slaves, not distributed generally over the Union, but localized in the southern part of it. These slaves constituted a peculiar and powerful interest. All knew that this interest was somehow the cause of the war. To strengthen, perpetuate, and extend this interest was the object for which the insurgents would rend the Union even by war, while the Government claimed no right to do more than to restrict the territorial enlargement of it. Neither party expected for the war the magnitude or the duration which it has already attained. Neither anticipated that the cause of the conflict might cease with or even before the conflict itself should cease. Each looked for an easier triumph, and a result less fundamental and astounding. Both read the same Bible and prayed to the same God, and each invokes His aid against the other. It may seem strange that any men should dare to ask a just God's assistance in wringing their bread from the sweat of other men's faces, but let us judge not, that we be not judged. The prayers of both could not be answered. That of neither has been answered fully. The Almighty has His own purposes. "Woe unto the world because of offenses; for it must needs be that offenses come, but woe to that man by whom the offense cometh." If we shall suppose that American slavery is one of those offenses which, in the providence of God, must needs come, but which, having continued through His appointed time, He now wills to remove, and that He gives to both North and South this terrible war as the woe due to those by whom the offense came, shall we discern therein any departure from those divine attributes which the believers in a living God always ascribe to Him? Fondly, do we hope, fervently do we pray, that this mighty scourge of war may speedily pass away. Yet, if God wills that it continue until all the wealth piled by the bondsman's two hundred and fifty years of unrequited toil shall be sunk, and until every drop of blood drawn with the lash shall be paid by another drawn with the sword, as was said three thousand years ago, so still it must be said "the judgments of the Lord are true and righteous altogether."

> With malice toward none, with charity for all, with firmness in the right as God gives us to see the right, let us strive on to finish the work we are in, to bind up the nation's wounds, to care for him who shall have born the battle and for his widow and his orphan, to do all which may achieve and cherish a just and lasting peace among ourselves and with all nations.[333]

Finally, on April 9, 1865, General Lee surrendered his army at Appomattox Court House. The son of James and Elizabeth Vass, Reverend L.C. Vass (see the vignette "A Tisket, A Tasket, A Red and Yellow Basket"), was the Confederate Post Chaplain at Petersburg, Virginia. He ministered to the spiritual needs of the many wounded and dying soldiers in the Petersburg hospitals during the last days of the Confederacy. After the surrender, Vass continued in the city for some time giving care to the soldiers and writing in his diary. "How anxious we have been about Gen. Lee. We would not believe the first reports about his surrender. Men cried when told on their beds that Gen. Lee had capitulated. Many would not believe it and scarcely credit it now (five days) after it has occurred."[334]

> *The ancient village [Falmouth] has, by the devastations of war, been almost obliterated from the earth.*
>
> _____Moncure Conway

O CAPTAIN! MY CAPTAIN!

President Abraham Lincoln visited Stafford County six times during the Civil War for a total of fourteen days.[335] It is not known if the President passed through the town of Falmouth. He did visit nearby Chatham. On April 14, 1865, the assassination of Abraham Lincoln took place, five days after General Lee surrendered the Army of Northern Virginia. Walt Whitman wrote a poem in tribute to the fallen President, the ex-slaves' Father Abraham. The poem first appeared in 1865 as an appendix to Whitman's ever expanding collection *Leaves of Grass*. Moncure Conway was Whitman's London agent who successfully promoted his poems to an English audience. Conway would officiate at Whitman's funeral in 1892 upon the death of the "Good Grey Poet."

O Captain! My Captain!

O Captain! My Captain! Our fearful trip is done,
The ship has weather'd every rack, the prize we sought is won,
The port is near, the bells I hear, the people all exulting,
While follow eyes the steady keel, the vessel grim and daring;
But O heart! heart! heart!
O the bleeding drops of red,
Where on the deck my Captain lies,
Fallen cold and dead.

O Captain! my Captain! Rise up and hear the bells;
Rise up—for you the flag is flung—for you the bugle trills,
For you bouquets and ribbon'd wreaths—for you the shores a-crowding,
For you they call, the swaying mass, their eager faces turning;
Here Captain! dear father!
This arm beneath your head! It is some dream that on the deck,
You've fallen cold and dead.

My Captain does not answer, his lips are pale and still,
My father does not feel my arm, he has no pulse nor will,
The ship is anchor'd safe and sound, its voyage closed and done,
From fearful trip the victor ship comes in with object won;
Exult O shores, and ring O bells!
But I with mournful tread,
Walk the deck my Captain lies,
Fallen cold and dead.

The first reading of the Emancipation Proclamation before the cabinet. From the original painting at the White House.
Courtesy LOC

PART IV

FALMOUTH AFTER THE WAR

Moncure Conway wrote, "Virginia became the chief battlefield on which the civil war was waged, and the struggle left her a desolate and scarred memorial of the retribution that violated justice can bring upon a state . . ."[336]

The Civil War was followed by a period in United States history known as Reconstruction, which historians generally view as dating from 1865 to 1877. Like much of the South, Falmouth suffered indelibly from the war. Property values in town were significantly reduced by 1865, and little new construction occurred after the war. The "violated justice," referred to by Conway, brought ". . . the iniquity of the fathers upon the children unto the third and fourth generation . . ."[337] Falmouth, and all of Stafford County, entered a bleak and unproductive period that lasted for 80 years. The census of 1860 recorded the county's population as 8,555; in 1870, that number had fallen to 6,420. Not until the Second World War did the county surpass its pre-Civil War growth.[338]

During Reconstruction, some African Americans who left during the war returned to Stafford County and Falmouth. Of those that stayed, some exercised new freedoms while others left for good. Life was generally hard as farmland left fallow during the war had to be reclaimed by clearing away the undergrowth which had taken over. Religion and education played an important roll in the lives of the ex-slaves in Falmouth. They built their own church and began educating their children. The winds of change gently blew upon the town and separated the shadows. In 1870, the Fifteenth Amendment gave African Americans the right to vote.

During this period, the Southern states passed numerous laws aimed at restricting the new freedoms of African Americans. These laws were called "Black Codes." Virginia's laws were modest in comparison with those of the other states in the deeper South. In some cases, Virginia law reinforced the rights of African Americans but did nothing to eliminate racism. African Americans survived in Falmouth by looking after one another and by exercising a firm commitment in faith.

NOT YET MAN

In *Testimonies Concerning Slavery*, Conway expounded on his childhood experiences and observations in Falmouth and used these to relate to the British audience the repugnant evil of slavery in America. While in England, Conway was a frequent visitor at the home of Thomas Carlyle, a highly influential man of letters in British political and economic affairs. Mrs. Carlyle, ". . . was well read, intelligent, witty, full of sensibility . . ."[339]

Thomas Carlyle, elected Lord Rector
of Edinburgh University.
Courtesy LOC

Conway wrote, "In a modest old mansion, apart from the great whirl of fashion, resided Carlyle, the man to whose wonderful genius more than to any other is to be attributed the intellectual and spiritual activity of his generation."[340] Conway further recorded one of his visits:

> When the Union war had nearly closed, Carlyle spoke so stormily against emancipation that Mrs. Carlyle—the only other present—interrupted him. "Carlyle," she said, "you ought not to talk so much against a cause to a man who has suffered and made sacrifices for it." Carlyle, who always took his wife's reproof meekly, turned to me and said softly, "You will be patient with me. All the worth you have put into your cause will be returned to you personally; but the America for which you are hoping you will never see: and you will never see the whites and blacks in the South dwelling together as equals in peace."[341]

Human Unity. Men we have; but not yet Man.

———————Moncure Conway

AND NOT THIS MAN

"Is not the negro a man?" The question was posed by a Union soldier writing from Falmouth in April 1862. "Warmed by the same sun, hurt with the same weapons, having the same feelings, affections, aspirations that the white man has?"[342]

The word "franchise" possesses a much older definition than the one which generally comes to mind in today's culture. We think of franchise in terms of association with modern business. The original meaning being to set free, freedom, liberty, the full right of citizenship, and the franchise of every citizen to vote.[343] After the war, a great question faced the nation: would African Americans, especially those who fought in the nation's epic Civil War, be granted a franchise in the Republic?

Negro Battle Hymn

Chorus—
    They look like men,
    They look like men,
    They look like men of war.

    The National Union League was very active in the South during Reconstruction. Established in 1862, the National Union League was a Northern patriotic organization that supported loyalty to the Union and the policies of Abraham Lincoln. After the war, the National Union League mobilized the Freedmen to vote.[344] Carlyle's pessimism of white and black equality was evident in the preceding vignette. In 1865, *Harpers Weekly* published a drawing by Thomas Nast entitled "Franchise." Nast depicts Columbia with her hand on the shoulder of a black soldier who lost a leg in the war. As if responding to Conway's rhetorical, "But not yet Man," Columbia ask, "And Not this Man?"

"FRANCHISE. And Not This Man?" A great question faced the nation, would African Americans be granted a "franchise" in the Republic?
Courtesy LOC

The Freedmen's Bureau

The Freedmen and Southern Society Project was established in 1976 to "capture the essence" of emancipation by transcribing, organizing, and annotating some 50,000 selected documents dealing with slavery. The Project writers stated, "In the United States, emancipation accompanied the defeat of the world's most powerful slaveholding class and freed a larger number of slaves than did the end of slavery in all other New World societies combined. Clothed in the rhetoric of biblical prophecy and national destiny and born of a bloody civil war, it accomplished a profound social revolution."[345]

On March 3, 1865, before the war had ended, President Lincoln signed into law a new Federal agency, the Bureau of Refugees, Freedmen, and Abandoned Lands. The Bureau was backed by military force. It was part of the War Department, and General O.O. Howard was its first commissioner. It provided rations, schooling, accessibility to courts, and medical care to freed African Americans. The Bureau regulated labor policies for freed slaves to work on former plantation lands under pay scales fixed by the Bureau.

Like the US Army itself, the Bureau was organized into Districts. The headquarters of the Virginia Freedmen's Bureau was located in Richmond. On June 6, 1865, Major General A.H. Terry, who commanded the Department of Virginia, issued General Order No. 77 from the former Capital of the Confederacy:

> The laws of the State of Virginia ... made to restrain the personal liberty of free colored persons were designed for the Government of such persons while living amid a population of colored slaves. They were enacted for the security of slave property: they were substantially parts of the Slave Code. Slavery has been abolished in Virginia and therefore upon the principle that where the reason of the law ceases, the law itself ceases. These Laws and Ordinances have become obsolete. People of color will henceforth enjoy the same personal liberty that other citizens and inhabitants enjoy.[346]

The Virginia Freedmen's Bureau was divided into Sub Districts. The Sixth Sub District, 1st Division, included the jurisdictions of the City of Fredericksburg and the Counties of Stafford, King George, and Spotsylvania. Its headquarters was located in the Farmer's Bank building in Fredericksburg. African Americans living in Stafford County and Falmouth had to go to Fredericksburg to conduct their business. By February 1866, there was a school, church, "Sabbath School," and hospital operating in Fredericksburg for the freedmen in the city "and surrounding counties."[347]

In order to gain perspective on the operations of the Freedmen's Bureau in Falmouth, one must look to the Bureau's reports pertaining to Stafford County. On February 16, 1866, the Bureau's Sixth Sub District Commissioner, Brevet Captain Hector Sears, commented on the social dynamics in Stafford County: "In reference to the 'feeling existing between the whites and blacks' I have to state that the whites have not a kindly feeling or do they show good will toward the blacks ... they have been threatened and fear violence, and my observations warrant me in expressing fears that in some cases these threats would be executed were it not for the military." Another report was filed on February 28, "The whites appear to really hate the Freedmen . . ."[348]

The Freedmen's Bureau by Alfred Waud
and illustrated in *Harpers Weekly*.
Courtesy LOC

The Bureau's Circular 10, dated March 12, 1866, restored control of Freedmen's criminal cases to the civil authorities. On May 31, 1866, from his headquarters in Fredericksburg, Superintendent James Johnson of the 10th Bureau District, which included the Sixth Sub District, expressed his concern to Brevet Brigadier General Orlando Brown, Assistant Commissioner of the Freedmen's Bureau of Virginia:

> My impressions are however that in the event that the protection now afforded should be withdrawn—a portion of the Blacks (most especially those who left during the War and have since returned, a large portion of them being of this class) would suffer severe punishments at the hands of the Civil Authorities for trifling offences—and that Whites will scarcely be held for trial for crimes committed against the Blacks except in exceedingly aggravated cases.[349]

Now that the Freedmen's cases were returned to civil authority, there was the fear that if protection offered by military presence were withdrawn also, the courts would render injustice toward the Freedmen.

It is of interest to note "a large portion" left during the war and returned. It is very likely, those Blacks who returned found farmlands and homes abandoned. Bureau offices were often located in cities and tended to draw African Americans away from the countryside. Naturally they would gravitate to Fredericksburg, where food and medical assistance could be obtained. Falmouth was just across the river. The Bureau alluded to a race riot in Falmouth, which occurred June 29, 1866, and reported via Military Telegraph from Fredericksburg to Richmond.[350]

The withdrawal of Bureau control over the justice system appears to have warranted the fears of Superintendent Johnson. On January 31, 1867, Commissioner Hector Sears reported that ". . . Duff Green a Magistrate of Stafford County Va. stated to me a short time since—words to the effect—that he did not intend to pay any more attention to the Freedmens Bureau . . ." On February 28, the Commissioner reported, "Same as before . . . essentially the whites and blacks don't trust each other, and the freedmen have no faith in the civil courts."[351] On November 30, 1867, Commissioner Sears reported a civil case demonstrating the inequity in justice faced by African Americans:

> Charles H. and Nathaniel Lucas brought suit against James L. Green of Stafford County for Ten dollars, damages done their crop by said Green's cattle, the case was tried at Falmouth by Justice F.B. Stone the judgment was, that Lucas should recover one dollar and fifty cents damages and pay his own costs [of court] which amounted to three dollars and seventy cents, bringing Lucas two dollars and twenty cents in debt besides loosing his corn.[352]

At the start of 1868, General Order No.102, HQ First Military Division, Richmond, Virginia, went into effect. From then on, the City of Fredericksburg and the Counties of Caroline, King George, and Spotsylvania became part of the 14th Division, Sub District of Richmond. Stafford County, including Falmouth was moved into the 19th Division, Sub District of Alexandria.[353] Freedmen in Stafford wishing to report a grievance or needing to conduct business with the Bureau would have to travel to Alexandria, almost fifty miles to the north. Not enough information exists to know if moving Stafford into another Sub District affected the Freedmen's nascent rights. Almost nothing about the Freedman's Bureau exists in Black oral history in Stafford County.

On February 29, 1868, the Bureau reported a case wherein, "James Moxley of Stafford County on the 16th inst. Committed an outrage upon a colored boy 11 years old named James King, by cruelly whipping said child, first stripping off the boys Coat tying his hands, then strapping them to a log in a stable or barn." According to a follow up report on May 30, "A White man was tried in Stafford for inhumanly whipping a small colored boy, he was fined one dollar and costs [of court]."[354] The Moxleys of Stafford were very poor and uneducated in contrast to the affluent and well-educated Greens of Falmouth (see "The Beating"). Their actions indicate that racial hatred and violence against African Americans knew no social boundaries in Stafford County's white society.

By June 1872, the Freedmen's Bureau activities were officially terminated by Congress. The agency had suffered corruption, inefficiency, and charges of misappropriated funds. Those who politically opposed the Radical Republican Party viewed the Freedmen's Bureau as a tool to help maintain Republican control of the states occupied by Federal troops.

The future in the United States of the African Race. Among the problems connected with the future destiny of our country, this is one of the most important.

_____Dr. Samuel Gridley Howe

Gathering Bones

The first known African American association with Falmouth is through their influence in pottery formed from out of the clay. On the recent Civil War battlefields, the bones of the dead cry out the sacred words of Job, "I also am formed out of the clay."[355] Following the war, the US Government ordered the remains of the Union's fallen dead exhumed for re-internment in newly established national cemeteries. African Americans provided the labor to perform this gruesome task as part of the US Burial Corps.

In Falmouth, the Union Church Cemetery had been used as a burial ground for soldiers who had died from wounds and disease. The church itself and nearby Conway House were utilized as hospitals. Beginning in 1866 and continuing through 1869, the remains gathered from Falmouth, Fredericksburg, and the surrounding area were deposited in the National Cemetery in Fredericksburg. More than 15,000 Union dead were recovered from the area, but most of the remains were never identified.

Gathering bones on a Virginia battlefield.
Courtesy LOC

Excerpts from *The Golden Hour*, Moncure Conway's second book written during the Civil War, form a fitting epitaph for the Union soldiers who gave their lives to bring an end to the oppressive system of slavery in the United States.

> *It may be that Liberty shall have to say presently to the slumbering sentinels, "Sleep on now: my hour is come";—and must needs pass to its resurrection through the dark portals of her chosen nation's grave.*
>
> *Who can appraise the hours which arrive, one by one . . . each proffering the sacred volumes in which the victorious destiny of a Free Republic is written?*
>
> *Thus they listen, thus they watch, more than they that watch for the morning . . .* [356]

In 1875, during Conway's return visit to the area, an unidentified "negro housemaid . . . sent me a beautiful bouquet gathered from the [new national] cemetery where lie the bodies of the Northern soldiers . . ."[357] Starting in 1867, local African Americans observed Memorial Day by placing flowers upon the Union dead in the National Cemetery in Fredericksburg. This they continued doing until 1884, when Union and Confederate veteran organizations excluded blacks from participating in commemorating the graves.[358]

THE LOOK OF FREEDOM

When the Union army occupied Falmouth during the war, many of its former businesses and buildings were taken over and turned into "grog shops" and saloons. Camp followers and traveling entrepreneurs took every opportunity to relieve the soldiers of their pay. An officer in the Second Regiment Pennsylvania Reserve Volunteers wrote of Falmouth, " . . . the town was filled with our sutlers, storekeepers and photographers . . ."[359]

In 2012, a remarkable photograph of an unknown African American surfaced in the Fredericksburg area. Very little information accompanied this amazing image. It could be from the Civil War period, or after the war.[360] The image merits closer observation. The plain canvas backdrop (with its pole curled at the bottom) is typical of those used by traveling photographers. The clothing appears to be Civil War period, but African Americans wore old style clothes (cast offs) long after the war.

A young man with the look of freedom.
Author's Collection

Could the subject be a freed slave who found employment by a Union officer? In most respects, a photographer's sitting would have been unaffordable by an African American. The subject in the image probably did not have two nickels to rub together. Perhaps a benefactor's generosity paid for the photograph. We may never know the circumstances which occasioned the photograph or the identity of the young man. One observation is certain; he has the look of freedom.

And they sung as it were a new song . . .

————————Revelation 14:3

The Congregation

Prior to the Civil War, Falmouth's Union Church was used by several denominations on a rotating basis. African Americans were allowed to attend services but were segregated from the white worshipers. To what extent African Americans attended these services remains unknown. Moncure Conway, however, suggests African Americans in Falmouth were familiar with the preaching of white ministers:

> Our own kitchen-fireside was nightly the scene of religious exercises and conversations which were very fascinating to me, and from which I had to be dragged with each returning bed-time. The dreams, visions, and ecstasies there related were as gorgeous as those of the *Pilgrim's Progress*; for these humble and ignorant souls, denied the reading of the Bible, had conceived a symbolism of their own, and burdens of prophecy, and had changed the fields on which they toiled into the pavements of the New Jerusalem, glorified with spirits arrayed in white. The cant phrases of the white preachers whom they listened to had become alive to them, and mingled strangely in their speech and hymns.[361]

The years of war that saw the Union Church used as a Federal military hospital and soldier's billet left the building ravaged. All of the church's interior woodwork and pews had been cut up for fire wood, and the church bell had been removed, most likely to be melted down in a northern foundry to make cannon.[362]

Soon after the war, the white citizens of Falmouth reclaimed their community's house of worship. In 1868, Falmouth officials executed a new deed for the church property. The deed required trustees to be appointed to carry out repairs to the church so that rotating services could resume among Episcopalian, Presbyterian, Methodist, and Baptist congregations. The deed is also very clear about who may not use the church. ". . . that the Congregation above mentioned as entitled to the use of said church shall be the white congregation of the respective denominations above named and shall not [be] construed to include any colored or black congregation."[363] Among the names signed on the document as one of the original six trustees is a name seen before, Duff Green.

Services were held in the Union church until 1935. The church fell into disrepair and was severely damaged in a storm in 1950. The narthex is all that remains of the sanctuary. The 1868 deed stands as a legal document at Stafford Court House and still governs the property, but its applicability regarding use is now moot.

THE UNION BRANCH OF THE TRUE VINE

The Union Branch of the True Vine was an African American organization created in Stafford County soon after the Civil War. It provided a form of community support and insurance to its local members:

> From the end of slavery, 1865, to approximately 1945, a period of eighty years, Union Branch of the True Vine provided an extremely valuable association for assurance and support for Former Slaves and Blacks in Southeastern Stafford County, Virginia... It has always been a service organization where its members assisted each other in times of need. Most of its members were farmers. If one member was unable to work his or her crops, the healthy members would get together and arrange to work the disabled member's crops. When a member died, the other members would assist the family of the deceased with the funeral and burial arrangements. There was no other form of insurance available to Black farmers.[364]

No doubt the work of this organization became even more significant after General Order No.102 was issued from Richmond in December 1867. The order shifted Stafford County along with Falmouth out of a Sub District of the Freedmen's Bureau with its headquarters in Fredericksburg, to another Sub District with its headquarters in distant Alexandria. In the region southeast of Falmouth, the Union Branch of the True Vine remains deeply woven into Black oral history.

The absence of early documentation for this organization may be attributed to post-war hardships when people were busy just making a living and trying to put food on the table. Given the hardships of everyday life and long days of work, no time was left for writing anything down by those who were literate. The first historical record of the organization dates to 1903 with its incorporation.[365] The organization appears to have operated mainly among the farming and rural African American families just beyond Falmouth's environs and out several miles to the east around White Oak. "Servant" was the title given to the person in charge of the organization, which continues today to conduct important community programs and provide a leadership role in the Black community.

We do know that there were prominent African Americans living in Falmouth during the Reconstruction period who would have been leaders in the Black community. In 1867, a "Report on Prominent Whites and Freedmen" by a Commissioner of the Freedman's Bureau included five names from Falmouth. These were Joseph B. Ficklen, a "Conservative Union" white; "York Johnson, colored; Charles H. Lears or Leavis, colored; Dorie Cartice [Dora Curtis], colored; and James Pryor [Prior], colored."[366]

As seen in a previous vignette, James Prior was a former Conway slave who lived in Falmouth after the war. It is interesting to note included among the names was that of a woman, Dora Curtis. She was a free black who owned property at the northern end of Falmouth. Dora is included in the 1830 Stafford census as free and is in the personal property tax records 1840 and 1841 when she paid on one horse. She is listed in the 1860 census as a 53 year old "black carpenter." Dora may have worked for John Moncure who sold to her Lot 61 in Falmouth, where she lived from 1840 until her death around 1873.[367]

Of special interest is York Johnson. His name appears along with the other individuals in the Freedmen's Bureau report identified as being from Falmouth, but the report indicates he is in Fredericksburg under the care of Dr. Hugh Morson. Fortunately, we do know more about York Johnson. He was the first pastor of Bethlehem Primitive Baptist Church, which still serves today as the "home church" of The Union Branch of the True Vine. In 1868, this church was organized out of White Oak Church when York Johnson was chosen as "Preacher" from among 27 "colored members" who "desire separate organization."[368]

Having been listed as a prominent Stafford citizen by the Freedmen's Bureau, it is quite possible that York Johnson was instrumental in starting The Union Branch of the True Vine and Bethlehem Primitive Baptist Church, with assistance from the Freedmen's Bureau.[369]

York Johnson's obituary appears in the *Fredericksburg Star* on April 29, 1885. It reads, "DEATH OF AN OLD COLORED MINISTER. York Johnson, a respected old colored Baptist minister, died at the residence of Jane Taylor, in Stafford County, on the 23rd instant at the advanced age of 88 years. He was widely known and bore a good character. He was once the slave of Dr. Hugh Morson, and had his full confidence."

Including the statement that York Johnson was once a slave having the "full confidence" of his master reminds us of "Faithful Servant" on the gravestone of the slave Osborne Merricks (seen previously). As in the excommunication of Anthony Burns from the Union Church, it demonstrates the power once held by the old mindset that slavery was sanctioned in Biblical scripture; a view perpetuated before the war by the proponents of slavery and one to be embraced by the dutiful slave as well.[370]

At the same time in May 1868 that Bethlehem Primitive Baptist Church was being formed, 59 "colored members" of White Oak Church moved to Alexandria and chose Fielding Robinson from among their number to serve as "Preacher." One wonders if Alexandria was chosen because it was the headquarters of the new Sub Division of the Freedmen's Bureau in which Stafford County was placed effective January 1, 1868. Certainly there would have been better employment opportunities, a black social network developing around Washington, D.C., and possibly friends and family there who had moved up during the war. With 32 more members who went to Alexandria, it appears that the majority of the black congregants of White Oak Church decided to leave Stafford forever.[371] For those that stayed, the work of The Union Branch of the True Vine filled a vital role within the African American community.

NEW FREEDOM

Beginning in 1785, the General Assembly of Virginia enacted a series of laws aimed at preventing slaves from assembling freely. Those caught breaking the laws "were punishable by whipping."[372] The laws did not seem to apply to labor-related or religious gatherings, as long as a white overseer or minister was present.

After the Civil War, African Americans gathered publicly in Falmouth as seen in a 1870s photograph of one of Falmouth's more prominent dwellings, the Forbes House. The photograph shows a few whites and a small group of African Americans to the right side of the front of the house.[373]

Forbes House, where African Americans can
be seen freely gathered on a public street.
Courtesy of National Park Service, Fredericksburg, VA

The Forbes House fronted on Willow Street (originally named Caroline Street). In the first quarter of the 20th century, Willow ran to the east end of town where it became little more that a wagon path. Bill Butler, a free black even before the Civil War, had a house just outside this end of town. Bill is thought to be a son of Elizah Butler (see the vignette "Elizah followed by a "B"). As Falmouth grew, Willow Street was extended and became known to the locals as "Bill Butler Road."[374] The name Willow was dropped. The African Americans captured in the 1870s photograph could not have guessed that the new freedom they exercised that day took place on what would become Butler Road, now a busy thoroughfare named after an African American.

Yet in America it seems that those who have known that race most intimately, have found in it resources and feelings rich enough to make its story the romance of this generation.
_____Moncure Conway

A Bush Arbor

With one exception, black churches in Stafford County did not come into being until after the Civil War.[375] No "official" African American church existed in Falmouth prior to the war. African Americans displaying ingenuity and unlimited faith did have a distinct form of worship. Before slavery ended in the South, African Americans avoided white-controlled churches by secretly meeting in "hush harbors." The meetings, which provided a psychological refuge from slavery as well, were announced by communicating with coded signals and messages not discernable by the whites. This was often done in song such as "There's a Meeting Here Tonight" and "Steal Away."[376] There was a fear held by the white slave owners that unsupervised meetings would be used for planning a revolt. If caught attending a "hush harbor," slaves could be severely punished by whipping or sold. Secret codes and signals that were used for "hush harbors" had enough time to be perfected and spread, with the continued selling of slaves from plantation to plantation, to be use on the Underground Railroad.

> Steal away, steal away,
> Stael away to Jesus!
> Steal away, steal away home,
> I ain't got long to stay here.

The antebellum "hush harbors" evolved into the "bush arbor" or "bresh arbor." Bush arbors were gathering places for African Americans to hold religious services in Stafford County during Reconstruction. Ex-slaves may have continued to feel the psychological need to assemble in hidden places due to the punishment stigmatized with the "hush harbors." The name "bush arbor" was termed by African Americans themselves to identify their own unique and humble place of worship. In thickly tangled woods where shrubs could be cut out, African Americans were able to create an open yet secluded space where they could gather. Inside the "bush arbor," preaching and worship could be conducted away from white supervision or direction. The indigenous box shrubs out of which the arbors were made can still be found growing in Falmouth today. Frank White, African American historian, provides more details from oral history:

> I have never heard of "hush harbors." I have heard of something with a similar name called "hush arbors." Hush arbors were secret places deep in the woods where slaves used to go at night to practice religion. In doing this they took grave risk because if the slave owner found out about them, the slave involved would be whipped or harshly punished. To avoid being discovered, they had lookouts, took measures to deaden the sound of the singing, preaching, and other activities, and they used code words to notify other slaves about the dates, times and locations of the meetings. An outgrowth of this was bush arbors. After slavery when the slaves could legally worship, and they had little or no money to build a church, they built bush arbors to worship in. These bush arbors were in a way symbolic of the hush arbors. About 30 years ago, I had an opportunity to see a bush arbor. An African American church in Orange County was celebrating its 125th anniversary. This church had started in a bush arbor. As a part of their anniversary celebration, some of the elderly gentlemen in the church had gone down into the woods, cut down some tree limbs and bushes and used them to construct a bush arbor . . . I had a long conversation with a couple

of the gentlemen who built the bush arbor. I couldn't attempt to tell you how they built it, but they did a good job . . . They are probably both deceased by this time.[377]

The birth of the "Black Church" in the United States took place in the 19th century. In 1895, the National Baptist Convention was organized by African Americans meeting in Atlanta, Georgia. It remains the largest Black religious organization in the United States. Some present day African American congregations and churches in Stafford County owe their origins to the humble "bush arbor."

Neither do men light a candle, and put it under a bushel, but . . . let your light so shine before men . . .
_____Matthew 5:15-16

Old Path

After the Civil War, an African American "primitive church" seems to have existed in Falmouth called the Ironside Baptist Church, which reportedly had fifteen members.[378] A "primitive church" is one adhering to strict worship services. Such a church was sometimes referred to as "old path" or "old school." Singing hymns was allowed but playing music on instruments was prohibited, which included the piano. Women could not conduct the singing. Men and women were seated on separate sides of the sanctuary. If a woman wanted to know anything, she was to "keep quiet" until home and ask her husband.

Leadership roles were viewed as belonging to males only. Both white and black churches respected women; however, the view was held that if women assumed leadership roles, men would take a back seat and not step up to be responsible leaders. In a historical perspective, this view would have carried much weight during the Reconstruction era when leadership was vital. Although women were not recognized in a role of authority, they organized the children's classes, did accounting, counted offerings, and preformed other duties behind the scenes, as they usually possessed higher educational skills than the men.

The Virginia Historical Society has stated, "Spiritual life has been especially important to African Americans not only because slavery and inequality restricted social and political life, but also because, after emancipation, churches were the primary instruments of autonomous black culture and community."[379]

When black churches first formed in Stafford County after the Civil War, they met only once a month. A black preacher could be the minister for several churches. When a church did not hold services, the members attended another black church in the area and vice versa until all the black churches in the locality were able to have their own minister and hold service each Sunday.

In the day when I cried thou answeredst me, and strengthenedst me with strength in my soul.

_____Psalms 138:3

LITTLE SHILOH

Not much is known about Ironside Baptist Church. Its small congregation may have met in the home of Dora Curtis, listed by the Freedmen's Bureau as a prominent Black living in Falmouth, who owned Lot 61. In 1873, the lot was sold at public auction after Dora's death. Judy Brown was the highest bidder.[380] That same year, land was purchased for a primitive church on the east side of Cambridge Street (present day US Route 1) in the northern part of Falmouth. This was the same Lot 61, acquired from Judy Brown for $25.00 to "build thereon a suitable house to be used for public worship and school for the exclusive use of the colored people." The original three trustees were Thomas Pool, James Pool, and James Rowzey.[381] The name of the church was Little Shiloh Baptist Church. Baptisms were performed in the Rappahannock River.

After the Civil War, the African American community moved to establish its own educational institutions. It was common practice for black churches to be responsible for the education of black children.[382] Little Shiloh was the school for Falmouth's African American children and perhaps the first black school in Falmouth. In 1871, there were three white schools in Falmouth and no black school.[383] Little Shiloh's single room served as a classroom during the week and a sanctuary on Sunday. Black schools with grades first through sixth or seventh were taught on average six months out of the year, but had no high school classes.[384] This would have been the case at Little Shiloh. Women filled the role of educating the children.

Reverend Cornelius S. Lucas was a minister of Little Shiloh Baptist Church. He was ordained in 1882, and it is believed that he became minister of Little Shiloh that same year. Reverend Lucas remained active in this church until his death in 1927 at the age of 82 (Reverend Lucas will later be seen in the vignette "Pap Lucas").

Some nights the congregation would walk down to the "sand beach" (now the Historic Port of Falmouth Park). They carried homemade kerosene lights and held "festivals" on the shore of the Rappahannock River. They brought food and conducted little games for the children. There was no singing or baptism in the river during these festivals. A white man, St. Clair Brooks of Falmouth, owned the sand beach at the time and allowed the African Americans to gather there without anyone bothering them.[385]

. . . Negro Christianity. It is something of a very definite and touching character—all forgiving, all believing, making a decided religious impression of its own . . .

_____Julia Ward Howe

NOT HERE

In 1866, a Freedmen's Bureau report on "Bureau Affairs" in Stafford County stated, ". . . they [whites] are very much opposed to the education of the negroes." In a following Bureau report, "The whites in most cases are opposed to educating the Freedmen."[386] Eight years later, a notice for "Colored School Established" appeared in the *Fredericksburg Herald* on October 22, 1874. "The School Trustees of Falmouth township, in Stafford County, have established a colored school which will be opened on Monday. It is the first colored school established in that township." Just nine years after the Civil War, this bold announcement would appear to be to the town's credit. Around the same time, a little black school of which little is known opened in one of the town's more respectable houses. It is unknown what relationship this little school may have had, if any, with a "Colored School Established." In Falmouth there is an old clapboard house with an English gambrel roof, built around 1780. It is referred to as the Barnes House after its mid-19th century owner, Harrison Brockenbrough Barnes. His five sisters—the Misses Lucy, Fannie, Balsora, Margaret, and Bettie—did not marry and lived with their brother. Harrison's wife was the sister of Walker P. Conway. Imagine one man living in a house with so many women! A little school for African American children was opened in the basement of the Barnes House and oral tradition maintains it was taught by the Barnes sisters.[387] The Barnes House was located on Washington Street, in a predominately white section of old Falmouth. It is not known how long the school lasted until the surrounding white residents said, "Not here!"

When the last sister, Bettie, died in 1892, a life tenancy was given to "an old and faithful friend." This friend was Annie Duncan Lucas, who had been a servant for the Barnes family before the Civil War and remained with the family after freedom. She and her husband, Daniel Lucas, who may have been a Barnes' slave also, lived in the Barnes House. Daniel held an appointment to what was an important position in the community at that time. For many years, he worked as the "faithful" mail carrier between Fredericksburg and Falmouth.[388] Daniel Lucas died in November 1904. Believed to have been in her eighty-fifth year, Annie died in January 1919. The heirs of Harrison B. Barnes sold the Barnes House the following year.[389]

LETTER FROM VIRGINIA

"At length I was at the old Virginia home again! Of the young men in Falmouth who had compelled me to leave the place because of my abolitionism in 1854, hardly one was left; they were in Confederate graves." So wrote Moncure Conway of his return trip to America in 1875, which included a visit to Falmouth. Conway left America in 1863 to gain the support of the English people for the cause of abolition in America. The abolitionists in America realized it would be detrimental to the United States' war effort and the Emancipation Proclamation if England recognized the Confederate States as a legitimate government.

Conway went on Britain's lecture circuit, which included London's prestigious Exeter Hall. He suffered an embarrassing diplomatic affair with the Confederate envoy to Great Britain, James Murray Mason, who had drafted the Fugitive Slave Law of 1850.[390] In the following year of 1864, Conway became minister of London's South Place Chapel, one of the oldest free thought organizations in Great Britain.[391] He decided to remain in England. During his return visit to America, Conway wrote a "Letter from Virginia."

> My old Virginian home . . . From this place I departed 17 years ago under circumstances more grievous than any physical cloud or storm. I had offended against the despot Slavery by thought and word, and the kindness of a few could not save me from the bitterness and wrath of the many. Under the threats of some who had once been my playmates and schoolmates I was compelled to leave the home of my parents, the land of my birth; and as I sailed away that day on the broad Potomac, and looked back on the state I passionately loved, its beauty was darkened by a sense of that impending tragedy which since has fallen upon it. On that soil of Virginia from which I was driven with heart full of love for those I was leaving, hosts were soon gathered with rifle and cannon. On the banks of that gentle and silvery river which to my childish eyes seemed far away from the great world, are now thirty thousand graves of young men who might have loved each other but for the remorseless decree of that fell power which held neither love nor life of value compared with its wild and guilty phantasy that man could hold property in man. These events have never changed my feeling towards my early home, my kindred, or even those who threatened me. I was never accustomed to look upon them in any other light than as more unhappy victims of a hereditary evil than I was. Their anger and alienation from me I traced beyond themselves to the tyrant institution which swayed with perpetual terror. It was perfectly true that even my poor presence was a danger. If human beings

were to be held in bondage no one hostile to the wrong could move among them without danger of exciting the slaves to some outbreak. Fear can turn even soft hearts to stone. But I knew these hearts from infancy; and I knew that when the wrong was gone, and the danger, and the fear, they would again beat warm with love and generosity. And it was under this conviction that there drew within me that longing to revisit my old home which, for a space, has parted me from you . . .[392]

Conway visited his parents in 1875. His hope for warmer hearts after the war appears to have been substantiated by his own father:

I learned from leading gentlemen that during all the "reconstruction" time, when the negroes were required to have an official representative, those of Fredericksburg unanimously elected my father. Other offices were offered him, but this alone he agreed to accept. Without any salary he served them with justice. "When your father entered the board," said a friend, "his first speech was, 'Gentlemen, henceforth I know neither white men nor black.'"[393]

As I was wandering in the deep woods on the bank of the Rappahannock, on the brightest of summer days, I lay down to rest beneath the shade of a tree.

_____"Letter from Virginia"

A Certain Youth

As a minister, Moncure Conway had a chance to meet, and influence, hundreds of people. Through his writing, Conway fondly relates the story of "a certain youth" he had known in Washington, D.C., who died in the war. The young man, Gerald FitzGerald, attended Harvard and served in the 2nd Massachusetts Regiment. He was buried in an unknown grave and lies on the opposite side of the Rappahannock

River from his friend and mentor's childhood home in Falmouth. Conway's description of FitzGerald is a powerful statement about the worth and loss of one young man to his friends, his nation, and his cause. In his 1904 autobiography, Conway reflects on the post-war years and eulogizes "a certain youth:"

> Of all that swarm of officials, congressmen, officers, not one face now emerges with the clearness and radiance of a certain youth unknown to fame who tried to share my burden of the world-woe, and under it perished. This youth, Gerald Fitz-Gerald, was about eighteen when I settled in Washington. I believe the family were Catholics, but he was the lover of a very attractive and spirituelle young lady of my church, and this had brought him into contact with new ideas. He became my devoted friend, he took to heart my every sermon, and a determination grew in him to enter the ministry. I did not influence him in the least, personally, but even had some misgivings,—presentiments perhaps of my own approaching troubles. He was very handsome, not to say beautiful; he was intellectually brilliant without conceit; he had a charming voice, fine humor,—every quality that might make a successful minister. So it was arranged to that he should study at the Divinity School, Cambridge.
>
> Then came on the war,—that damnable double-tongued war that lured the best youth to their graves with promises now broken. Just on the threshold of a career already radiant Gerald uplifted the ensign of liberation of both negro and nation from slavery, and went forth as a foot-soldier. It would not have been difficult, with his influential friends, to secure for him a chaplaincy or some other position in the army, but he sought it not.

Gerald FitzGerald, a certain youth.
Courtesy US Army Heritage and Education Center

None of us ever saw Gerald again. Two soldiers reported that they found him dying of a wound on the field and bore him to the shade of a tree. The place of his burial is unknown. Before me is a strangely sweet poem of several pages, privately circulated, but by an unknown writer, which is headed: "Gerald FitzGerald. Killed in Battle on the Rappahannock, May, 1863." So vague were the rumors about his end that I long cherished a hope that Gerald might be in some kindly cabin recovering life, and might yet surprise the circle in Washington that so deeply mourned his loss. But in these last years I have felt it some compensation that the noble youth died with the full assurance that the fair ideal America, and peace never to be broken, would arise out of the blood he had shed,—his own, and blood of adversaries just as brave. Knowing well Gerald's sensitive heart, I feel sure that even had he returned from the work of slaughter he could never have smiled in the old way. Had he lived to this day he would find himself amid phantoms asking, "Was it well then to shed our blood in order that the negro might be freely lynched? . . ."

Rest in your peaceful unknown grave beside the Rappahannock, O my friend! For you no tears, no heartbreaks, no harrowing reflection that your chivalry was in vain, and the war mere manslaughter! These are for me, who found you a happy youth clinging to me with boyish affection, and from my pulpit helped to lay on you the burden of the world.[394]

Here let us end this sad chapter, as painful to him who wrote it as to any who shall read it.

_____Moncure Conway

PART V

THE LATE 19TH AND EARLY 20TH CENTURY

By the 1880s, Falmouth had become a rural village. Time and events had passed it by. Its former industry and trade were gone. Its old mills and canal walls were crumbling. Their materials were salvaged and reused in the construction of new structures in the more prosperous city of Fredericksburg across the river. In 1898, a cousin of Moncure Conway wrote, "And the old Falmouth that we knew has gone down into the ocean of the past forever."[395]

Most of the leading white families of Falmouth had relocated to Fredericksburg. A few remained, such as the O'Bannon sisters at Carlton, Judge Wallace at Clearview, and the Ficklen family until they sold Belmont to renowned artist Gari Melchers. The number of African American head of households also declined as life in general continued amidst the charm of decay.

"Northern migration" began just before World War I. The Civil War and three amendments to the United States Constitution had given African Americans the freedom they had been denied for more than 250 years, but only slowly would the record and memories of the slaves' accomplishments and importance to the history of this nation be brought out of the shadows.

Lucas is Walking Tonight

I found this story difficult to relate. This vignette may disturb some readers and I suggest that an adult be available to talk afterward with children who may read it. It concerns a man named John "Jack" Maurice O'Bannon, a brutal human being by all accounts. Moncure Conway wrote, "Near my father's estate was one owned by a certain 'captain,' who was one of the worst of men, and who had a face naturally belonging to the worst of men."[396]

The O'Bannon family lived at Carlton, a plantation house built in the late 1700s, perched on a high hill overlooking Falmouth in the valley below. Before the Civil War, "Captain" Jack O'Bannon had been elected twice to represent Stafford County in the Virginia Legislature.[397] O'Bannon was a demagogue of Virginia's "slaveology" within that governing body.

Some years before the war, one of O'Bannon's slaves ran away and was caught. "Captain" Jack O'Bannon had him tied to a tree and beat him to death with a black snake whip.[398] According to a slave named Dolly, the beating lasted all day and continued into the night, O'Bannon swearing "that he wouldn' leave bref in him."[399]

Carlton sits atop the hill in this c.1920s photogtaph. The old Dunbar Kitchen, now a residence, is in the foreground.
Courtesy LOC

The murdered slave was "Big Jim" Lucas. He was a young man who had run away at least once before because of beatings. Local oral history indicates that O'Bannon would sometimes cut the slaves' legs and rub salt in the wound, a punishment awarded to slaves who had attempted to run away.[400] Caught and returned to O'Bannon, Lucas was murdered in cold blood by his master. His fate was tragically sealed in slavery, he did not live to see the Union Army arrive in Falmouth in 1862, or to self-emancipate himself as did John Washington and so many other slaves from the area.

Lucas's death created a stir in Falmouth and Stafford County. Moncure Conway wrote of the incident, "A certain man who dishonored the name of a reputable family by lashing his slave so severely that he soon after died, so shocked the county that the tradition of that manslaughter remains to this day." Conway continued, referring to his father, the Stafford County magistrate. "I remember well my father's efforts to bring the manslayer to justice,—unavailing because only slaves witnessed the tragedy."[401] Under the laws of Virginia, the testimony of African American slaves who witnessed a murder was not permissible in court. An elderly slave from Falmouth simply known as "Uncle" remarked, "Bless ye, chile! Niggers seein' a thing ain't more'n so many pine-trees."[402]

The exact date of Lucas's murder is unknown. It occurred while Moncure Conway was growing up in Falmouth. As surely as the Scriptures saith, "sin lieth at the door," the murder may have been the subject of a sermon taken from Falmouth's doorstep.[403] In 1854 (see the vignette "The Father's Letter"), the abolitionist minister Reverend Moncure Conway delivered a sermon, "The poor African, thy brother, where is he? Alas! How often our reply is in the tone of the first murderer," a reference to Cain, who slew his brother Abel. Like Cain, who hid the body of Abel, O'Bannon buried the body of Lucas underneath the floor of the Carlton stables.[404] It is said that in the cool of the evening, when the whip-poor-wills begin to call, Lucas walks in the meadow below Carlton and by the trickling waters of Falls Run.

O'Bannon's ruthless treatment of his slaves was well known in Falmouth. Residents had to close their windows at night due to the screams. After the beatings were over, more screams would follow as the bleeding backs were doused with salt brine to prevent infection.

Marion Brooks Robinson, a member of a white family well-established in Falmouth, related this story:

> My grandparents and other old people in the town remembered the screams of anguish coming from the beatings of slaves at Carlton. The plantation house still stands on a hill overlooking Falmouth and Falls Run. Irish immigrant Jack O'Bannon used slaves to farm his corn and sorghum on the hills and in the meadows surrounding the mansion. My grandfather, Wes Brooks, told my father that as a young boy, he had witnessed O'Bannon beating a slave until the blood streamed from his back. The slave was then doused in salt brine, which stopped the bleeding and aided healing—you did not want to lose too many work days.[405]

During the Civil War, the O'Bannon slaves were likely among the first to leave when Union forces occupied Falmouth in the spring of 1862. Union soldiers quartered inside the Carlton mansion. O'Bannon's rage over losing his slaves, and the war, was plainly evident. When he returned to Carlton after the war, he decreed that no one could sleep in the beds slept in by Yankees. He threw the bedsteads, with their elegant hand-carved posts, and the bedding, out of a second story window onto the front lawn and ordered it burned.

O'Bannon had two daughters. Local tradition relates that whenever a suitor attempted to court one of the girls, the father would run off the young man at the point of a shotgun:[406]

> Older residents said that once he [O'Bannon] no longer had black slaves, he proceeded to enslave his two daughters Ellen and Nannie . . . The hard-drinking, bitter O'Bannon handed the upkeep of the stables and grounds to Miss Nannie and the housekeeping to Miss Ellen. The two women stayed on at Carlton, never marrying because their father would never allow either daughter to receive young men. According to my family, one of my father's uncles had dared to call on Miss Ellen and had been severely beaten about the

head and shoulders with a buggy whip. I remember the two sisters during the '30's . . . dressed in ankle-length dresses and seemed to ignore all passing of time after the death of their father in the 1870's."[407]

An elderly resident of Falmouth remembers seeing the two spinsters driving a stylish old black buggy pulled by a single white horse into town to buy some groceries. Ellen "wouldn't say much" but Nannie "was very mouthy and bossyfied. They never got over the Civil War. Because they were land owners, they thought they were supposed to run everything, acted like men and wore long dresses."[408]

At Carlton, all three resided together, Ellen, Nannie, and Lucas, although the "ghost" was never talked about. Nannie, who kept the stables, avoided walking over a certain spot in the floor. Falmouth's townspeople were well acquainted with Lucas. He would be seen walking about barefooted with his shirt torn almost off. Just as sundown approached and when the whip-poor-wills began calling in the evening, the older residents would say, "Lucas is walking tonight."

During the 1930s, a "row of small slave houses, each with its own door, like five or six little jails," still stood on the Carlton property.[409] The large barn stables accidentally burned in the 1950s when a brush fire was fanned by a change in the wind. Today, the Carlton mansion, a kitchen, a couple outbuildings, and a slave graveyard remain.

What hast thou done? the voice of thy brother's blood crieth unto me from the ground.

_____Genesis 4:10

THE CONFEDERATE SECRETARY OF WAR AND AN EX-SLAVE

James Alexander Seddon was the Confederate Secretary of War. He was a descendant of William Alexander, Earl of Stirling, and the Seddon family had old ties to Stafford County, Virginia. The Seddons lived in a house which stood on Lot 83, described as "pleasantly situated in a retired part of the Town."[410] In 1815, Henry Minor, about 30 years of age, was able to save enough money to buy his freedom from James's father. Henry was born and raised in Fredericksburg. When freed, he had been living in Falmouth for about ten years and was a barber. Henry couldn't afford to purchase his wife and children, who remained in slavery.[411]

On July 13, in the same year that Henry Minor bought his freedom, James Seddon was born in Falmouth. Due to his frail health, James was educated primarily at home. He attended the University of Virginia Law School at age twenty-one and was admitted to the bar in 1838. He then established a successful practice in Richmond. James's father, Thomas Seddon, had moved across the river to Fredericksburg and entered into banking. Thomas, along with being a merchant, had inherited a 500 acre farm four and a half miles to the northeast of Falmouth, in the direction of Brooke. The 500 acre Seddon farm was reduced by 1831, the year that Thomas died. The family sold the remaining portion, known as "Valley View," around 1850.

James A. Seddon served as a US Representative from Virginia in 1845-1847, and again from 1849-1851. Due to poor health, he remained retired for the next few years at his estate, "Sabot Hill," on the James River above Richmond. Seddon also co-owned two Louisiana plantations. One produced sugar, the other cotton. One wonders if slaves from Falmouth or Stafford County may have been transported down South to labor on these plantations.

Prior to the outbreak of the Civil War, Seddon was a member of the failed Washington Peace Conference, which worked to find a resolution to the crisis and the impending war. He was a delegate from Virginia to the Confederate Provisional Congress in 1861. Confederate President Jefferson Davis appointed Seddon Secretary of War on November 21, 1862. As the fortunes of the Confederacy turned for the worse, accusations from Congress resulted in his resignation from office on February 6, 1865. As befell many ex-Confederate officials, Seddon was captured and arrested. He was imprisoned at Fort Pulaski, Georgia, until November 23, 1865. Released upon signing a loyalty oath to the United States of America, he returned to "Sabot Hill" in Goochland County. He died there on August 19, 1880.

The same year, Manuel Johnson bought "Valley View." Johnson was a former slave of Charles Tackett of Stafford County. Because Johnson was disobedient, Tackett sold Johnson to the highest bidder and he was transported down South. He remained in slavery until the war was over. Johnson was probably part of a slave coffle and a victim of the inter-state slave trade. It is not known where Johnson labored as chattel, but once free, he returned to Stafford County. Johnson lived and worked elsewhere in the county until he purchased "Valley View" in 1880. There he spent the remaining days of his life. Johnson left the farm to his daughter, Salley Johnson Gray.[412]

It may be a fascinating irony that an ex-slave became owner of the former family farm of the Confederate Secretary of War, or simply a local example of the sweeping changes brought about by the Civil War. African American historian Frank White says, "Some of the Johnson descendants still live in Brooke. I talked to an elderly lady a few years back who remembered Valley View and knew where it was. I think she either lived on or near there during her childhood. Valley View Farm is all overgrown with woods now, but there are still some people in Brooke who knew where it was and can take you to the vicinity of Valley View Farm."[413]

From Slave to a Contraband, from a Contraband to a Citizen

On May 24, 1882, the New York *Jefferson County Journal* carried an obituary: "Peter Booker, colored, died last Thursday . . . Peter was formerly held as a slave in Virginia, and during the rebellion escaped into the Union lines . . ."[414] Actual names of individuals seeking their freedom in the spring and summer of 1862 are scarce.[415] One of the many slaves to find his freedom and subsequent employment by a Union officer was Peter Booker. His employment began at Falmouth on July 24, 1862. The officer was Captain Sidney J. Mendell of the 35th New York Infantry, the "Jefferson County Regiment." Booker is believed to have been 45 years old at the time. He performed his duties until the end of the war, when the Captain, promoted to a Major, returned to his hometown of Adams and brought Peter north. On December 30, 1874, the *Jefferson County Journal* carried a story entitled, "A Lessen in Politeness:"

> Peter Booker, our industrious negro Cartman was in the Lockwood house on Monday, and while there a fellow from the country took occasion to call him a "d____d black nigger" and kindred terms. Peter remarked to the individual that "he didn't allow anyone to talk to him in that way more than once," and upon the fellow repeating the offence he told him to come out doors and he would lick him. The fellow followed Peter out doors and Peter took him down and gave him a good pounding. After letting him up Peter gave him a parting salute with the toe of his boot, and the victim retreated towards the hotel barn with his respect for the colored race improved. Booker at once proceeded to the office of Justice J. W. Penny and told him that "a fellow had called him a black son of a b___h," and "here was a dollar he was willing to pay for his little enjoyment." The Justice took the fine and discharged Peter.

For 20 years Peter lived in the village of Adams, where it appears his main occupation was selling and delivering ice. His obituary continued with, "Peter was a pleasant, jovial man and well liked in the community. This makes the fifth death in the Booker family within the past year." Upon learning of Peter's death, Major Mandell said that Peter made the "transition from 'slave' to a 'contraband,' from a contraband to a citizen."[416] Upon further passing of the years, Major Mendell reminisced about his friend Peter:

> Peter Booker came home with me from the war. He was a truly, capable, efficient servant and became a respected and useful citizen of Adams; married, bought a house and lot, reared a large and smart family, successful in business . . . He kept his children in school, and they scored high in their studies. Excelling in declamations and competitions . . . pestilence came to his home, the dreaded diphtheria taking Peter and four or five of his children to another world. There are many still living in Adams who well remember him, his family and the fatal sickness that overtook them.[417]

"... Peter, raised his hat with that grace and ease I never saw before."

_____Major Sidney J. Mendell

HER MASTER WAS A REBEL CONGRESSMAN

Major Mendell, appearing in the preceding vignette, inadvertently provided the name of yet another freedom seeker. Among his writings, which he contributed to the *Jefferson County Journal*, the Major relates an incident that occurred while the regiment was in camp near Falmouth in 1863. During the army's winter months of inactivity, high ranking officers sometimes would invite their wives to join them for an extended visit in camp. The Major's wife had consented to such a visit and was soon expected to arrive:

> [Peter Booker] brought to my office a bright, clean, sprightly colored girl, some nineteen years, and wanted a pass for Washington. She gave her name as Eliza Gordon; her master was a rebel congressman, and she had always worked indoors for her mistress, washing, cooking, and caring for the children. I asked her to stay and assist Peter in his manifold duties till my wife came and then aid her as we were going to keep house, and when she left for home accompanying her to Washington, and suggested she might like Mrs. M. so well would be glad to go home with her. She consented to stay ... Some three weeks were spent very pleasantly in our temporary home, making trips to Falmouth and other points, visiting camps near by, Company G in particular, and often dining out with officers of the 35th and other regiments.

The arrangement must have been an agreeable one. Eliza not only consented to stay during Mrs. Mendell's visit, she also accompanied the Major's wife back to Adams, New York. The Major wrote, "In closing just a few words about the 'contrabands' we brought home from the army—the sad sequel of their lives." He was referring to Eliza Gordon and Peter Booker. As noted in the previous vignette, Peter lost most of his family and his own life to diphtheria. The Major continued with some detail about Eliza's life after the war:

> We sent Eliza to school; did not know a letter. She made great proficiency in her studies—studying spelling, reading, arithmetic, geography and grammar, and wrote nice letters. She remained with us till we went west [Iowa]. She remained and married a shiftless colored man; bought a home, and in her effort to pay for it overtaxed her strength and endurance and death came to her relief.[418]

INCIDENT AT SPOUT HILL AND THE COLORED BELLE OF FALMOUTH

One of Falmouth's more famous springs was named Spout Hill. Noted for its dependability and its refreshing clear cool water (see "Clear Water from the Spring"), the spring was located halfway up Gordon Street not far from the Falmouth Bridge. This bridge was also known as Ficklen's Bridge, since he was the owner of the bridge and charged a toll for crossing it. In 1884, on Easter Day in Falmouth, Spout Hill was the scene of a "Probable Fatal Shooting" described in the *Fredericksburg Star*:

> On Monday afternoon a party consisting of Enoch Johnson, Robert Ross, Tom Lawson, Mary Washington and sister Sallie Prior and Lucy Long—all colored, and from Stafford county, took an Easter promenade around the Falls, and were having a good time generally. On returning, when near the spring just above Ficklen's bridge, Enoch Johnson and Robt. Ross got into an altercation, when Johnson drew a pistol and shot Ross, the ball penetrating the stomach. The women began to scream, which attracted the attention of Mr. Cloe, the bridge-keeper, and he having heard the shot, called to Mr. Wm. F. Ficklen, and both repaired to where the

shooting took place. They found Ross lying on the ground wounded, and being told by the women that Johnson did the shooting, immediately arrested him, and carried him into the office of the Bridgewater Mills, and searched him, finding on his person a large knife and a 32-calibre nickel-plated pistol, all the chambers except one being empty. Officers Stone and Gore were sent for and arrested Johnson and locked him up in the Corporation jail.

We learn that the trouble between the combatants arose from jealousy, Martha Washington being the object of their affections, and who is said to be the colored society belle of Falmouth.

We also learn Johnson attempted to fire the second time, and but for Tom Lawson knocking his pistol down Ross would have received another bullet in his body.

Albert Crutchfield and Tom Lawson placed Ross in a spring wagon and conveyed him to the house of an old colored woman living in Falmouth named Juda Morris. Dr. Ashton was sent for and attended the wounded man. Up to this printing the ball is still in the body of Ross, and the chances for his recovery, we are informed, are very slim. Johnson and Ross are quite young men, probably neither of them over twenty years of age.[419]

Robert Ross was a son of Alexander Morson Green and his cook, Nancy Ross (see "The Beating"). Ten days after the shooting, another Fredericksburg paper reported, "Robt. Ross, (coloured,) who was shot with a pistol in the hands of Enoch Johnson, another coloured man, near Falmouth Bridge, on the 14th instant, and who has been lying in a very precarious condition, died this morning at 3 o'clock, in Falmouth."[420]

An African American Cemetery

About halfway down the hill from the Union Church Cemetery and facing the Rappahannock River, there is an African American cemetery. Several black families lived in the area during the early 20th century, and among them were the Russells. The only marked grave bears the name of John W. Russell, who died when he was 22 years old in 1902. His small marble headstone is almost lying flat under the fallen leaves. The cemetery is on a wooded knoll which provides a serene view across the meadow below to the river. There are an unknown number of unmarked graves present.

The cemetery is located in an extreme end of town where the terrain drops steeply down to a small creek called Cady's Gut. This creek marked the original southeast boundary of Falmouth when it was created in 1727. During the 20th century, the retired industrialist John Lee Pratt of Chatham reportedly owned the land in this area. According to oral history, "he allowed the black people to live there and never bothered them."[421] Today, the cemetery is abandoned and extensively overgrown.

Walk around Zion, and go round about her: tell the towers thereof. Mark ye well her bulwarks, consider her palaces; that ye may tell it to the generation following.

_____Psalms 48:12-13

A True Soul

The abolitionist Moncure Conway's life was one of great contrast to that of Falmouth's Captain O'Bannon and Chatham's Major Lacy. Both O'Bannon and Lacy served in the Virginia Legislature. On the other hand, Conway was exiled. The student of Southern sociology will find Falmouth presents a case of extreme opposing beliefs and actions emanating from the same small Southern town. Conway wrote, "I need not attempt to repeat the execrations which returned to me from Virginia when it was reported that I had become an Abolitionist, or the expressions of terror and grief from my relations, many of whom declared that they had rather have heard of my death." He recorded his experience when he wished to visit Falmouth prior to the Civil War:

> I returned, with all hope and eagerness to my home in Virginia. Alas, it was to find that thenceforth I had no home there for ever; it was to be chilled by the sneers and coldness of those who once loved me; to find that my most intimate friends of former days would not appear with me in the street; and that many of those whose blood I shared regarded me as a leper. As soon as it was known in the town that I had arrived, I was confronted in the street by a company of young men, most of them my former schoolmates and friends, who told me that I was spared tar and feathers only for the sake of my father and other relatives, and on the condition that I should leave the State for ever . . . I was exiled from the spot where I was born, simply for an honest conviction that Freedom was better than Slavery.[422]

Moncure Conway described himself as a "witness to developments and events which have made momentous chapters of history." As an "old author uttering his last words to mankind," Conway expounded, "The wisdom or unwisdom of a new generation must largely depend on its knowledge and interpretation of the facts and forces that operated in the generation preceding . . ."[423] In 1900, Conway attended the Paris Peace Convention and presented a pamphlet suggesting a world peace-keeping process that later became the basic tenets of the League of Nations and its successor, the United Nations. Closing his 1904 autobiography, Conway wrote, "Implore Peace, O my reader, from whom I now part. Farewell!"

Moncure Conway in 1906.
Author's Collection

In January 1907, Conway expressed to friends in America his hope of returning to Virginia and attending the Jamestown Exposition.[424] Conway did not return, however, to rest once more in the Virginia Shade. He died alone in his Paris apartment in the early morning hours of November 15, 1907.

Andrew Carnegie, who attended the funeral service, wrote, "He has passed, but he has left behind him a precious legacy to all who were so fortunate as to be able to call him friend. They are better men and women because Moncure Conway has lived and entered into their lives."[425]

One week prior to Conway's death, the *Yellow Springs News* published an article about Conway. The article began, "Moncure D. Conway, a man of high culture and advanced thought and for many years a writer and lecturer of celebrity, came of a wealthy family of strong slave holding proclivities in Stafford county, Virginia in that part of the state where wealth, refinement and ease had long existed. His father [Walker] Peyton Conway, owned broad estates and many slaves, he was an aristocrat of the true Virginia type."[426]

After the death of an older brother in 1852, it befell upon Moncure Daniel Conway the important status of "eldest son" and heir to Southern aristocratic birth. As such, he stood to inherit the family estates, fortunes, Conway House, and 50 to 60 slaves. Recalling the earlier vignette, "An Ancient and a Modern Compromise," the tempter speaks, "All this power will I give the, and the glory of them . . ."[427] Conway could have easily embraced slavery. He could have easily chosen a privileged life among his peers. He could have easily remained safe within his own culture. He could have enjoyed the power and glory of such a birthright. Moncure Conway chose rather to follow what Emerson termed his "true soul," and stepped out of the Virginia shade, a "precious legacy" that challenges America's future generations.[428]

Let us follow his example. The rest is silence.

_____ Andrew Carnegie

BORN IN VIRGINIA

Alexander "Alec" Morson Green was born in Falmouth on September 7, 1827. He was the son of Duff Green, previously noted as a prominent merchant of Falmouth in the vignette "The Beating." Alexander Green attended the Virginia Military Institute, class of 1848, but resigned without graduating. Before the Civil War, he owned 12 slaves and during the war, like his brothers, served in the Confederate army. Green never married, but had a large family by his African American cook, Nancy Ross. Two of the nine children were born into slavery: William Carter Ross, born in 1856; and Mary Ross, born in 1859. The mother, Nancy, who could read and write, is believed to have been born in 1837. Green and Nancy lived on a farm farther out in Stafford County and above Falmouth.[429]

On August 3, 1878, at age 21, William "Willie" Carter Ross enlisted in Troop K, 9th US Cavalry. The 9th and 10th US Cavalry were composed of black enlisted men with white officers. The plains Indians called them "Buffalo soldiers" because their hair and skin resembled the buffalo. He served in the field at Animas City, Colorado Territory, took part in the Ute Campaign in 1879, and at different locations in

New Mexico. On August 2, 1883, First Sergeant Ross mustered out at Fort Supply, Oklahoma Territory.[430]

In the spring of 1883, Ross married a Cheyenne-Arapaho woman named Ans-chis. The marriage ceremony was according to Native American custom. Ross was then adopted into the tribe. In 1886, the couple married again with the ceremony preformed by Captain Jesse M. Lee, according to the custom of the white world. They had four children whose names were Dusty Bull, Standing Twenty, Margaret M. "Maggie," and Alexander Morson. Dusty Bull, who was given the name Marcus Aurelius by his father, who had been exposed to the Classics by his father, died in his fourth year. Standing Twenty, a daughter, died at age two. The other two children lived to adulthood. In January, 1896, Ans-chis died of pneumonia.[431]

Alexander Morson Green in 1902.
Courtesy Gene Wiles

William Carter Ross, Troop K, 9th US Cavalry, c.1880.
Courtesy Gene Wiles

Ans-chis, wife of W.C. Ross, with their son, Dusty Bull.
Courtesy Gene Wiles

The Late 19th And Early 20th Century

William Carter Ross, Buffalo Soldier.
Courtesy Gene Wiles

Mary Ross, second child of Alexander M. Green and Nancy Ross, born into slavery.
Courtesy Gene Wiles

The same year that Ans-chis died, Ross married his deceased wife's "best friend," Mina Schoonover Ashford. They had seven children. Dennis Collins wrote about William Carter Ross in *The Indians' Last Fight or the Dull Knife Raid*:

> W.C. Ross, through his foresight and good business management, succeeded in locating his family allotments in close proximity to the City of El Reno . . . his location proved to be one of the most valuable in the Canadian Valley. By its increase in value, due to its location, and by his knowledge of farming, he has placed himself and his family above the reach of want. He is educating his sons and daughters . . . and they have proved themselves good students. Their native talents developed in such surroundings, show that they are or will be capable of fulfilling the duties of responsible positions in the very near future.[432]

In 1915, W.C. Ross died and was buried in El Reno Cemetery, Canadian County, Oklahoma. His obituary states, "He was prominently identified as one of Oklahoma's pioneers and did his share towards upbuilding [sic] the new country."[433] His grave marker is inscribed, "Born in Virginia."[434]

I'm so glad I live now and not then, but then is very interesting to me now.

_____Gene Wiles, W.C. Ross descendent

A BEACON LIGHT IN FALMOUTH

On January 11, 1917, *The New York Age* published a letter to the editor written by Mary (surname unknown), an African American from Falmouth. *The Age* was a black newspaper founded by Timothy Thomas Fortune, a former slave. By 1880, the paper first appeared as *The Globe*, later renamed *The Freeman*, and finally *The New York Age*. Mary's mind was eager to know the world outside of Falmouth. She was also interested in social issues involving African Americans. She relates to the paper's editor her concerns over the treatment of African Americans by one another in Falmouth. Unfortunately the paper did not provide Mary's complete name:

> Inclosed [sic] is my check to pay for a year's subscription. *The Age* grows more interesting all the time, so I feel as though I cannot well do without it. I was much impressed by what customers said were some of the reasons why they could not patronize their own merchants. I know, from experience, that they are true. Our people must learn that they are not to be patronized simply because they are colored, but because they [merchants] are able to furnish what the people want and keep as clean places as others and treat their own race with at least as much politeness as the members of the white race do. I often wonder why we cannot be more respectful to our people, instead of less so . . . I wish *The Age* a Happy New Year and much prosperity. May it live long to espouse the case of the just and to be a beacon light to the race."[435]

Uncle Jim

James "Uncle Jim" Rowser lived on Union Street in Falmouth. This street was below the town's white Union Church. When Uncle Jim lived there it was simply known as "the lane," the older name of Union Street having long been forgotten. It was later re-named Rowser Road. Uncle Jim did farming and odd jobs for people when needed. On the weekends, he would dress-up and be gone for several hours of the day. When he returned it was not prudent to ask about where he had been. Family members assumed he had been socializing with friends in Falmouth, which probably included a social drink with his friend Gari Melchers, the American impressionist who had moved to Belmont in 1916.

Around 1918, Melchers painted *Uncle Jim*. In 1920, it was put on exhibition in the Montross Gallery in New York. The painting was accompanied by an article in *The New York Times* that described the work as a study made "con amore." Loosely translated, it meant "a friend painted with affection." The article stated, "Northern talents subjected to the influence of the South respond with a peculiar graciousness . . . the long, narrow panel immortalizing Uncle Jim." Uncle Jim's grandson related that, "When asked if Uncle Jim ever talked about the painting or Melchers, according to his daughter, 'he was very secretive about the painting.'"[436]

Uncle Jim, Gari Melchers, oil on panel, ca. 1918.
Courtesy Gari Melchers Home and Studio,
Fredericksburg, VA

Uncle Jim Rowser.
Courtesy Lucas Collection

PAP LUCAS

Cornelius S. Lucas was a slave to the Pollock family of Stafford County. The Pollock farm, Rumford, lay along the Rappahannock River below Falmouth. During the Civil War, the Pollock's eldest son joined a regiment of soldiers raised from Stafford County and Falmouth. Captain William G. Pollock served in Company H, 47th Virginia Infantry. Cornelius Lucas was the faithful body servant of Captain William Pollock. On January 1, 1865, William Pollock was granted furlough because he was greatly debilitated and unfit for duty. He died just two days before the surrender at Appomattox as a result of chronic diarrhea.[437] At some time during the war, perhaps after Captain Pollock went home, Lucas served as a cook for William's younger brother, Captain John Gray Pollock, of the Fredericksburg Artillery. Cornelius Lucas remained a faithful family servant throughout all four years of war.

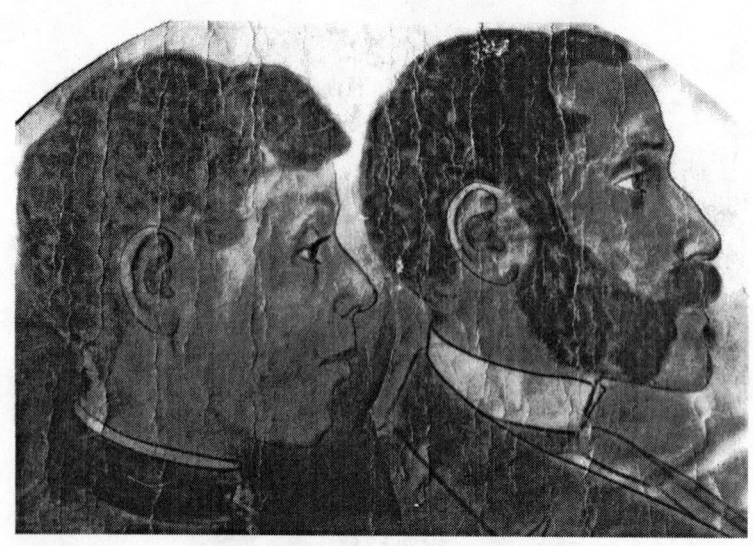

Cornelius S. Lucas and his wife, Maria.
Courtesy of L. Reginald Lucas

After the war, Cornelius Lucas became the minister of Little Shiloh Baptist Church in Falmouth. He lived in Fredericksburg, where he ran a coffeehouse and store. On April 9, 1919, Reverend Lucas received a certificate from the United Daughters of the Confederacy for his "valuable service to the Confederate States during the four years of the War Between the States" and "to show its appreciation of his faithfulness and devotion." In 1925, he received a Confederate pension. Reverend Lucas died at his home on Douglas Street in Fredericksburg on May 13, 1927. He and his wife, Maria, are buried in Shiloh Baptist Cemetery in Fredericksburg. L. Reginald Lucas, grandson of Cornelius Lucas, wrote an account of his grandfather during the years following the Civil War:

> He worked to improve the moral, intellectual, economic and cultural conditions of the black people. One of his greatest contributions was to instill in the black race the desire to be better citizens of Fredericksburg, Va. He knew that he could not do this by himself so he sought the help of the white community who readily assisted him. The rewards from his work have been noticed through generations. All of this work was done

for the good of the community and no self-gain for himself.

Rev. Lucas was a Christian man and he lived to help other people by giving them food from his store when they had no money; seeing that they had oil for their stoves so their children could be warm in the winter. He lived on Douglas Street and he earned the nickname "Pap Lucas" because he was always trying to be a father to the children in the area. The first Church he pastored was a missionary Baptist church. Rev. Lucas was very active in civic affairs. He worked with his many white friends to get improvements for the black race such as housing and voting rights.[438]

THE STUD

Willie P. Roots was born in 1878. He married Mary L. Nelson, who was known as "Lottie." They lived and raised their family on Washington Street in Falmouth. Willie was described as a "big man," better than six feet tall, and weighing between 275 and 300 pounds. A Falmouth resident remembered watching him moving a piano by himself and observing the large muscles in his arms ripple in the sunlight. Another resident remembered, "He carried coal on his back in a big bag especially made for that purpose and delivered it to peoples' houses. It was told in Falmouth his father was a slave stud back in the days of slavery."[439]

YES AND NO

As mentioned previously, African American women in Falmouth carried tubs and buckets on their heads prior to the Civil War. This practice continued into the early 20th century. African American women in Falmouth were seen carrying large baskets of "wash" on their heads. White residents were amazed to witness the black women shake their heads "yes" and "no" while balancing a heavy load effortlessly. Sallie

Byrd was remembered especially for her ability to carry great bundles in this fashion and shake her head during conversation.[440]

The practice of using one's head to transport objects is traditional in Africa. Even today, African children begin to "practice" at five or six years of age. By the time they are seven, they are well skilled. Paula Royster, founder of The Center for African American Genealogical Research, Inc., observed while visiting Ghana, "They do it as a practical matter: to leave their hands free, to transport their food and items for sale or trade." If something is dropped, they "pick it up and never even reach to hold the basket steady. It was as if there was nothing on top of the head."[441]

The image of African American women with baskets and bundles on their heads conjures up a romantic picture of bygone days. However, the reality was one of toil and labor. During the Civil War, a Union drummer boy in Falmouth watched "a group of black women carrying baskets of manure on their heads to a local pumpkin field . . ."[442]

KNOW THEIR PLACE

The Jim Crow era was a period of racial discrimination against and segregation of African Americans in the South from 1876 to 1965. Like other places in the South and Virginia, Falmouth had its share of social and personal prejudice. As long as Falmouth's African Americans knew their place, the white residents treated them well. When a black "outsider" entered Falmouth, that person was subject to discriminatory remarks. In the "Falmouth bottom," an older section of town, only blacks who were residents were allowed to be there. Unknown African Americans were accosted or run out of "the bottom," with physical force if necessary. On one occasion on Washington Street, five black "outsiders" were beaten for not leaving promptly.[443]

White children in Falmouth were instructed by their parents never to address older blacks by their first name. They were to be called "Mr." or "Mrs." in contrast to the antebellum days when it was customarily to address them as "uncle" or "aunt." A white woman in Falmouth, Sarah Coppedge, "made medicines out of herbs and gave them to the colored people who really liked her."[444] No lynchings took place in Falmouth, although some white boys were known to hang dogs for sport. One favorite dog of the boys was named "Nig."[445] Times were hard and the people were tough. When it was determined that a white boy should know how to swim, the men of the town would throw him in the river or leave the boy on an isolated rock surrounded by deep water.[446] In April 1926, the town's Union Church received a monetary gift from the Ku Klux Klan after robed members attended the services there.[447] In such circumstances, one can imagine the pressures on African Americans "to behave."

One very kind lady of Falmouth remarked, "I think it's so nice when black people know their place."[448] This well-intended statement exemplified the social conscience, or lack thereof, during this deplorable period in American history. Jim Crow was coined from an early Negro minstrel song by that name. State-sponsored school segregation was declared unconstitutional by the US Supreme Court in 1954 in <u>Brown v. Board of Education</u>. Generally, the remaining Jim Crow laws were overturned by the <u>Civil Rights Act of 1964</u> and the <u>Voting Rights Act of 1965</u>. Stafford County's school system started the integration process in September 1961. Innumerable injustices were done to African Americans during the Jim Crow era. Like most southern towns, Falmouth struggled through Jim Crow.

We are to be tested in our patience, our forbearance, our perseverance, to acquire and use skill, in our ability to compete, [and] to succeed . . .

_____Booker T. Washington

COLOR

Among the older homes in Falmouth is Belmont. Gari Melchers, an American impressionist painter, and his wife Corinne, desired a countryside home away from the city and its hectic lifestyle. They purchased the house and estate from the Ficklen family in 1916. Gari Melchers was an academician of the National Academy of Design and a member of the American Academy of Arts and Letters.[449] Melchers built himself a studio on the estate grounds in 1924. Around 1928, Melchers created a painting he titled *Color*. In the painting, an African

American girl sits alongside a very large flower arrangement. The identity of the girl is not given.

Adjacent to the Belmont estate was a modest frame house, the home of Mary and Willie P. Roots.[450] Their daughter Fannie was likely the African American girl in the painting *Color*. She was apparently in her teens at the time.[451] The flowers in the arrangement were from Corinne Melcher's gardens, which Fannie may have helped tend.

Color, Gari Melchers (American, 1860-1932), oil on canvas, ca.1928. The painting remains among the collection at Belmont and has shown at the Corcoran Gallery in Washington, D.C.
Courtesy Gari Melchers Home and Studio, Fredericksburg, VA

Fannie Roots in front of Falmouth Baptist Church
(old site).
Courtesy Lucas Collection

Fannie was employed as Mrs. Melcher's maid. She served at the parties given at Belmont dressed in formal maid's attire. Remarkably, at the astonishing age of sixteen, Fannie became president of the county taxpayers' association, Stafford County Citizens' Alliance, and was known with distinction as "Miss Roots." Fannie never married. She said, "Nobody would have me. They didn't know it, but I didn't want them, either."[452] Corinne Melchers enjoyed Fannie's companionship for many years. After Mrs. Melcher's death in 1955, Fannie continued living in her parent's little house on Washington Street. She passed away in 2004. A Falmouth icon, she was the last African American resident of the old town. Truly, she added "color" to Falmouth.

A HILLY RELATIONSHIP

According to an 1870 Virginia law, "white and colored persons shall not be taught in the same school but in separate schools . . ."[453] Around 1925, Stafford County built the Falmouth Elementary School on the heights beyond the Union Church Cemetery. Only white children were permitted to attend this school. Within ten years, the county built the Falmouth Colored School. It was located along River Road, in the floodplain of the Rappahannock River, and at the foot of the hill below the white children's school.

According to historian Frank White, "The black kids could only go halfway up the hill and the white kids were allowed to go only halfway down the hill, but they were not supposed to play with each other."[454] The white boys held the high ground, and the advantage. They could throw rocks down the hill at the black children, despite the teachers prohibiting such behavior.[455] There were claims and counter-claims about fights between the white and black boys on the hillside. One former white student says, "I have talked with two friends who attended Falmouth about the time I did. They confirm that not a single interaction took place between the schools. In fact one friend said she wasn't even aware the [black] school was there . . ."[456]

The Falmouth Colored School went only to the sixth or seventh grade. In 1937, a major flood lifted the Falmouth Colored School off its foundation. St. Clair Brooks tried to save the school by enlisting the aid of other white men in Falmouth to tie the building to trees with ropes. No one was willing to assist. Either the effort was viewed as futile or the white residents did not care. Little James Lucas, who lived on "Rowser Lane," stood with others on the hill where the Union Church is, and watched Falmouth Colored School float away.[457]

Falmouth Colored School, floated away in
a flood of the Rappahannock River.
Courtesy Shirley Heim

Pick it Up, Brother

The church was the social epicenter of the African American community. To Falmouth's white citizens, Little Shiloh Baptist Church, just a short distance north of the Falmouth Baptist Church (first site), was simply known as the "colored church." On special occasions, some of Falmouth's African Americans worshiped with the white congregation of Falmouth Baptist Church.

An amusing story is part of Falmouth's folklore. In 1939 or 1940, on a particularly cold autumn day, the worshipers at the colored church became enraptured in singing praises and were so moved by the Spirit as to cause the top of the old cast iron stove to fall off onto the floor. The preacher hollered, "Pick it up, brother! It's not hot." A congregant grabbed the top. Quickly replacing it on top of the stove, he exclaimed loudly, "The hell it won't!"[458]

By 1951, the name Little Shiloh Baptist Church was changed to Mt. Pisgah. The name refers to the Biblical peak upon which God told

Moses to, "Get the up into the top of Pisgah, and lift up thine eyes westward, and northward, and southward, and eastward, and behold it [the Promised Land] with thine eyes."[459] Reverend Roger J. Poindexter was the minister at the time. He had been a chaplain in the military and trained in the Pentecostal faith. He and his family lived in Mayfield, an upper class African American community of Fredericksburg. Mt. Pisgah was a Pentecostal church and known at the time as a "Fire Baptized Holiness" church. The congregation numbered 25 to 30. Sunday services continued till 2:00 or 3:00 o'clock in the afternoon. Baptismal service would be preformed in another larger church, not in the river as had been the previous practice at Little Shiloh.[460]

Little Shiloh Church, later named Mt. Pisgah Church.
Photograph by the author

Congregation of Little Shiloh Baptist Church.
Courtesy Lucas Collection

Falmouth's African American residents also attended Shiloh "Old Site" Baptist Church in Fredericksburg across the river. A number of Falmouth's African Americans are buried in Shiloh Church Cemetery. The African American community in Falmouth seems to have been well connected with its Fredericksburg counterpart, especially in regard to their shared religious faith.

THE FAITHFUL FRIEND

For years, Helen Turner, in her capacity as midwife, delivered many of the white children born in Falmouth. Helen, who gave her birth year as 1874, lived with the Brooks family. She received her food and board, but no pay. Known as Mammy Helen within the Brooks family, she was nanny to the Brooks children and would stay with anyone in the extended Brooks family who fell ill. She once told little Marion Brooks, "Hush that mouth and eat this dinner, I don't want to clean those dishes after midnight."[461] Despite her scoldings, Mammy Helen was adored as a member of the family.

One of the little Brooks boys, whose grandparents had died, once said, "I have a black grandmother, Mammy Helen!" On one occasion, St. Clair Brooks knew the Nelson Payne family in Falmouth needed help with a sick child. He suggested to Mammy Helen that she could earn some money by attending the child. Mammy Helen's response was emphatic: "Mr. Clair, I belong to the Brooks family and I don't work for money!" Helen felt degraded by the suggestion.

Around 1920, artist Gari Melchers completed a work called *Ironing*. It brilliantly captures the determined toil of an African American domestic. The subject portrayed is believed to be Helen Turner.[462]

Ironing, Gari Melchers, charcoal,
pastel and gouache, ca.1920.
Courtesy Gari Melchers Home and Studio,
Fredericksburg, VA

Mammy Helen, sitting on the Geneva Brooks House porch.
Courtesy LOC

When their beloved mammy died around 1931, the Brooks family buried Helen Turner in their family plot in the Union Church Cemetery. Some years later, "a relative" complained about the arrangement. Mammy Helen's remains were removed from the family plot and reinterred in a distant corner of the cemetery.[463] Her original grave marker disappeared. A new marker reads, "Helen Turner, Faithful Friend." The relationship between white and black had evolved from "faithful servant" on the gravestone of Uncle Osborne Merricks, coachman to the Forbes family before the Civil War, to one of "faithful friend."

EVIL SPIRITS

During the Colonial period, a common practice prevailed concerning doors and hinges. The front of the door would appear much like a modern door, but the back side omitted the molded edge around the panels. This created the appearance of a Cross at the top of the door and an open Bible below. The hinge, made by an H joined with an L, represented the "Holy Lord." The purpose of a "Cross and Bible" door combined with H and L hinges was to keep evil spirits from entering the room. If any spirits did get through, a remedy was to hinge the door from the opposite side, reversing the way it opened. This was to "fool" the spirits by confusing them how to enter.[464]

Like the English and European emigrants to the new world, Africans brought and maintained, to a degree, their own cultural and spiritual beliefs. Examples can be traced to Falmouth's African Americans during the 20th century. White and black residents alike reported Eva Gunn did "practices." One such practice was the sprinkling of flour meal around her house to keep away unwanted people.

As noted in the vignette "Charms," blue beads were used as an item of adornment and possessed cultural meaning reflective of West African beliefs. Wearing the color blue could also deflect ill wishes—such as when someone gave you the "evil eye"—back upon an antagonist. The Southern slang word "haint," a variant of "haunt," refers to those evil, restless spirits of the dead. Since it was believed that haints could not cross water, some African Americans used blue paint around doors, on window trim, or shutters to imitate water and "fool" the haints from "crossing" into the house. Blue paint used in this way was termed "haint blue." For a greater part of the 20th century until her death in 2004, Fannie Roots, like her father before her, kept the modest Roots house painted white, but the doors and windows had a bright blue border painted around them. This was Fannie's way of keeping out the "evil spirits."[465]

Fannie Roots House, with haint blue to kept out evil spirits.
Photograph by the author

THE GATE POSTS

During the 1930s, Reuben Roots was the newspaper delivery boy in Falmouth. One stop near the end of his run was the house of a little girl who possessed an inquisitive mind and wanted to know anything and everything. In front of the house where she lived were two gateposts made of stone. She would sit atop one of the posts and wait for the paper boy every evening, for he had all the news. Before Reuben reached this house, his route took him through most of Falmouth and he picked up all the local gossip along the way. This is just what the little girl wanted to hear—not the world news, but the town news!

When Reuben reached the little girl's house he would perch himself upon the top of the opposite gatepost and the two would talk. Every evening was a delight until the day when the little girl's mother kindly told her to bring Reuben into the backyard where they could sit in chairs behind the house. "It did not look good to have a black friend out where everyone could see." The little girl's feelings were so badly hurt all she could tell Reuben was, "I can't talk anymore." Each heart was broken.[466]

   . . . thy nobler children [shall] rear for thee the tabernacles of the Past, the Present, and the Future.

_____Moncure Conway

EARLY 1920s AND 30s PHOTOGRAPHS

Courtesy Lucas Collection

Fannie Roots and friend with Union Church in the background.

Julia Russell sits in the tripod for a Civil War Sibley tent.

Julia Russell and Peter Alexander

Taylor Lucas on right, Mary Lucas center, an unknown visiting friend on left. The photo was taken on River Road.

Uncle Jim's House, Billy Rollins dressed as cowboy and Taylor Lucas.

The Late 19th And Early 20th Century

The Woodpile

Mary Lucas at Falmouth Beach.

James Lucas

PART VI

THE MODERN ERA

    The history of Falmouth is the history of many different people and cultures. It has been the home of Native Americans living at the falls of the Rappahannock River, colonists and entrepreneurs from England, Scotland, Wales, and Ireland, and enslaved and free Africans and African Americans. The town rose to prominence as a busy port, slipped quietly into decline, was wrenched awake by the Civil War, and then left alone to recast itself as a small rural village. Such was Falmouth's character in the early 20th century.

    After World War II, Falmouth began to lose its identity as a distinct place and became a suburb of Fredericksburg. A booming national economy, affordable housing and automobiles brought new social and economic freedoms to African Americans in Falmouth. Mass ownership of the automobile enabled the next generation of African Americans to leave. The elder members of the town's established black families—Lucas, Wheeler, Gunn, Long, Rowser, Russel, and Roots—died out, and the younger members moved away. No one came to replace them.

The Best Place

There was no single part of Falmouth identifiable as a "black section." African Americans lived at the north, southeast, and west ends of town. Their properties were generally the less desirable parcels in each section of town. North of town on US Route 1 were the Gunn, Long, and Wheeler families, and some Clarks; at the southeast end of town along River Road lived the Rowser, Lucas, and Russell families, Peter Alexander, and Ham Coon; and at the west end along Washington Street were the Roots and another Lucas family. Each of these three areas produced at least one African American who stood out as a prominent figure. Perhaps most notable was the colorful Miss Fannie Roots, the attractive Mrs. Julia Russell, who looked as if she had "just stepped out of Macy's," and the entrepreneur Mr. Robert Wheeler.[467]

Julia Russell is helping the bride with her veil, November 20, 1954, wedding day inside Conway House.
Courtesy Shirley Payne Alfred

The Modern Era

Engineer Lt. William (Billy) R. Rollins, son of Julia Russell. He is wearing the famous Corcoran jump boots.
Courtesy Lucas Collection

Robert Wheeler (fifth in line), Monroe and Berry Store in Falmouth.
Courtesy Harrison Berry

Around 1941, the highway department built a new, straight road into Falmouth. The new US Route 17 cut into Falmouth on the west, dramatically altering the landscape and sense of space between Washington Street and Carlton. The four-way intersection created by the addition of US Route 17 shifted the commercial focus of the town away from the river. The area north of the intersection along US Route 1 became an integrated community. This was the northern-most boundary of the original 1727 town of Falmouth, a place where free African Americans had settled early in the town's history. African Americans and whites lived, worked, and worshiped intermixed. This community had a white church, an African American church, a white store, and an African American store.[468]

Thomas Jefferson wrote of his misgivings that "deep-rooted prejudices entertained by whites" and "ten thousand recollections, by the blacks, of the injuries they have sustained," would keep the races from living together after emancipation.[469] It has been suggested that black and white residents of Falmouth got along together so well after the Civil War because everyone was so poor. A humorous bit of Falmouth's folklore suggests the people were so poor that they ate dried apples for breakfast and drank a glass of water for dinner. At supper, they sat around the table and waited for the dried apples to swell up![470]

In the 1940s and 1950s, an integrated community such as existed in Falmouth was remarkable. One former African American resident of Falmouth recalled, "It was the best place could ever live in and haven't felt that since." Former resident, Lawrence Wheeler related, "The white and black children played together and sometimes slept over at each other's house. The community took care of each other with disregard to the color of its citizens. If one were not seen for several days, someone came looking for you to see if you were alright. No one ever went uncared for when sick. No one ever went hungry when in need."[471]

I knew these hearts from infancy; and I knew that when the wrong was gone, and the danger, and the fear, they would again beat warm with love and generosity.

_____Moncure Conway

Goosey Goose

There were three, perhaps four, meat or slaughter houses in Falmouth. These provided employment for local African Americans, some of whom were very skilled butchers. In the slaughter houses, an animal was killed by hitting it in the head with a sledge hammer and immediately cutting the throat. Although this sounds cruel, a worker skilled at this task could perform it quicker and more humanely than by modern methods.

Robert Wheeler, an African American resident of Falmouth, worked for years as a meat cutter at Monroe and Berry Store in town. In 1947, Wheeler was able to open his own store on the east side of US Route 1, just north of the intersection with Butler Road and next to Mt. Pisgah Church. The cinder block building was locally known as Robert Wheeler's Store, Wheeler's Store, and Wheeler's, but the correct name was originally "Wheeler's Market." Wheeler and his family lived behind the church in a house which many years earlier was originally an old log cabin. Robert built additions to the house while living there.

One day, a little white girl named Gloria Payne, about seven years old, entered Wheeler's Market with her favorite pet goose under her arm. As the little girl wished to look around inside, she sat "Goosey Goose" on the top of the store's very clean counter. No sooner had this been done than Goosey Goose dropped its business on Mr. Wheeler's spotless countertop. This prompted some rather serious remarks from Mr. Wheeler. For the store's patrons, it was the cause of much amusement and hilarious conversation. Due to the market owner's good graces, Goosey Goose was spared that day. Goosey's final fate came sometime later, as the main course at the little girl's family dinner table.[472]

The AMOCO Connection

The age of modern transportation changed the Falmouth landscape. Just as the King's Highway brought Colonial travelers to Falmouth, the automobile brought modern travelers and a new industry of service stations and garages. Just north of the town traveling along US Route 1 to the Falmouth Bridge, there were no less than seven service stations.

During the 1930s, Odham's AMOCO service station was located on the northeast corner of the town's major intersection. In 1952, the station was operated by a new owner, Linwood Bourne. Although a FLYING A and an ESSO station were in close proximity, African Americans patronized the AMOCO station.

At the time, many businesses displayed signs, "whites only." Service stations were no exception in discriminating against blacks. Pulling into a service station in the South could be very intimidating. When African Americans traveled, it was a common practice to carry their food with them. It could prove difficult finding a restaurant that would serve blacks.

As seen in previous vignettes, slaves used coded words, sometimes in song, for communicating secretly. Signals and coded messages announced a meeting at a hush arbor and were used on the Underground Railroad. Oral history provides an example in the story about stitches made in the inside lapel of coats worn by two boys being conducted through Virginia to freedom. African Americans along the way interpreted the meaning of the stitches and knew where to send the boys. The boys themselves did not know what the stitches meant.[473] In a similar but reversed situation, after blacks migrated north, children were sometimes put on the train and sent back south to visit grandparents and family. A piece of paper was pinned to the inside of their coat lapel with their name and destination. The black porters, who knew where to look for the pieces of paper, would see the children safely off at the right station where family members would be waiting for their arrival.[474]

Since the days of slavery, African Americans communicated information among themselves of which whites were unaware. African Americans traveling Virginia's highways spread the word that the AMOCO station in Falmouth was a safe place to stop. At Bourne's AMOCO, everyone was treated the same, regardless if they were black or white. Local black teens could use a small car wash at the station. Sometimes Mr. Bourne charged them a quarter for the water they used. US Route 1 was the main thoroughfare until Interstate Route 95 opened in Virginia in 1964. Mr. Bourne provided a place to one side of his station where African American travelers could park and eat the food they would bring with them. Blacks used the restrooms and water fountain like everyone else.[475] As they traveled back and forth to visit family, attend funerals, or church home-comings, the AMOCO connection was established in Falmouth.

CARLTON SLAVE GRAVEYARD

Charles Emery Stevens, the biographer of Anthony Burns, provides a description of African American burials on a plantation. Stevens obtained his information directly from interviewing Burns, who was an "exhorter," or unofficially ordained black preacher, in Falmouth, where it sometimes fell on Burns to conduct the burial service for the dead. Stevens' account may in some regard describe the burial of slaves at Carlton (see "Lucas is Walking Tonight"):

> If a slave died during the week, no funeral was allowed to interrupt the daily toil of the plantation. The body... was deposited in the ground without ceremony or delay, and a few shovelfuls of earth were thrown in, while the bereaved kindred went about their toil as usual. But on the following Sabbath, the whole body of slaves, attended by the master or the overseer, assembled to "sod the grave." With prayers, exhortations, and much singing of hymns... this final ceremony was completed. In death, as in life, the social distinctions of slavery are carefully maintained... the dead bodies of slaves never mingle their dust with that of the sovereign race. No monument, inscribed with the name of the deceased, ever marks the spot where he lies, as no legal sanction was ever given his name while he lived. A rough stone, gathered from the wayside, or a branch of cedar, soon to die, is his only monument.[476]

A few outbuildings survive at Carlton, including a prominent brick kitchen and a dairy. Away from these and the "big house" is a gently sloping field where a row of slave cabins once stood. Beyond the field, thick woods and tangled undergrowth cover an unassuming hillside, where some unknown world sleeps deep below. On this obscured slope is the slave graveyard of Carlton.

The overgrown hillside gives the appearance that it was chosen for a graveyard because it was impractical terrain for farming or any other productive use, and because it was hidden from sight of the "big house" and farmstead. If the white owners of Carlton intended that the location of the graveyard should convey that slaves were of no human value, that slaves were simply property to be disposed of as unwanted refuse, they succeeded. The graveyard may contain 150 or more unmarked graves.[477] Today the site conveys the feeling of utter isolation—as if the graveyard was in its own grave.

Local oral history speaks indirectly of the burial place. It has been said of Carlton's owner, Captain O'Bannon, that when a slave made him angry he would just shoot them and tell the other slaves to bury the body.[478] Moncure Conway, the primary source of information about O'Bannon's murder of his slave Lucas, does not record anything about O'Bannon shooting his slaves. In fact, the author was unable to find any primary source material that could substantiate the stories about shootings. This does not mean, however, that the shootings did not occur. As Conway wrote in *Testimonies Concerning Slavery*: "'Breaking their spirit' is a phrase as frequently used with regard to slaves as horses. Sometimes a slave must be killed, that the mastery of a hundred others may be secured. No large body of slaves could be held securely, unless it was understood that there would be no hesitation in shooting any who should rebel."[479] Carlton's slave graveyard lies buried with,

. . . blood-dripping wounds and psalms of the dead.

_____Walt Whitman

Behold, I Show You a Mystery

A 1739 Anglican hymn, one probably sung in the old Falmouth Anglican Church, remains popular today. It is known as the "Easter Hymn."

Made like Him, like Him we rise,
Alleluia
Ours the cross, the grave, the skies,
Alleluia

The Union Church Cemetery in Falmouth dates to the Anglican period of Virginia's history. In 1727, the Virginia General Assembly set aside land for a church and cemetery in the newly created town of Falmouth. A high prominence was chosen to inspire the lower classes with awe and reverence toward a state supported religion.[480] By the Civil War, local residents knew the cemetery as the old Revolutionary burying-ground, which was described by ex-slave John Washington as containing some of the earliest graves in Virginia.

The location of the old cemetery and Union Church became known as "Church Hill." The south side of the hill sloped sharply downward toward the Rappahannock River. This less-desirable hillside in the back of the cemetery was used for the burial of African Americans. Many of those graves may have been unmarked.

When the cemetery was running out of burial space in the mid 20th century, fill dirt was added to the hillside. This built up the south side of the cemetery to provide additional burial plots. White graves are now located in this portion of the cemetery in the fill dirt, above unmarked black graves further down.[481] Christians believe in a bodily resurrection from the grave, as based on teachings in New Testament scripture:

> Behold, I show you a mystery; we shall not all sleep, but we shall all be changed, in a moment, in the twinkling of an eye, at the last trump: for the trumpet shall sound, and the dead shall be raised incorruptible, and we shall be changed. For The Lord himself shall descend from Heaven with a shout, with the voice of the archangel, and with the trump of God: and the dead in Christ shall rise first. Then we which are alive and remain shall be caught up together with them in the clouds, to meet the Lord in the air: and so shall we ever be with the Lord.[482]

Theologians explain "the dead in Christ shall rise first" because they have six feet further up to travel "to meet the Lord in the air." Given this premise, the African Americans buried in the Union Church Cemetery will rise ahead of the whites. They are buried further below and have a greater distance to travel!

And, Behold, There Are Last Which Shall Be First, And There Are First Which Shall Be Last.

_____Luke 13:30

A New Century

From the humble beginnings of a broken clay pot, the author indiscriminately used the date 1660 extending to the 1960s Civil Rights Movement to establish roughly 300 years of African American history in Falmouth.[483] Falmouth played no significant role during the Civil Rights Movement of the 20th century. Stafford County was not without its recognizable contribution to important events during that movement, but I leave this for others to chronicle. Today, Falmouth is surrounded by residential development, crisscrossed by two US highways, and often the scene of oppressive commuter traffic. But the town and its stories remain resilient, waiting to be explored and rediscovered. Perhaps an even greater chapter is yet to be written about Falmouth, a place we now call historic, a place of slavery, war, and injustice, a place which has slowly emerged from the shadows of the past three centuries.

I have seen a land right merry with the sun; where children sing, and rolling hills lie like passioned women, wanton with harvest. And there in the King's Highway sat and sits a figure, veiled and bowed, by which the traveler's footsteps hasten as they go. On the tainted air broods fear. Three centuries' thought has been the raising and unveiling of that bowed human heart, and now, behold, my fellows, a century new for the duty and deed.

_____W.E.B. Du Bois

The End

EPILOGUE

A Secret

In the 1870s, a monument to General Robert E. Lee was commissioned to be built. On May 29, 1890, the Lee Monument was unveiled in Richmond, Virginia, attended by 150,000 exuberant white southerners. It stands today on Monument Avenue. Moncure Conway's comments about the memorialization of Lee and others during this period are circumspect:

> There are secrets withheld from the mighty but revealed unto the lowly,—revealed unto babes . . . the Virginians were erecting a monument to the great General Lee who led the Confederate Army; but I could not help reflecting that all the military ability of Lee and his generals—and all the statesmanship of the South—had done less for it than it could have got by trusting the simple faith in God and right of the poor negro, in whose breast was mapped out the march of destiny—the inviolable advance of justice—wars against which may never be won.[484]

Civil Liberty

Julia Ward Howe was previously mentioned (see "The Divine Idea") as visiting the Falmouth area in 1863. She was a contemporary and friend of Moncure Conway. Like Emerson, Thoreau, Parker, Phillips, Garrison, and Conway, she held the Universalist belief in the worth of each individual in a free society. Julia Ward Howe wrote in her private journal after the Civil War:

Civil liberty is that which the one cannot have without the many, or the many without the one. The liberty of the State, like its solvency, concerns and affects all its citizens. Equal sacredness of rights is its political side, equal stringency of duties its moral side. The virtue of single individuals will not give them civil liberty in a despotic state, but the only safeguard of civil liberty to all is the virtue of each individual.[485]

The greatest man in history never owned a slave, yet they called Him, Master.

_____Anonymous

APPENDIX A

TRAIN RIDE TO FREEDOM IN CONWAY'S OWN WORDS

The Train Ride to Freedom in Conway's own words, excerpted from *Moncure Daniel Conway, Autobiography, Memories, and Experiences*, Cambridge: Houghton, Mifflin and Company, The Riverside Press, 1904, Vol. I, 355-362:

Before leaving for the East we went to pass some weeks with our intimate friends, Mr. and Mrs. Oriel Eaton, at their summer cottage, Yellow Springs. I found there enough repose even to indulge myself in an occasional game of chess, Dr. Phillip Meredith, president of the Chess Club, being within a mile of us. One day, however, when we were in the middle of a game I was sent for in haste by my wife. A note had arrived from my mother saying that two of my father's slaves had reached Washington, but most of them were wandering helplessly in Stafford within the lines of the Northern army. I started the same evening, and after a wearisome journey of nearly three days on irregular trains crowded with soldiers reached Washington. After some searching I found those I was looking for,—Dunmore Gwinn and his wife. They had set up a small candy-shop in Georgetown, taken in washing, and saved sixty dollars.

. . . None of our negroes had followed Dunmore Gwinn and his wife to Georgetown. I therefore resolved to go to Falmouth, if possible, and bring them all away. I consulted my old friend Secretary Chase, and formed a plan of settling our negroes at Yellow Springs, where I had friends.

Secretary Chase took me to see Secretary of War Stanton. I found him hard and narrow-minded. He said they did not want any more negroes in the District; and when I said that I would merely take them through the District, he said that the military situation in Stafford was too critical for him to give me the permit. I then visited President Lincoln and stated the entire case. He sympathized with my purpose and recognized that I had a right to look after my father's slaves. He warned me, however, of the personal danger in such a journey. I told him that I had considered that matter, and would be cautious; I also promised to be prudent in not connecting him or the administration with the affair. I simply needed practical suggestions as to the best means of doing a thing which, for the rest, would really relieve his officers in Virginia and ultimately the District from the care of fifty or sixty colored people. The President advised me to call on General Wadsworth. I think he must have communicated with his general, for the next day when I appealed to Wadsworth, in company with W.H. Channing, who determined to accompany me to Falmouth, he did not hesitate to give us the necessary orders.

HEADQUARTERS MILITARY DISTRICT OF WASHINTON,
WASHINGTON, D.C.

The Rev'd Mr. Conway will be allowed to go to Falmouth and return on Government Boat and R.R. train.

W. J. WADSWORTH,
Brig. Gen'l.

We were both staying at the house of our friends Mrs. Walter Johnson and her sister Miss Donaldson, always the antislavery saints of the Unitarian society. We had arranged to start at daybreak the next day. But during the evening I began to feel that my plans were too immature. If, as was probable, our negroes were in separate localities and far away from Falmouth, how could they be reached and collected—how could they be brought up to Washington? General Wadsworth's permit said nothing about negroes. I had provided myself with money, but might need the aid of Stafford negroes. But it had been many years since I had known the negroes there, and they might suspect any white man searching for coloured people.

After I had gone to bed I was seized with an impulse to consult an old mulatto whom I had known in boyhood and who now resided in the farthest suburb of Georgetown. He had helped many a slave to escape, and probably knew the principal negroes between Georgetown and Falmouth. He would be able to give me their names and some advice about my expedition. But the distance was five miles, and I was baffled by a terrible storm. I waited long for it to abate, but it only seemed to increase. I determined, however, to go, and without disturbing any one crept out into the darkness at about eleven o'clock. The thunder and lightning were fierce, the rain fell in torrents, the wind rendered an umbrella useless, the streets were flooded. As I approached Georgetown bridge the lights were few, but I knew every foot of the road leading to my old Methodist circuit. When I had got through Georgetown to the line of negro cabins a new difficulty confronted me; they were all dark—it was after midnight—and I could not identify the shanty sought. At length, however, I saw a glimmer of light in one little window, and to that I went. As I approached the door I heard negro voices within singing a hymn. When I knocked the voices ceased; there was perfect silence. On another knock a voice demanded, "Who is that?" I answered, "A friend! Moncure Conway." There was a wild shout, the door flew open, and there I found all my father's negroes.

They had just arrived, most of them in the storm. Through a weary way of near sixty miles they had been dragging themselves and their little ones, their coverlets and boxes. They were crammed into the two ground rooms, the children sleeping wherever they could find a place for their weary heads, and several mothers had babes at their breasts. The latest comers were wet. The elements had pursued them like bloodhounds; they were tossed about by destiny, but still able to raise their song in the night.

Many years had parted me from them, but when I entered all knew me on the instant. Old Maria, who had nursed me when I was a child, sprang forward and folded me in her arms as if I were still an infant. They pressed around me with their children, and clung to me as to a lifeboat in their storm. Far into the night we sat together; and they listened with glistening eyes as I told them of the region to which I meant to take them, where never should they feel oppression, never hear of war again.

Thus I was saved the danger and expense of going down into Stafford. But for all the gladness of this night, my troubles had scarcely begun. It was yet a question whether negroes situated like these were free to go North; for every coloured person taken over them the railroads exacted a bond of $3000, with security, for fear they might be sued by an owner for taking off his property. And there was still a potential proslavery and Confederate mob in Baltimore, through which at the time a journey to Ohio must be made. In Baltimore passengers going west were taken in omnibuses through many streets to another station. General Wadsworth, military governor of the district, was ready to see me safely on the road to Baltimore, but could not guarantee me transit through that city. Senator Sumner got together several congressmen to consult on the matter, and one of them—Giddings, I think—said the only safe way was for me to take a cowhide and drive the negroes through the Baltimore streets! But though such a ruse might, as he humorously said, bring all white Baltimore to my feet, it was suggested that it might have the reverse effect on the excited negroes there. Though my father was a Confederate, there was as yet no legal process by which the title of his slaves to freedom could be perfected. I was thus, in the eye of the law, a slaveholder! Although I could not obtain authority to convey these negroes to Ohio, Secretary Chase obtained a letter to General Wool, commander at Fort McHenry, which would authorize him to grant me protection if necessary in taking "my father's slaves" through Baltimore. This did not brighten the prospect much. General Wool was a good but infirm old man, not likely to interest himself in my affair, and the fort was a long distance from the centre of Baltimore, through which we had to pass.

At last we started out from Washington, a concourse of coloured people attending us. The terrors did not fail us when we were set down in the streets of Baltimore, with a small world of baggage and far from the other station. There were no arrangements to take any but white people from station to station. The sensation we caused was immediate; hundreds of negroes of all ages surrounded us and became so mixed up with mine, especially the children, that it was hard to distinguish them. For a few moments there was danger from these negroes. There had been rumors of Washington slaveholders hurrying their slave into Maryland to evade the Act of Emancipation in the District; and my Virginian physique being unmistakable, the dusky folk muttered and hissed around me and impeded my efforts. But some signs passed from "my contrabands" which suddenly transformed the angry crowd into friends; they were presently conveying us with our baggage in wagons, making a procession across the city. But the procession was too triumphal. It excited attention in every street, and when we reached the station we had an ugly crowd of whites to confront.

Alas, there was no westward train for three mortal hours! I took the negroes into the regular waiting-room, so completely had I forgotten the customs of slave States. Of course the railroad officials drove us angrily out. I asked for some room; they had "no room for niggers." I offered to pay for one, but could not get it. I asked to be permitted to take them into a car, but was told that the gate would not be unlocked for two hours. Meanwhile we were in the streets, and the crowd of whites was increasing every moment; and they saw, by the delight of the blacks, that it was an abolition movement. Uglier and uglier they became, glaring at me, and annoying the negroes under my protection until I had to restrain my men from resentment. I implored my people to be patient, and pointed out to the police the threatening aspect of affairs; but these sneeringly said it was my own affair, not theirs. Nevertheless, I took a bit of paper from my pocket, and I declared it would take the negroes through though it should bring the guns of Fort McHenry on the city. This imposing utterance had evident effect on some in the crowd. Yet they persisted in worrying my negroes, and, when I interfered, several called me "a damned abolitionist, who had brought on the war."

At length, much to my relief, the ticket-agent appeared at his window. I saw that, like the other officials, he was angry, but he was a fine-looking Marylander. He turned into flint as I approached; and when I asked the price of tickets, he said sharply, "I can't let those negroes go on this road at any price." I knew that he would have to let them go, but knew also that he could make things very uncomfortable for us. I silently presented my military order to the disagreeable and handsome agent, and he began to read it. He had read but two or three words of it when he looked up with astonishment, and said, "The paper says these are your father's slaves." "They are," I replied. "Why, sir, they would bring a good deal of money in Baltimore" "Possibly," I replied. Whereupon (moved probably by supposing that I was making a great sacrifice) he said, "By God, you shall have every car on this road if you want it!" Then having sold me the tickets, he gave his ticket-selling to a subordinate, and went out to secure us a car to ourselves; and from that moment the imprecations around us sank, and our way was made smooth.

It was late in the evening when we started, and we were to travel all night. I observed that the negroes would neither talk nor sleep. The mothers had put their children to sleep, but were themselves holding a silent watch. They were yet in a slave State, and every station at which the train paused was a possible danger. At last, when the name of a certain wooding-up station was called out, I observed that every eye danced, every tongue was loosened, and after some singing they all dropped off to sleep. It was not until next day that I learned that the station which had wrought such a transformation was the dividing line between the slave and the free States. How they knew it I cannot divine; it was a small place, but there the shadow of slavery ended.

Far into the night we sat together; and they listened with glistening eyes as I told them of the region to which I meant to take them . . .

_____M. D. Conway

APPENDIX B

NAMES OF THE CONWAY COLONY FREEDOM SEEKERS

Accounts vary as to the number of slaves Moncure Conway shepherded to Yellow Springs, Ohio, in 1862. They range from 31 to 70. Most often mentioned are 31 slaves described as "his father's slaves," those actually owned by Walker P. Conway. Slaves owned by a neighbor, Anna Dunbar, also made the journey, as did at least one slave owned by another neighbor, Dr. Rose.

In some accounts, the youngest children and babies may not have been counted. In *Testimonies Concerning Slavery*, Conway states the number as between forty and fifty, adding that most of the women had a baby at their breast and there were lots of children. The author, with the gracious assistance of Ms. Jean McKee, historian of the Conway Colony, has identified 50 individuals:

John Berk
Elizabeth Berk
Elizabeth S. Berk
William Berk
Emma Berk
Thornton Berk
William Bray
Susan Bray
Hannah Dunnaho, "Aunt Hannah"
Cuffee Dunnaho
Benjamin Grimes
Hannah Grimes
Eliza Gwinn, "Aunt Lizy"
Dunmore Gwinn

Alfred Gwinn
George Gwinn
Jacob Gwinn
Isabel Gwinn (Isabelle)
Nellie Gwinn
Evaline Gwinn
Richard Herod, coach driver for Dr. Rose
Nancy Gwinn Herod
Elizabeth Herod (Herood)
James Holmes
Luthenia Holmes
Maria Humstead, "Old Maria"
Churchill Humstead
John Humstead
Peter Humstead
Charles Morgan
Julia Gwinn Morgan
Mary Morgan
Alice Parker (soon went to Easton, Pennsylvania)
Clarissie Parker
James Parker, valet of Walker P. Conway
Adelaide Parker
Anna Parker
David Parker
Churchwill Taylor
Maria Taylor, wife
Anne Taylor
May Taylor
Maria Taylor, daughter
Lucy Taylor
Susan Taylor
Willard Taylor
Richard Taylor
Moncure Taylor
Maria Wormsley
Francis (last name unknown) and her two youngest children

Walker P. Conway is known to have engaged P.M. Tabb & Son, Negro Hirers and General Agents, in Richmond, Virginia. He owned between 50 and 60 slaves. Some were hired out and did not have the same opportunity to reach Georgetown in July 1862. From Moncure Conway's "Spouting Rock Letters" we learn, ". . . no sooner did the United States military lines reach Fredericksburg than every single one of my father's slaves not hired out below those lines asserted and gained his or her liberty . . . Some of their children hired at Richmond and elsewhere had to be left. There were many hardships in the way of leaving; yet these negroes . . . leaped at their liberty as soon as it came within reach."

Eliza and Dunmore reportedly brought nine of their children to Yellow Springs. The list of Gwinn names does not include all nine. Their son Peter Gwinn and another son (unidentified) each served as body servant for the two Conway brothers in the Confederate army. Peter did not go to Yellow Springs, and after the war lived in Washington, D.C.

James Parker, Walker P. Conway's valet, had a wife named Clarissa who, sometime before the Civil War, became mentally ill and was committed to an asylum in Baltimore. Walker P. Conway granted James an annual expense-paid visit to see his wife. It is not known what arrangements were made to bring her to Yellow Springs. The name, Clarissie Parker, turns up among the Conway Colony members.

On June 15, 2003, Ohio Governor Bob Taft signed a State Resolution establishing a new Ohio State Historical Marker to honor the Conway Colony and Moncure Daniel Conway. Ms. Lenetta Schools of Falmouth, and Mr. Frank White of Stafford County, Virginia, traveled to Yellow Springs to meet the Conway Colony descendants and attend the unveiling of the marker.

In 2004, a Virginia State Historical Marker honoring Moncure Daniel Conway was provided by The Commonwealth of Virginia. Descendants of the Conway Colony founders, who traveled from Ohio to Virginia, were the guests of honor in Falmouth. The same year, the National Park Service designated Conway House as a National Underground Railroad Network to Freedom Historical Site. A bronze plaque reads:

CONWAY HOUSE was the home of Moncure Conway who freed himself from the dogmas of his culture and became an abolitionist. He is the only descendent of one of our nation's Founding Fathers to actively lead escaping slaves to freedom, thereby taking the initial steps to correct what was not accomplished in the Constitutional Convention. Conway House makes a significant contribution to understanding the desire to achieve freedom of one's own self destiny.

APPENDIX C

LETTER FROM VIRGINIA

Previously, portions of Moncure Conway's "Letter from Virginia" have been quoted. An additional selection from "Letter from Virginia," located in Moncure Daniel Conway Special Collections, Rare Book and Manuscripts, Butler Library, Columbia University, provides a wonderful description of how Conway viewed post-war Falmouth. Conway was living abroad in London before his return visit to Virginia:

Nay, there had reached me across the sea intimations that a visit now would be welcomed; that hands once coldly withdrawn would be eagerly extended; that all could now recognize a true friend in one who had seemed a foe. These intimations have been more than fulfilled. For nearly a month now it has been my sweet privilege to know the joy of reunion and reconciliation. In the anxiety to remedy the injustice once done me even my notorious heresy has been overlooked, and the orthodox churches thrice thrown open that I might address the people.

As for the first time since I have been old enough to appreciate natural beauty I have wandered through this region, and as I now behold it free from the curse of Slavery—the white and black dwelling kindly together—I have realized how fair is the land from which I was banished. Nowhere—not even in Ireland, Scotland, or Switzerland, have I beheld a more picturesque region than that in which I write this letter. For a month the skies have spread their soft azure over river, glen and hill, while the blossoms of summer have passed to the brighter hues of early autumn. It is now the Indian Summer, which diffuses a shimmer of blue mist through the balmy air, a season which the red men called "the smile of the great spirit." Through the glowing atmosphere the sweet gum and maple are burning like embers; the hickory, ash, and saxifrage are sending up a leafy spray of gold; the red sumac decorates every field. The Virginia creeper winds over every field, like a throng of firry serpents; and the Virginia nightingale flashes torch like through the bowers of evergreen, or the woods festooned with grapevines. The golden maize stands uplifting its bounty by every roadside. The chinquapin nuts peep out like bright black eyes from their burrs, and seem to say, "Old friend, how many times have you scratched your hands in trying to get sweet things since you used to gather us in the Saturday afternoons?" I tasted them when on my way to visit some former schoolmates, and they were delicious as of old, and happy young faces appeared around them with merry laughter; but when I had seen the schoolmates and was returning, their old taste was changed, and gray-haired men and women seemed to be silently passing the chinquapin bushes without pausing or inviting me to pause. Ah, how strange it is to meet again those whom we knew as blooming boys and little maidens, and try to recover them and recognize them in pale gray-haired fathers and mothers! Time touches us by such slight degrees, we grow old so insensibly, that we only learn our own age when we see its effects summed up in others without the intervening graduations. To me it is laughing childhood transformed at a stroke to maturity, youth and beauty to wrinkled age, as it were in a single night.

As I was wandering in the deep woods on the bank of the Rappahannock, on the brightest of summer days, I lay down to rest beneath the shade of a tree. Suddenly a melody broke forth in the air, and to it I listened breathlessly—charmed, enchanted, unconscious of the passing hours. Then I rose and returned home. I found the house in dilapidation, the garden overgrown with weeds, the trees cut down and withered, its inmates scattered. The desolations of time, revolution, war, have passed over the scene. I seek those whom I left and find some grown aged, some in their graves, over their breast their children planting flowers. Slowly it dawns on me that I have been listening twenty-five years to that melody which seemed only the charm of a happy morning.

So seemed at first; but long since I knew that it was the song of liberation sung at the grated windows of a prisoner. Destiny had lavished on my lot everything but freedom. Pint up in a narrow creed, taught to hold my own soul evil and Nature accursed, moving through a weary round of prayer-meetings, listening to dull sermons, hearing of the great world beyond our village only as a vast empire over which Satan reigned supreme, I had lived in one of the fairest regions of the earth as in a wilderness or desert; until that day when the gracious theme of liberty began to steal into my breast. The flowers bursting into bloom whispered, "Break thy bonds", and the flying cloud said "Be free!" The strain was taken up by the winds, I heard it in the ebb and flow of the tide, and to it moved the stars in their courses. At last I went forth into the world, a homeless wanderer but a free man. Later I learned that this music of freedom meant also the purpose and order of the world. Ere long that theme which I heard from flowers and streams was breaking loud over the land in the thunders of war; amid the howl of shot and shell and the wild cries of anguish there was still a music—a music of the breaking of millions of fetters, the hymns of slaves set free, and, not less sweet, of slaveholders set free. The destiny of nations is bound to the conscience of a child.

_____Moncure Daniel Conway, October 1875

APPENDIX D

African Americans from Falmouth of the late-19th to mid-20th centuries, with Comments from Oral History

The following names from Falmouth were not taken from official records. I leave that pursuit to future scholars. I "collected" these names during my personal interviews with those who have now grown old, who graciously shared with me their recollections and memories. The names are all the more precious because they were recalled from the heart rather than a census record or court document. The information is sometimes sensitive. I have tried to phrase the comments as closely as they were spoken to me during the interviews. The list below is not, of course, inclusive of every African American who lived in Falmouth after the Civil War.

The past moves me and with me, although I remove myself from it. Its light often shines on this night traveler; and when it does, I scribble it down. Whatever pleasure is in it I need pass on. That's happiness.

_____Virginia Hamilton

Peter Alexander, originally from Fredericksburg. He separated from his wife and moved to Falmouth, where he lived along River Road with Julia Russell for thirty years.

Aunt Sarah, no last name, may have been Rowser. She was a midwife for the Payne Family (white). She would live with the family when a child was born and move from Payne Family home to home as she was needed.

Sallie Byrd, may have lived on Rowser Road. She is well remembered as one who could skillfully balance large workloads on her head. While doing this she could shake her head yes and no during a conversation as if nothing were on top of her head.

Fannie Churchill, talked in a whisper because she had something wrong with her voice box. She moved to Fredericksburg as an elderly woman. White men from Falmouth would go over to do chores for her that she could not do for herself. Whenever they went, Sam Berry [a white store owner] always sent her a basket of groceries.

Daisy Clark, mother of Dave, Edward, and Rufus Clark. The Clark family lived on US Route 17. Daisy later married John Long and lived on US Route 1.

Dave (Davie or Dana) Clark, lived on US Route 1 across from the old Falmouth Fire Station.

Edward Clark, brother of Dave and Rufus Clark.

Rufus Clark, drove a school bus in the 1940s. He lived near Olde Forge on US Route 17.

Ham Coon, lived up in the ravine called Cady's Gut in a shack. At one time he had a grave marker with his name on it in the Union Church Cemetery, but now the marker is gone. The name may also have been spelled Coons.

Rose Donavan, white. She married Lawrence Wheeler. The Donavan family lived in the old frame Thompson Sullivan house down a lane behind the "colored church" (Mt. Pisgah) on US Route 1. Rose's sisters were Anna and Lilly Mae. The girls sometimes had their black girlfriends spend the night "sleeping over" at the Donavan house.

Eva Gunn, did "practices," such as sprinkling flour meal around her house to keep people away. She may have been the mother of Willie Ann Gunn.

Willie Ann Gunn (b. 1899, d. 1986), washed cloths, curtains and drapes, ironed, did household chores for people, and cooked for parties and weddings. She also did some upholstery work. When little white girls were playing and stayed out too late before dark, she would say, "You best to get along home now girls!" Described in nature as a lovely woman who helped everyone (white and black), she lived with the Wheeler family and was the half sister of Robert Wheeler.

In the 1940s, she baked the weeding cake for a Falmouth white couple and attended the church wedding but was not allowed in the main body of the sanctuary. Rather, she was seated in the balcony. Many years later the bride explained that no prejudice was intended, this being what was acceptable at the time. Willie Ann married David Southerland and lived in Fredericksburg. Her funeral was held at Shiloh Old Site Church in Fredericksburg and attended by a large crowd. She is buried in Shiloh Church Cemetery in Fredericksburg.

John Long, 5'5" tall, a laborer, had chickens. He lived with his mother Lucie Long for many years. He was a very "private man." As he got older he lost his hearing and white boys would throw rocks at his house for fun. He went to the doctor and was given an early model hearing aid. In the latter four or five years of his life he married Daisy Clark. John died in 1948 or 1949 and is buried in the Union Church Cemetery.

Lucie Long, may have been the mother of John Long. Lucie is believed to be buried in the Union Church Cemetery.

Pricilla Long, sister of John Long. She died June 5, 1925, and is buried in the Union Church Cemetery. Pricilla was thought by some to be the mother of John Long due to John having been possibly born out of wedlock, but John always introduced her to others as his sister.

Annie Duncan Lucas (b. ca. 1834, d. 1919), married to Daniel Lucas. She was a servant at the Barnes House and a Barnes family slave before the Civil War.

Archie Lucas, was the son of Sarah Lucas, cook for the Melchers at Belmont. Mrs. Melchers gave money to provide Archie with a college education. He became an educator and died about the year 2007.

Betty Lucas (b.1889, d.1929). Her grave is in the Union Church Cemetery. It is not clear if she was white or part of an African American family named Lucas.

Corbin Lucas, son of Nannie Rowser Lucas and Taylor Corbin Lucas. As a boy of 14 or 15, Corbin drowned about the year 1943 or 1944 in Hazel Run in Fredericksburg. He is buried in the "Black Cemetery," Shiloh Church Cemetery in Fredericksburg.

Cornelius S. Lucas, a slave, he was an aide (body servant) to a Confederate officer during the Civil War. He lived in Fredericksburg after the war and operated a store and coffee house. Ordained in 1882, Lucas became minister of the Little Shiloh Baptist Church in Falmouth and remained active there till his death in 1927. He and his wife Maria Yates Lucas are buried together in Shiloh Church Cemetery in Fredericksburg. L. Reginald Lucas of Spotsylvania is his grandson.

Daniel "Danny" Lucas, married to Annie Duncan Lucas, may have been a Barnes family slave before the Civil War. His obituary appearing in the Fredericksburg *Free Lance*, November 15, 1904, states: "Daniel Lucas, colored, aged about 70 years died at his home in Falmouth Friday night. Daniel was thoroughly reliable and respected by all who knew him. For many years he had been the faithful mail carrier between this city [Fredericksburg] and Falmouth."

James "Luke" Lucas, lived on Rowser Lane [Road] until the 1937 flood. His mother was Nannie Rowser and his father was Taylor Corbin Lucas. His maternal grandfather was "Uncle Jim" Rowser, the subject of a painting by Gari Melchers. As a child, James watched the Falmouth Colored School being washed away during the 1937 flood of the Rappahannock River.

Nannie O. Rowser Lucas, married Taylor Corbin Lucas. A small woman, she worked as a housekeeper for different people in Fredericksburg. Nannie had two sons, James and Corbin. The latter drowned when he was young. They lived at the end of Rowser Road and relocated in Fredericksburg after the 1937 flood. "Uncle Jim" Rowser, was her father. Nannie is buried in Shiloh Church Cemetery in Fredericksburg.

Sarah (or Sara) Lucas, was the cook for the Melchers at Belmont. She lived in a small house on the north side of Washington Street near Falls Run. This house was known as the "Lucas House," and was said by St. Clair Brooks to have originally been a slave quarters (today the house has undergone much change). Sarah may have worked for the Ficklens prior to the Melchers purchasing the Belmont estate. Her son was Archie Lucas.

Taylor Corbin Lucas, originally from Corbin in Essex County, Virginia, he went by the name "Taylor" and married Nannie O. Rowser. Taylor is buried in Shiloh Church Cemetery in Fredericksburg.

Ramous (no last name), a boy who lived with the Geneva Brooks Family after the Civil War. The Brooks home was the "Old Cotton Warehouse." To avoid work and keep from being found, Ramous would jump in a briar patch and stay there all day.

William "Billy" R. Rollins (b. 1917, d. 1995), son of Julia Russell. As a child growing up in Falmouth, he was called Billy. He served in the US Army as a 2nd Lieutenant in World War II and as a 1st Lieutenant in the Korean Conflict. On December 3, 1941, he returned home to Falmouth on leave. His leave was cut short once the Japanese attacked Pearl Harbor four days later. Rollins retired from the US Army in 1962 as a Lt. Colonel and lived in Washington, D.C., until his death. Billy's first wife was Bertha Young of Fredericksburg. They had no children. Bertha died while Billy was in the service. His second wife for 30 years was Ethel Lenora Rollins. Billy Rollins is buried in Arlington National Cemetery.

Adrian Roots, brother of Willie P. Roots, never married.

Ethel M. Roots, daughter of Mary and Willie P. Roots.

Fannie L. Roots (b. 1914, d. 2004), a daughter of Mary Roots and Willie P. Roots. She was Mrs. Melchers' maid at Belmont and served at parties dressed in formal "maid outfits." Fannie never married. She was an active member of the Stafford County Citizens' Alliance for many years and is buried in the Nelson Family Cemetery near Hartwood in Stafford County.

Hawk "Hawky" Roots (given name may have been Charles), a brother of Willie P. Roots. Hawk lived in Falmouth but kept a shanty just outside of town where the Clearview Heights subdivision is today. On voting day in Falmouth, "Noodles" Cox (white) voted a second time using the name of Hawk Roots, who had just died and was still lying in his casket. Cox was ridiculed for his fraudulent act.

James "Jimmy" E. Roots, a son of Mary and Willie P. Roots. He married Alice Lee. They lived on US Route 17.

Mary G. Roots, a daughter of Mary and Willie P. Roots. She married a Lewis.

Mary (Lettie) Nelson Roots, wife of Willie P. Roots. They supposedly had eight children. A daughter, Fannie Roots, stated there were six children. Census records indicate only six. Possibly two grandchildren were raised in the Roots' household as a son and daughter. Mary was part Native American, a descendant of Rappahannock Indians.

Nelson C. Roots, a son of Mary and Willie P. Roots.

Rachael Roots, a daughter (or granddaughter) of Mary and Willie P. Roots. She married young and went to live in Fredericksburg.

Reuben Roots, a son (or grandson) of Mary and Willie P. Roots. He was a newspaper boy in Falmouth. As a boy, he would go to the Falmouth post office to pick up Mrs. Melcher's mail for her. He did this until Mrs. Melcher's chauffeur assumed the responsibility.

William Carroll Roots, a son of Mary and Willie P. Roots. He went by the name "Caroll."

William "Willie" Peyton Roots (b. 1878, d. 1944), his grave marker placed sometime later gives the year of death as 1943 (believed to be an error). Falmouth lore maintains his father was a slave stud. Willie worked for C.H. Montgomery Coal Co. and Seed Co. in Fredericksburg. His marked grave is in the Union Church Cemetery. Willie married Mary L. Nelson from Hartwood in 1893. Nelson, Jimmy, Caroll, and Reuben were their sons, Ethel, Fannie, Mary, and Rachael were daughters (Reuben and Rachael may have been grandchildren raised in the household as their own children).

Rosie (no last name), helped the Payne Family (white) with domestic chores. She moved away from Falmouth. After many years, she contacted the Payne family and asked them to visit her in the hospital in Fairfax (which they did). She said she wanted to see them one last time before she died.

Chester Rowser, a son of Thomas B. and Laura Bundy Rowser. The family lived on "Rowser Lane" now Rowser Road.

James "Uncle Jim" Rowser, lived on "Rowser Lane." Uncle Jim was the subject of one of Gari Melchers' paintings. The painting was done around 1918. He is reported to be buried in the "Black Cemetery," Shiloh Church Cemetery in Fredericksburg.

Wilbert J. Rowser, a son of Thomas B. and Laura Bundy Rowser. He married Ella Mae Randall of Hampton, Virginia, in 1947. Ella Rowser was a well known and longtime African American educator in Stafford County. The old H.H. Poole School building in Stafford was renamed in her honor as the Rowser Building. It is currently utilized by Stafford County Parks and Recreation. Wilbert and Billy Rollins both entered military service in the US Army on the same day prior to the outbreak of World War II. Wilbert relocated to Fredericksburg. He died December 13, 2005, at the age of 90. He was known for having "a keen sense of humor and an infectious smile to share with everyone."

Hannah Russell, is the name associated with the lot occupied by Julia Russell and her son William "Billy" R. Rollins. Property taxes were not paid after 1997 and the "Hannah Russell Estate" was sold at public auction by Stafford County. No additional information was found on Hannah Russell.

John W. Russell (b. March 15, 1880, d. Dec. 15, 1902). John Russell's grave is in a secluded wooded area of Falmouth known as the Hannah

Russell Estate. The grave is marked by a small headstone, partially buried.

Julia (Juliet) Russell (b. 1896, d. 1972). She married William Rollins but they separated when she was still young. She and Peter Alexander lived together for thirty years. A local seamstress, she made her own clothes and hats. She was very attractive, always well dressed and looked as if she had just stepped out of Macy's. Julia was later referred to as "Aunt Julia" by both white and black people. At some point Julia moved to Washington, D.C., and lived with her only son, William "Billy" R. Rollins. Julia was "light skinned." She is buried in Shiloh Church Cemetery in Fredericksburg.

Louise and Mathew Taylor, they had four children; Terry, Donnell, Monica, and Dianne. They lived on Rowser Road in the house previously occupied by the Lucas family, which moved to Fredericksburg in 1937. The family was said to be originally from Brooke. After Louise's death, the family moved back to Brooke.

Helen "Mammy Helen" Turner, midwife to many of the Brooks children born in Falmouth. She lived with the Brooks family (white) and in her later years lived with Geneva Brooks in the Old Cotton Warehouse. Her grave in the Union Church Cemetery is marked "Helen Turner Faithful Friend" without dates of birth or death. Helen is said to have been born in 1874, the year remembered as the one she herself gave.

Betty Wheeler, was the mother of Clarence, Elizabeth, Eustace, Robert, and Thomas Wheeler. Described as caring and helpful, she was highly regarded by the white community.

Clarence Wheeler (b. 1904, d. 1963). He ran a slaughter house in Falmouth and would sometimes go to other people's houses to butcher hogs at hog killing time. He was going to have a "late night tonight" when he went to cut down a very large oak tree belonging to Hanson Able (white). The tree accidentally fell on top of him and killed him. One account says that he had cut one tree and it fell into another. When he went to cut that tree down, one of them fell on him. Clarence is buried in Shiloh Church Cemetery in Fredericksburg.

Coleman "Coman" Wheeler, son of Helen and Clarence Wheeler. Coleman and his mother were both long-time teachers in Stafford County. Either or both of them taught at Berea, Concord, and Stafford Training School (later known as H.H. Poole School and the Rowser Building). Coleman taught at Drew Middle School until he retired.

Elizabeth Wheeler Alexander, sister of Clarence, Eustace, Robert, and Thomas Wheeler. Elizabeth died in 2009 at the age of 103.

Ethel L. Wheeler, wife of Robert Simpson Wheeler. Ethel sold Avon products and is remembered as always smiling and being kind to others.

James Eustace Wheeler (b. 1910, d. 1937), went by "Eustace." Eustace is buried in Shiloh Church Cemetery in Fredericksburg.

Fielding "Fee" Wheeler, married to Hattie Wheeler. Fee worked for Mrs. Melchers at Belmont. He was the chauffer and "nearest thing to a butler." He is buried in Sunset Cemetery in Fredericksburg. A white resident of Falmouth related that the "only time I ever saw my father cry was at Fee's funeral."

Fielding Wheeler, Jr., son of Fielding and Hattie Wheeler.

Hattie Wheeler, wife of Fielding Wheeler.

Helen Wheeler, wife of Clarence Wheeler. Helen was a long-time teacher in Stafford County.

Lawrence Wheeler, son of Ethel Wheeler and stepson of Robert Wheeler. Lawrence walked on crutches due to a spinal defect at birth. He married Rose Donavan.

Robert "Robby" Simpson Wheeler, married to Ethel L. Wheeler. He worked at Monroe and Berry Store as a meat cutter. In 1947, he opened his own store built of cinderblock. It was robbed three times at night through the same window and closed within three or four years. He was described as a "showy person" who "bought a horse when black people should not have had one and the white people did not like it." He later owned a number of horses and hired someone just to take care of them. Robert was a trustee of Mt. Pisgah Church in Falmouth. He and his family lived behind the church.

Thomas "Tom" A. Wheeler (b. 1907, d. 1986). Tom is buried in Shiloh Church Cemetery in Fredericksburg.

Vara Jane Wheeler, daughter of Fielding and Hattie Wheeler.

Wheeler, Roots, Rowser, and Lucas descendants still live in the Fredericksburg area. The surname Lucas appears frequently among African Americans from Fredericksburg and Falmouth. In some instances no relationship exists. The name Lucas is also found among early whites who once lived in the Falmouth area.

Historian Frank White provides the names of several African Americans living within two miles of Falmouth. Members of the Juggins family still live in their home place next to Falmouth Elementary School. Lewis Johnson lived with his father, mother, and other siblings, near Olde Forge on US Route 17. The family relocated to Stafford when Fort A.P. Hill acquired property in Caroline County. The French family also lived in the area of Olde Forge. On US Route 17, Boyd and Betsy Washington lived next door to Jimmy and Alice Roots. Norman and Anne Lee lived near Jimmy Roots, and the Scotts, who later moved to Philadelphia.

APPENDIX E

MONCURE CONWAY AFTER THE AMERICAN CIVIL WAR

LONDON

In 1863, with Conway's repulsion for the horrific warfare waged in America, London appeared more suited to his literary and intellectual pursuits. After lecturing in Great Britain on the American cause for emancipation, Conway wrote, "London had cordially offered me what my native country had not—a field for the exercise of the ministry for which my strange pilgrimage from slaveholding Virginia and Methodism to freedom and rationalism had trained me." Deciding to remain in London where he was joined by his wife and children, he became minister in 1866 through 1885, of that city's most distinguished free thought congregation, South Place Ethical Society. In 1870, during the Franco-Prussian War, he was a field correspondent for the *New York World*.

Lecturing abroad and in America, Conway regularly contributed to leading periodicals such as the *Atlantic Monthly* and the *North American Review*. While writing for *Harper's* and the *Cincinnati Commercial* his "London Letters" interpreted England for America. With letters from an "American Minister in London" and writing for *Fraser's* and *The Fortnightly Review*, Conway interpreted America for England. Conway was the London literary agent for Walt Whitman, Mark Twain, Louisa May Alcott, and Elizabeth Cady Stanton. He was the American agent for Robert Browning.

Conway's spiritual journey moved from theism to a reverential agnosticism. In London, he was among the late-Victorian intellectuals who affected change in established religion and morality. Conway endeavored to humanize knowledge for all classes through the arts. Acquainted with most of the eminent men and women of his time, his friendships included Carlyle, Rossetti, Annie Besant, Charles Darwin, Agassiz, Herbert Spencer, and Robert Collyer.

AMERICA

In 1884, Conway became the first president of the Thomas Paine National Historical Association in New Rochelle, New York. In 1885, Conway moved to New York City, where he resided for the next seven years. There he wrote some of his most noted works of history, including those related to his beloved Virginia. Related are *Omitted Chapters of History Disclosed in the Life and Papers of Edmund Randolph* (1888), *George Washington and Mount Vernon* (1889), *George Washington's Rules of Civility* (1890), and *Barons of the Potomac and Rappahannock* (1892). In 1892, Conway was awarded an honorary Doctorate of Literature and History by Dickinson College.

In 1892, Conway returned to London and resumed his ministerial position at South Place Ethical Society. He returned to New York City in 1897. His wife Ellen died of cancer on Christmas Day, 1897. The following year, Conway left the United States in opposition to "spreadeagleism" and the Spanish-American War.

PARIS

Conway did not return to Britain, but rather chose to reside in Paris, France. There he championed the cause of world peace. In 1904, his friend Andrew Carnegie donated money for a building at Dickinson College to be named Conway Hall in his honor. During his lifetime he had sixty-six major works published. In 1907, Moncure Conway died in Paris.

Born in a "lonely corner of the world," Conway later engaged Europe's most progressive thinkers and his literary works articulated the highest levels of human endeavor. As an expatriate, one who had to leave Virginia's "sacred soil," Conway contributed to the diversity, equality, and freedom all Virginians enjoy regardless of color, religion, or political beliefs.

Conway knew what, at their best, Melville, and Steinbeck, and Kevonac knew—that Americans live up to their destiny not by staying close to home but by leaving it . . .

—————John d'Entremont

APPENDIX F

Union Branch of the True Vine Covenant

UBTV was founded shortly after the Civil War and incorporated in the early 20th century.

UBTV is associated with, but independent of Bethlehem Primitive Baptist Church (BPBC).

Having been led, as we believe, by the Spirit of God to receive the Lord Jesus Christ as our Savior, and on the profession of our faith, having been baptized of the Father, and of the Son, and of the Holy Ghost we do now, in the presence of God and angels, most solemnly and joyfully enter in the covenant with one another as one body of Christ.

We engage, therefore, by the aid of the Holy Spirit, to walk together in Christian love;

To strive for the advancement of this church in knowledge, holiness and comfort;

To promote its prosperity and spirituality;

To sustain its worship, ordinance, discipline, and doctrines;

To give it a sacred and a highest preeminence over all institutions of human origin;

To participate enthusiastically in UBTV activities, and to contribute cheerfully and regularly to the support, ministries and expenses of a home church, the relief of the poor, and the spread of the gospel through all nations. (BPBC) is UBTV'S home church. One may be a member of UBTV and another Christian Church.)

We also engage to maintain family and secret devotions;

To religiously educate our children;

To seek the salvation of our kindred and acquaintances;

To walk circumspectly in the world;

To be just in our dealings, faithful in our engagements and exemplary in deportment;

To avoid all tattling, backbiting and excessive anger;

To abstain from abusing intoxicating drugs or other substances (liquids and solids), and be zealous in our efforts to advance the kingdom of our Savior;

We further engage to watch over one another in brotherly love;

To remember each other in prayer;

To aid each other in sickness and distress;

To cultivate Christian sympathy in feeling and courtesy in speech;

To be slow to take offense, but always ready for reconciliation and mindful of the rules of our Savior, to secure it without delay;

We moreover state, that if moved from UBTV, we will remain united with a Christian Church, where we can carry out the spirit of the covenant and the principals of God's word.

NOTES

1. Miriam Haynie, *The Stronghold, A Story of Historic Northern Neck of Virginia and Its People* (Richmond, Virginia: The Dietz Press, Incorporated, 1959), 21-22.
2. Kerry Ogata, "African American Women and Medicine: Expanding Interpretations of Colono Ware" (Master's thesis, Department of Anthropology, University of South Carolina, Columbia, 1995). See Chapter Two, "Colono Ware and Models of Cultural Contact."
3. "Historic Resources at the Falls of the Rappahannock River," Department of Planning and Community Development, City of Fredericksburg, Fredericksburg, Virginia (2001), 36.
4. Found by Brian Schools. The Colono Ware shard was picked up on the grounds of the Conway House in 2000. The shard is 1 1/4 by 1 5/8 inches, gray black in color, and well burnished. It is now in the Conway House Collections, Falmouth, Virginia. Colono Ware shards tan or brown in color have been found at Ferry Farm on the Rappahannock River below Falmouth. Lora Galke, interview by author, Ferry Farm Foundation, May 2009.
5. Ogata, Chapter One, "Introduction." See also Chapter Four, "African American Women and the Function of Colono Ware."
6. Shirley Virginia Parrish, "The Fur and Skin Trade of Colonial Virginia" (Master thesis, Department of History, Old Dominion University, 1972), 67.
7. Oscar H. Darter, *Colonial Fredericksburg and Neighborhood in Perspective* (New York: Twayne Publishers, 1957), 48.
8. Cadwallader Jones Map, 1687, showing the vast distances traveled in the trade, courtesy of Wayne Morris of Fredericksburg, Virginia.
9. Parrish, 133.
10. Ibid., 123.
11. Margaret L. Smith, "1720 Falmouth, Va.," Garden Club of Falmouth, Va. (1922).

[12] Moncure Daniel Conway, *Moncure Daniel Conway, Autobiography, Memories, and Experiences* (Cambridge: The Riverside Press, 1904), Vol. I, 35. The name Hogtown is generally known in oral history among the older residents. The nickname became a point of derision among Fredericksburg residents. A well-known former resident of Falmouth, Pina Brooks Swift, delighted in relating the story of Falmouth's nickname (interview by author, 2003). Another resident, Ed Resio, related that there was a pecking order with "upper Hogtown" and "lower Hogtown" (interview by author, 2010).

[13] Hogs were a main food staple in Colonial Virginia and afterward. The meat was cured in salt brine and smoked to keep it preserved throughout the year till the next killing season during late fall. When the meat was prepared for smoking, it was hung in the smokehouse with a fire in an open pit in the floor. A boy slave, eight or nine years old, would be locked inside the smokehouse for three days at a time to keep the fire going. On large plantations the process might last for as many as 14 days.

[14] Duncan, "Falmouth," *Virginia Gazette*, Norfolk, April 20, 1775, and Green, "Ten Dollars Reward. Ranaway" *Virginia Herald*, Fredericksburg, September 25, 1795. Tom Costa, and The Rectors and Visitors of the University of Virginia "The Geography of Slavery in Virginia," University of Virginia (2005), http://www2.vcdh.virginia.edu/gos/index.html.

[15] Ruth Coder Fitzgerald, "African-American History of Stafford County," Stafford County Tourism Brochure, Library Point, Central Rappahannock Regional Library (2002), http://librarypoint.org/african_american_history_of_stafford_virginia.

[16] Remnants of the wharf, specifically the large cut stones and iron mooring rings, were seen by Falmouth residents in their younger years when the river receded after a major flood. In particular this was related to the author by Frank Shelton, Sr. in 1999 and Herbert Brooks in 2009 who were "brought up on the river."

[17] Conway, *Autobiography*, Vol. I, 22-23.

[18] The King's Highway generally followed the routes of present day US Route 1 from Alexandria to Fredericksburg and State Route 2 leading to Bowling Green. Today this is designated a segment of the Washington Rochambeau Revolutionary Route.

Notes

19 Fairfax Harrison, *Landmarks of Old Prince William*, Volume I and II (Baltimore, Maryland: Gateway Press, Inc., 1987), 445-446. "Stafford duly appointed surveyors for the Potomac Path in three districts.... This would bring us to Aquia, whereupon, in 1666, the cleared road was extended 'from Aquia to Chopawamsic.'"

20 The King's Highway was an important road to Williamsburg, which served as Virginia's colonial capital until 1779, when it was moved to Richmond. One historian has suggested that King Street in Falmouth was named after Robert "King" Carter and not the King of England.

21 The spelling is consistently "King's Street" as it appears in the Falmouth Trustees' Minutes Book.

22 William Waller Hening, *Laws of Virginia* (Richmond: Franklin Press, 1820), 165, 297. "That all roads which heretofore have, or hereafter shall be ordered by the general court, or county court, to be laid out, and cleared, for the use and conveniency of the inhabitants of the country or county, shall be cleared and maintained by the surveyors appointed by the courts, and the inhabitants contiguous thereto."

23 Jerrilynn Eby MacGreggor, email to author, 26 January 2012.

24 Paula S. Felder, "The Falmouth Story, A View from the Twentieth Century," The Town Plan of Falmouth, and Part Two (no date), Virginiana Room, Rappahannock Regional Library, Fredericksburg, Virginia. The original town plan has been lost.

25 Hening, *Laws of Virginia*, 132-133.

26 Tom Costa, "Runaway Slaves and Servants in Colonial Virginia," ed. Brendan Wolfe, Virginia Foundation for the Humanities (January 18, 2012), http://encyclopediavirginia.org/Runaway_Slaves_and_Servants_in_Colonial_Virginia.

27 Anita Wills, *Notes And Documents of Free Persons of Color* (Raleigh, North Carolina: Lulu Publishing Company, 2003), 78.

28 T.M. Devine, ed., *A Scottish Firm in Virginia 1767-1777 W. Cuninghame and Co.* (Scottish History Society, Edinburgh: Clark Constable 1984), xv-xvi.

29 Ibid., 4-5.

30 Ibid., 211-212. See also Samuel Eliot Morison and Henry Steele Commager, William E. Leuchtenburg, *The Growth of the American Republic: Volume 1*, Seventh Edition (New York: Oxford University Press, 1980), 168. "A Declaration of the Causes and Necessity of Taking Up Arms.... We have pursued every temperate, every respectful

measure; we have even proceeded to break off our commercial intercourse with our fellow-subjects, as the last peaceable admonition, that our attachment to no nation upon earth should supplant our attachment to liberty."

31 Morison, *The Growth of the American Republic: Volume 1*, 168. "With hearts fortified with animating reflections, we most solemnly, before God and the world, declare, that, exerting the utmost energy of those powers, which our beneficent Creator hath graciously bestowed upon us, the arms we have been compelled by our enemies to assume, we will, in defiance of every hazard, with unabating firmness and perseverance employ for the preservation of our liberties; being with one mind resolved to die freemen rather than to live as slaves."

32 "Route of the French Army Wagon Train from Annapolis, Maryland, to Yorktown, Virginia, in 1781," Expedition Particuliere Commemorative Cantonment Society, Mount Vernon, Virginia (2010), http://xenophongroup.com/mcjoynt/wagon.htm. See also "The Washington-Rochambeau Revolutionary Route," National Park Service (2003), http://www.nps.gov/revwar/pdf/Significance%20 Report-Screen.pdf.

33 Hayes, "A Young likely Negro Man," *Virginia Gazette*, September 28, 1782, "The Geography of Slavery in Virginia."

34 Dixon & Hunter, "Five Dollars Reward," *Virginia Gazette*, Williamsburg, May 2, 1777, in "The Geography of Slavery in Virginia."

35 Jerrilynn Eby, *Laying the Hoe, A Century of Iron Manufacturing in Stafford County, Virginia* (Westminster, Maryland: Willow Bend Books, 2003), 193, 199, 215.

36 Ibid., 200.

37 June Purcell Guild, *Black Laws of Virginia, A Summary Of The Legislative Acts Of Virginia Concerning Negroes From Earliest Times To The Present* (Lovettsville, Virginia: Willow Bend Books, 1996). See generally the "Introduction," "Black Laws After the Revolutionary War, Emancipation."

38 Culpepper Minute Men Patriots, "Marking Revolutionary War Patriots' Graves," National Society, Sons of the American Revolution (2011), http://www.cmmsar.com/graves.html. The name appears as John D. Baptist or John DeBaptist.

39 It has been suggested that John DeBaptiste was related to a contemporary, Jean Baptiste Pointe du Sable from St. Domingue (now

Haiti). The latter was the first person of African descent and the first non-indigenous settler in what is now Chicago, Illinois, and popularly known as "The Father of Chicago." No connection was found between the two men.

40   G. MacLaren Bryden, *A Sketch of the Colonial History of Saint Paul's, Hanover, and Brunswick Parishes, King George County, Virginia, 1916* (Library of Virginia), 32.

41   Marion Brooks Robinson, interview by author, Falmouth, Virginia, 2009.

42   Shirley Payne Alfred and Brenda Payne Snellings, interview by author, Falmouth, Virginia, 2009. Payne family members maintain Burley Payne won "a bet" by breaking off a piece of the DeBaptiste gravestone.

43   Jerrilynn Eby, *They Called Stafford Home: The Development of Stafford County, Virginia, from 1600 until 1865* (Bowie, Maryland: Heritage Books, Inc., 1997), 278.

44   Ruth Coder Fitzgerald, *A Different Story, A Black History Of Fredericksburg, Stafford, and Spotsylvania, Virginia* (Morris Plains, New Jersey: Unicorn Publishing House, 1979), 65. The death of Bussell was reported on January 8, 1805, in the *Virginia Herald*. For more information on Fitzhugh slaves see "Collected material on Fitzhugh, Chatham, and Chatham Slaves," compiled by Julian Burke, Bound Volume 351-18, Fredericksburg and Spotsylvania National Military Park. Included is an 1810 inventory with the names of William Fitzhugh's 232 slaves.

45   Jane Howison Beale, *The Journal of Jane Howison Beale, Fredericksburg, Virginia 1850-1862* (Fredericksburg, Virginia: Historic Fredericksburg Foundation, Inc., 1995), 20.

46   "Slave Holdings Listed in Falmouth 1815 Personal Property Tax List," Mary Washington University, http://departments.umw.edu/hipr/www/Falmouth/1815pp/falmouth1815pp.htm. "Above 16 years old: 974; Between 12 & 16 years: 183; 9 to 12 years: 139." The tax was intended to help pay the costs of the War of 1812.

47   Fitzgerald, "African-American History of Stafford County," http://librarypoint.org/african_american_history_of_stafford_virginia.

48   John Janney Johnson, "Fredericksburg's Early Entrepreneurs," *Fredericksburg Times*, (October 1995), 20-24.

49   James Vass wrote to Dr. James Carmichael in Fredericksburg in a note dated June 7, 1820. "Dear Sir, Davenport continuing to be very

unwell you will be good enough to ride over & visit him." Carmichael Collection, University of Virginia.

50 "Notes to the VASS—MAURY Chart," p. 1, No. 8. Vass family descendants provided a copy of this family genealogy and "Chart" to the author in 2003 (Conway House Collections). Winifred K. and Lachlan C. Vass III, *The Lapsley Saga* (Providence House Publishers, 1997), relates Lachlan C. Vass II as a missionary. Winifred and L.C. Vass III were missionaries in the Belgian Congo from 1940 until 1970.

51 Virginia Historic Landmarks Staff, *Clearview National Register Nomination*, Stafford County, Virginia (1975). The original Buchanan letter is in the Conway House Collections.

52 Baron de Montlezun, *Voyage Fait dans les Annees 1816 et 1817, de New-Yorck a la Nouvelle-Orleans, et de L'Orenoque Au Missippi, par les Petites et les Grandes-Antilles* (Paris: Librarie de Gide Fils, 1818), 40.

53 On a plantation, slaves would "go by the horn" or a large bell may have been rung to announce morning rise, summons to work, noon, and "knock off." If the "big house" bell was heard during an odd time of the day, this was a signal for distress or fire. Horns were more practical for a town environment. The signal for alarm or fire was made by ringing the church bell.

54 John T. Goolrick, *The Story of Stafford, A Narrative History of Stafford County, Virginia* (Fredericksburg, Virginia: Cardinal Press, Inc., 1976), 81.

55 Charles Emery Stevens, *Anthony Burns: A History* (Boston: John P. Jewett and Company, 1856), 165. Although the Union Church is not named, the account refers to the "Baptist church at Falmouth." At that time, the only church in Falmouth was the Union Church.

56 Frederick Douglass, *Narrative of the Life of Frederick Douglass, An American Slave* (Boston: Anti-Slavery Office, 1845), 118-120, 122.

57 Guild, 178-179. Chapter 120 of the Criminal Code of 1848 states, "It is an unlawful assembly of slaves, free Negroes or mulattoes for the purpose of religious worship when such worship is conducted by a slave, free Negro, or mulatto . . . ."

58 Conway, *Autobiography*, Vol. I, 23. Conway noted that, "George Washington mentions without comment the use of an iron ring at Mount Vernon to cure Patsy Custis."

59 Jerrilynn Eby MacGregor, research notes concerning tax records for Stafford citizens owning slaves, personal collection, 2009. The historic tax records are held at the Virginiana Room of the Central

Rappahannock Regional Library, Fredericksburg, Virginia. John Frogget, a free black in 1809, also may have been a blacksmith in Falmouth. Freeman William Huntsman, a blacksmith in Falmouth who worked with Abram Howard, likewise owned slaves.

60   Jerrilynn Eby MacGregor, email to author, 28 April 2009.

61   Guild, Introduction. In 1832, the Virginia General Assembly passed a law curtailing the ability of free blacks to own slaves themselves and "... after this date, no free Negro would be able to acquire ownership of any slave, except through inheritance . . . ." Local folklore indicates that down river from Falmouth lived a free black woman who owned slaves, including her husband. After an argument she sold her husband. When she later regretted doing this, she could not buy him back.

62   Ibid., 86. See General Assembly 1840, Chapter 61of the Criminal Code.

63   Conway, *Autobiography*, Vol. I, 28.

64   Moncure Daniel Conway, *Testimonies Concerning Slavery* (London: Chapman and Hall, 1864), 12.

65   Lydia Crain, "Falmouth, A Virginia Village in the 'Forties' from a Child's Point of View," *Fredericksburg Free Lance,* March 15, 1898. Lydia Crain was a cousin of the Conway children. She often stayed with them and was describing scenes and servants at Conway House.

66   In 1807, Congress passed an Act Prohibiting Importation of Slaves effective January 1, 1808. The "native African" king would have arrived in the United States prior to that date.

67   Crain, "Falmouth, A Virginia Village in the 'Forties' from a Child's Point of View."

68   John T. Goolrick, *The Story of Stafford, A Narrative History of Stafford County, Virginia*, 9.

69   Conway, *Autobiography*, Vol. I, 27-28. Conway adds, "White converts were immersed separately from the negroes . . . ."

70   Wills, *Notes And Documents of Free Persons of Color*, 197-198.

71   The leftover liquid was very rich in Vitamins C and K, and minerals including iron. Mothers would be sent to work in the fields on a plantation. Children were cared for by an old woman who would feed pot likker to the slave children twice a day. The broth could be from a mixture of vegetables and seasoned with fatback and salt. Each child was given a wooden spoon which they dipped into a wooden trough where the pot likker was poured. Children too young to hold a spoon were fed by the older children.

72 Frank White, email to author, 21 July 2011(Conway House Collections).
73 Larry Evans, "Freedom meant something different to black people," *Free Lance Star*, Fredericksburg, August 14, 1976. Larry Evans, email to author, 7 July 2010. The quote used was by David J. Mays in his biography of *Edmund Pendleton*. Pendleton, a patriot of the American Revolution, attended the First Continental Congress and later served as first President of the Supreme Court of Virginia. Slaves who repeatedly ran away were branded on the cheek with an "R."
74 David W. Blight, *A Slave No More*, (Orlando, Florida: Harcourt, Inc., 2007), 186. The ex-slave was John Washington from Fredericksburg who was in Richmond at the time he referred to the slave jail whippings.
75 Conway, *Autobiography*, Vol. I, 28-29n1. The neighbor who complained was probably Miss Anna Dunbar, described by townsfolk as a "queer old lady" who lived behind the Forbes House.
76 Conway, *Testimonies Concerning Slavery*, 16-17.
77 Conway, *Autobiography*, Vol. I, 29.
78 Ibid., 12.
79 Conway, *Testimonies Concerning Slavery*, 4, 6.
80 Conway, *Autobiography*, Vol. I, 21.
81 When Thomas Stone died in 1787, his will's inventory of Goods and Chattels included twenty slaves. Charles County Will Book AH9 (1788), 489-94. Charles County Court House, LaPlata, Maryland.
82 Conway, *Autobiography*, Vol. I, 21.
83 Moncure Daniel Conway, "Letter from Virginia" (October 1875), 9. Moncure Daniel Conway Special Collections, Rare Books and Manuscripts, Butler Library, Columbia University.
84 Conway, *Autobiography*, Vol. I, 86. The dinner in Warrenton took place in September 1850.
85 Walt Whitman, *Blood Money* (*New York Daily Tribune*, March 22, 1850; *New York Evening Post*, April 30, 1850; and *Specimen Days*, 1882). Whitman wrote the poem using the pen name "Paumanok." Webster's speech was delivered on March 7, 1850. The Fugitive Slave Law was enacted by Congress on September 18, 1850.
86 Conway, *Autobiography*, Vol. I, 29, 125. A large rock was at one time located on the northwest corner of Butler Road and Carter Street in Falmouth. It was said to have been a slave auction block. No association with slaves was found. The rock was named "Dr. Jett's rock," after the

87 Conway, *Autobiography*, Vol. I, 128-129, 132-133.
88 F.B. Sanborn, *The Life of Henry David Thoreau: Including Many Essays Hitherto Unpublished, and Some Accounts of His Family and Friends* (Boston: Houghton Mifflin Company, 1917), 482, 485; also Conway, *Autobiography*, Vol. I, 141.
89 It is difficult to put together a timeline for Burns in Falmouth. He may have been born at Robinson's Quarry in northern Stafford County. Five of his sisters and brothers were sold when he was age 6. He seems to have first arrived in Falmouth at age 10. At age 12, he was hired out in Culpeper for one year, during which he returned to Falmouth to heal from a severe injury. With a disfigured hand, he was sent back to Culpeper to finish out the contract. He returned to Falmouth where he lived until age 16 or 17, during which time he was hired out to William Brent. He was then hired out in Fredericksburg for one year. Afterwards, Brent (Suttle's agent) hired him out in Richmond, from whence he made his escape.
90 Stevens, 165-166.
91 Conway, *Testimonies Concerning Slavery*, 43. Conway wrote, ". . . I had personally known him [Burns] and his master, C.F. Suttle, all my life."
92 Donald Yacovone, "A Covenant with Death and an Agreement with Hell," *The Massachusetts Historical Society* (2007); also Conway, *Autobiography*, Vol. I, 184-186.
93 John d'Entremont, *The Southern Emancipator, Moncure Conway: The American Years, 1832-1865* (New York Oxford: Oxford University Press, 1987), 86. The 2006 National Underground Railroad Network to Freedom plaque on the Conway House in Falmouth states in part that Moncure Conway was "the only descendent of one of our nation's Founding Fathers to actively lead escaping slaves to freedom, thereby taking the initial steps to correct what was not accomplished in the Constitutional Convention."
94 Mary Elizabeth Burtis, *Moncure Conway 1832-1907* (New Brunswick, New Jersey: Rutgers University Press, 1952), 46. See also, Conway, *Autobiography*, Vol. I, 187.
95 Conway, *Autobiography*, Vol. I, 187-188. The letter was dated September 18, 1854. For a contemporary Northern view on Southerners using religion to justify slavery, see "The Madness."

occupant who lived on the corner in what is today known as the Manor House.

96. Moncure Daniel Conway, *The Rejected Stone, or Insurrection vs. Resurrection in America* (Boston: Walker, Wise, and Company, 1861), 70.
97. Conway, *Autobiography*, Vol. I, 190-191.
98. Ibid., 191.
99. "Anthony Burns," *Oberlin Evangelist*, July 18, 1855, Oberlin College, Oberlin, Ohio. Burns was probably the first African American from Falmouth and Stafford County to attend college.
100. Elder John Clark was the pastor of three separate Baptist churches in Stafford County; Choppawamsic, White Oak, and Union. Having been a longtime resident of Stafford County, he relocated to Front Royal, which accounts for the letter signed by Clark appearing in the *Front Royal Gazette*.
101. The *Front Royal Gazette* identified the church as "The Church of Jesus Christ, At Union, Fauquier Co., Virginia." Either the editor of the newspaper or John Clark's clerk, William W. West, assumed incorrectly that Union Church was in Fauquier County, which adjoins Stafford County to the north. Charles Emery Stevens, *Anthony Burns: A History*, 165, states, ". . . he [Anthony Burns] was baptized and received into the Baptist church at Falmouth." Stevens' biography was based upon his personal interviews with Burns. The only Union Church in Fauquier County was organized after the Civil War.
102. Charles Emery Stevens, *Anthony Burns: A History*, 280-283.
103. Frank White, email to author, 13 June 2011 (Conway House Collections).
104. Martin Luther King, Jr., "Letter from a Birmingham Jail," African Studies Center, University of Pennsylvania (2010), http://www.africa.upenn.edu/Articles_Gen/Letter_Birmingham.html. Two of the most important quotes found in "Letter from a Birmingham Jail" are, "Injustice anywhere is a threat to justice everywhere." "Justice too long delayed is justice denied."
105. Hayes, "Ran Away," *Virginia Gazette*, Richmond, August 31, 1782, in "The Geography of Slavery in Virginia."
106. Richards, "Ran Away," *Virginia Journal and Alexandria Advertiser*, Alexandria, September 22, 1785, in "The Geography of Slavery in Virginia."
107. Timothy Green, "Ten Dollars Reward," *Virginia Herald*, Fredericksburg, November 12, 1789, in "The Geography of Slavery in Virginia."

108 Davis, "Committed . . . A Negro Woman," *Virginia Gazette*, Richmond, April 23, 1799, in "The Geography of Slavery in Virginia."

109 The date often associated with the beginning of the Underground Railroad is the early 1830s. Slavery was legal in most of Canada until 1834 when the Slavery Abolition Act of 1833 went into effect, after which it became a safe haven for freedom seekers. Underground Railroad as a metaphor appeared in the early 1840s.

110 Robert Stanton, introduction to *Underground Railroad*, National Park Service Handbook (Washington, D.C.: US Department of the Interior, 1998), 2.

111 Robert O. Norris, Jr., introduction to *The Stronghold, A Story of Historic Northern Neck of Virginia and Its People*, by Miriam Haynie, xvi.

112 Darter, *Colonial Fredericksburg and Neighborhood in Perspective*, 90.

113 A reward poster dated April 1, 1856, for Barnaby, Jim, and Billy describes each man and offers a $300.00 reward for all three or $100.00 each. The poster states, "Left Travellers' Rest Estate, in Stafford County, Virginia, three negro Men." Travellers' Rest was a farm south of Falmouth toward King George County on the Rappahannock River. A copy of the poster was provided by Frank White.

114 Louis Alexis Chamerovzow, "The Slave's Underground Railroad to Freedom," *Edinburgh Series of Anti-Slavery Tracts*, No. 1, 1 (between 1850 and 1861). Samuel J. May Anti-Slavery Collection, Cornell University. No date.

115 Moncure Daniel Conway, "An Ancient And A Modern Compromise," *House Divided*, Dickinson College, Carlisle, Pennsylvania (2007), http://hd.housedivided.dickinson.edu/node/668.

116 Conway, *Autobiography*, Vol. I, 358.

117 Ibid., 42. Conway continued with, "Chief Justice Moncure vehemently pronounced the decision contrary to both law and equity. His minority opinion is now supported by every jurist in Virginia. The case was decided not long before Secession, when the Southern people were infuriated, and to this feeling the injustice is generally ascribed. The outrageous wrong was reported in the Northern papers . . . ." For an example see "Emancipation of Slaves in Virginia," *Cleveland Herald*, June 16, 1858, "The Court delivered their decision, reviewing and confirming the doctrine decided by the case of Bayly and Poindexter—that the slave has in Virginia no civil rights or legal

capacity whatever; and consequently no power to make an election between freedom and slavery."

[118] Conway, *Testimonies Concerning Slavery*, 54-55.

[119] John Hennessy, email to author, 28 June 2010. Hennessy is Chief Historian, Fredericksburg and Spotsylvania National Military Park. He confirmed that, "Virginia was populated by more slaves than any other state in 1860: 490,865—31% of the population. There were 52,128 slave owning households in Virginia, about 26% of the total. While the number of slaves was the greatest, the percentage of slaves or slave-owning families in Virginia was no where near the highest. [In] Mississippi, for example, 49% of families owned slaves, and slaves comprised 55% of the population. It is likely, though, that the Tidewater and Piedmont areas were quite comparable to the lower South in densities, given that most of Western Virginia was populated by few slaves and few slave-holding families. In Spotsylvania, for example, slaves constituted nearly 60% of the population, and more than half the households owned slaves. In Stafford the percentages were around 40% for each."

[120] Betty Churchill Lacy, "Memories Of A Long Life," April, 1903, Betty C. Jones, http://homepages.rootsweb.ancestry.com/~elacey/chatham.htm. Of the 240 slaves, only two elderly slaves (husband and wife) remained with the Lacy family by the close of the Civil War.

[121] Smith, "1720 Falmouth, Va." "The old Dunbar house . . . was famous for its beautiful grounds and frontal gardens and conservatory, wood work and exquisite furniture. The last owner, of the name Miss Anna Dunbar, a great-granddaughter of Lady Spottswood, died there in extreme old age and it passed to others." The Dunbar House was destroyed in a fire, but the Dunbar Kitchen survives. Lady Spotswood was Anna Butler, daughter of Richard Brayne of Westminster, England, who in 1724 became the wife of Alexander Spotswood, the colonial Governor of Virginia. Anna Dunbar was a descendant of Lady Spotswood and her second husband, Reverend John Thompson. Their home was Salubria in Culpeper County. One of their grand daughters, Elizabeth Francis Thornton, married Robert Dunbar, a merchant of Falmouth. Elizabeth and Robert were Anna's parents.

[122] Crain, "Falmouth, A Virginia Village in the 'Forties' from a Child's Point of View." Anna's sister "dead long years before" was Julia.

[123] John d'Entremont, *The Southern Emancipator*, 118-119.

124 Ibid., 246n14.
125 Although the name of the girl's alleged father has been passed down through Gwinn family oral history, the author could not prove the relationship.
126 Ellen Dana Conway to "My Dear Miss Anthony," Inglewood, Bedford Park, Turnham Green, London, 4 February 1884. Elizabeth Cady Stanton, "Report of the Sixteenth Annual Washington Convention, March 4th, 5th, 6th and 7th, 1884: with reports of the Forty-eighth Congress, National American Woman Suffrage Association." Mrs. Conway's letter included in the report states, "Aim for the best, ask for the most, and if we fall short, try again."
127 Ellen died in New York City. Annie Besant's, "A Leaf on a Grave," tribute may be found in the Moncure Daniel Conway Archival Collection, Dickinson College, Carlisle, Pennsylvania. Moncure Conway wrote, "On Christmas morning, about dawn, she persuaded me that the death we had combated hour by hour for nineteen months must now be received as a friend.... The lines of pain were smoothed away. The face resumed its youth, under the halo of gray hair, and lilies of the valley were laid upon her breast.... Every day was fragrant with tokens of the affection she has inspired in all the hearts who knew her." Conway, Moncure Daniel, Letters to Andrew Ingalis Clark, Tasmania, 11 October 1883-2 December 1905, Tasmania Library Special and Rare Book Collection, University of Tasmania, Australia.
128 Moncure Daniel Conway, "An Ancient And A Modern Compromise," *House Divided*, Dickinson College, Carlisle, Pennsylvania (2007), http://hd.housedivided.dickinson.edu/node/668. The scripture source was Matthew 4:8-11.
129 Conway, *Autobiography*, Vol. I, 325.
130 On April 17, 1861, Virginia passed an Ordinance of Secession. This was ratified by the citizens of Virginia on May 23, 1861.
131 Julia Ward Howe, *Battle Hymn of the Republic* (November 1861). First published in *The Atlantic Monthly*, Vol. IX, No. LII (Boston,: Ticknor and Fields, February 1862). The song was an inspiration to Union soldiers fighting against slavery and is now regarded as a national anthem for freedom.
132 William Child, *A History of the Fifth Regiment, New Hampshire Volunteers, in the American Civil War, 1861-1865* (Bristol, New Hampshire: R.W. Musgrove 1893), 169.

133 "Spouting Rock Letters," August 10, 1862, *New York Tribune*, August 18, 1862. The author is not named, but is most certainly Moncure Conway.
134 Conway, "Letter from Virginia" (Oct., 1875), 10-12.
135 Conway, *Autobiography*, Vol. I, 344-346.
136 The President of the United States, The Emancipation Proclamation, January 1, 1863, Transcript, National Archives, Washington, D.C., http://www.archives.gov/exhibits/featured_documents/emancipation_proclamation/transcript.html.
137 d'Entremont, 166. The letter dated March 27, 1862, is in Moncure Daniel Conway Special Collections, Rare Books and Manuscripts, Butler Library, Columbia University.
138 Conway, *Testimonies Concerning Slavery*, 104. When Falmouth was occupied, Walker P. Conway took refuge in Fredericksburg. He returned to Falmouth at least once during April which coincides with an article appearing in, "Things at Fredericksburg [correspondence of the *New York Times*]," *Richmond Daily Dispatch*, May 9, 1862. Although no name is given, ". . . the gentleman who was within our lines to day [Falmouth], having first assured himself that his property would not be disturbed and that he would be protected from pillage, then professed his readiness to sacrifice every dollar of it to further the cause of the Confederacy." When Union troops occupied Fredericksburg, Walker P. Conway removed himself to Richmond as did many of the "good people of old Stafford."
139 George F. Noyes, Captain US Volunteers, *The Bivouac and the Battlefield; Or Campaign Sketches in Virginia And Maryland*, (New York: Harper & Brothers, Publishers, 1863), 22. Captain Noyes was an officer in the 76th NY Infantry Regiment.
140 The leading brigade commanded by General Augur received the order to advance about nightfall on April 15. The general point of departure on the 17th was from Catlett's Station on the Orange and Alexandria Railroad in Fauquier County, 28 miles above Falmouth.
141 Charles E. Morton letter to his Father, 20 April 1862, Albert Z. Conner Collection, Stafford, Virginia. Lt. Charles E. Morton was in the 2nd NY Harris Light Cavalry and further wrote, "Lieut. Decker from Orange Co. was gallantly leading his men, and coming up alongside a rebel officer, made a cut at him, when he turned and shot him with his

revolver through the heart." Lt. Decker was killed between 6:00 pm and 7:00 pm.

142 "Army Correspondence From McDowell's Advance," *Norwich Morning Bulletin*, Connecticut, April 26, 1862.

143 Bould Soger [pen name] to *Buffalo Morning Express*, reprinted in, J. Harrison Mills, *Chronicles of the Twenty-First Regimen* (Buffalo, New York: Gies and Co. Printers and Bookmakers, 1887), 172-173. The mother's letter was also published in "Our Martyred Heroes," *New York Times*, May 10, 1862.

144 "Our Martyred Heroes, The Death of Lieut. Decker—Resolutions of His Fellow Officers," *New York Times*, May 10, 1862. Lt. Decker's body was carried to the Union Church in Falmouth and buried in the church cemetery. The body was soon disinterred and sent home to the family cemetery in Wallkill, Orange County, New York.

145 Wyman S. White, *The Civil War Diary of Wyman S. White*, ed. Russell C. White (Baltimore: Butternut and Blue, 1993), 59.

146 Charles Teasdale Diary, Company E, 14th Brooklyn NY State Militia. The diary remains in possession of family descendants who provided the author with excerpts relating to Falmouth.

147 Ficklen's Hill was the farm and residence of Joseph B. Ficklen, which today is known as Belmont.

148 Washington Correspondent, "Contrabands in Washington," *New York Tribune*, July 26, 1862. The parentheses appear in the original. The date of the article coincides with Conway slaves arrival in Washington. Falmouth file, Chatham, Fredericksburg and Spotsylvania National Military Park, National Park Service.

149 John Hennessy, email to author, 19 October 2010. The population and activity in Falmouth had waned in the decades prior to the Civil War. The once-busy port town had become a smaller place. The English/Southern vernacular use of the term "town" carried over from the Colonial period. The term "village" is a "decidedly Yankee/European sort of term." Union soldiers referred to Falmouth as a "village." Both terms will appear interchangeably from this point forward.

150 Conway, *Testimonies Concerning Slavery*, 113.

151 Conway, "Spouting Rock Letters,"

152 Blight, 188. See also "The Army Before Fredericksburg," *Oswego Commercial Times*, May 8, 1862, the account given by a soldier in the 24th NY Infantry on April 25, which also related the Cuban threat.

"They tell great stories of the means used by their masters to intimidate them, to keep them from leaving, one of which was, by telling them that the northerners would take every one of them to Cuba and sell them . . . ."

153 White, 61-62.
154 Blight, 193.
155 W.W. Wright, Engineer and Superintendent US Military Railroad, correspondence to General Herman Haupt, 17 September 1862, *Official Records*, Series I, Vol. XII, Operations in N. VA., W. VA., and MD. Chapter XXIV, 816. "I think it safe to estimate the number of contrabands that have passed by this route since we took possession of the road at 10,000."
156 John Washington, "Memorys of the Past." Papers of John Washington (*TS* 1984), 89-90. Manuscript Division, Library of Congress. In 2010, an interpretive wayside marker was placed on the Falmouth side of the Rappahannock River to commemorate the site where John Washington crossed.
157 Blight, see the third page of illustrations, upper image, caption.
158 Conway, *Autobiography*, Vol. I, 355-356. The soldier who was shot is believed to be William Britton, Company C, 7th Wisconsin Volunteer Infantry. This unit did not enter Falmouth until a few days later; however, Britton was serving as a scout in the initial advance. He was severely wounded in the leg and discharged July 25, 1862, unable to perform further duty. It was later determined he was shot by friendly fire. Britton was originally from New York, New York.
159 The Peninsula Campaign refers to General George B. McClellan's advance on Richmond with the bulk of the Union army up the peninsula between the York and James Rivers. The campaign commenced March 17, 1862, and ended with McClellan's report for August 16, 1862: "Late in the afternoon of that day, when the last man had disappeared from the deserted camps, I followed with my personal staff in the track of the grand army of the Potomac; bidding farewell to the scenes still covered with the marks of its presence, and to be forever memorable in history as the vicinity of its most brilliant exploits."
160 When the Sharpshooters first entered Falmouth, they were armed with Colt revolving rifles, which they did not want. They had been promised Sharps breach loading rifles, which were issued to them in Falmouth on June 18th.

161 White, 63. There was no Ford House in Falmouth. Further research by historians of the US Sharpshooters in Falmouth substantiates that White was referring to the Forbes House.

162 Unknown Civilian, Letter "Fall hill" dated May 8, 1862, addressed to "My darling Will." US Army Military History Institute, Lewis Leigh Collection, Box 30. The letter is attributed to Mrs. Sallie Innes Thornton Forbes, wife of Murray Forbes.

163 White recorded that the other Forbes servants were waiting on Captain Caldwell, who had set himself up in the parlor and was very unpopular with the men of Company F. The arrangement did not last long. Shortly thereafter, the Captain became ill and the servants apparently abandoned the dislikeable Caldwell. Only one soldier attended him before he died.

164 Blight, 194.

165 Elizah paid taxes on Lot 67 from at least 1828-1880. She shared this lot with Polly Keyes, also African American. Elizah also held a joint interest in Lot 23 shared with Toby Fox and Nathaniel Lucas. Other free black landowners in 1865 were Dora Curtis, Lot 61, Armistead Bundy, Lot 66, and Benjamin Johnson, part of Lot 103.

166 Blight, 195-196.

167 "Official List of Killed and Wounded in the Affair Opposite Fredericksburg," *New York Times*, April 30, 1862. The list also contains the name of "John N. Davis, private, Co. H, Harris Light Cavalry; died 31 hours after being wounded." Davis, a member of the 2nd NY Cavalry, was captured and put on a train en route to prison in Richmond. He died at Ashland between Fredericksburg and Richmond.

168 Mills, 166.

169 Blight, 193-194. The 21st and the 30th regiments were among several New York infantry units in General Christopher Augur's Brigade, King's Division of McDowell's First Corps, and which were at Falmouth on the morning of April 18, 1862. Ladd was actually in Company H of the 30th New York. He survived the war and afterward with his wife Mary A. Ladd had two children, a son James R. Ladd (born 1868) and a daughter Jennie Ladd (born 1875). Originally from Hoosick, Ladd took up the harness-making trade and lived in Fulton County, New York.

170 "The Army Before Fredericksburg," *Oswego Commercial Times*, May 8, 1862.

171 William Ray, *Four Years with the Iron Brigade, The Civil War Journal of William Ray, Company F, Seventh Wisconsin Volunteers,* ed. Lance Herdegen and Sherry Murphy (Cambridge: Da Capo Press, 2002), 82. See the entry for April 25, 1862.

172 David W. Blight, *A Slave No More,* 198.

173 Rufus Robinson Dawes, *Service with the Sixth Wisconsin Volunteers* (Marietta, Ohio: E.R. Alderman & Sons, 1890), 40-41. Captain Dawes wrote the letter from "Camp opposite Fredericksburg" dated April 26, 1862.

174 Edmund J. Raus, Jr., *Banners South, A Northern Community at War* (Kent, Ohio: The Kent State University Press, 2005), 99-100.

175 It is not clear if Lt. Bouvier was with the 20th when it first entered Falmouth. He may have joined the regiment several days later via Aquia Landing and thence to Falmouth. On August 28, 1862, Lt. Bouvier was severely wounded. Shot through the body, the ball entered the left lung, passing out the back on the edge of the shoulder blade, leaving the lung almost entirely useless for the remainder of his life. He was captured on the day he was wounded and exchanged November 8, 1862. He was later promoted to Captain by brevet.

176 Theodore B. Gates, *The Ulster Guard and the War of the Rebellion* (New York: Benj. H. Tyrrel, 1879), 221.

177 "From McDowell's Corps Letter from the Second Regiment," *Milwaukee Sentinel,* May 9, 1862.

178 Mills, 166.

179 Conway, *Autobiography,* Vol. I, 328-329. The Battle of Bull Run, or Manassas, Virginia, was fought on July 21, 1861. The defeated Union army retreated to the safety of its defenses around Washington, D.C.

180 *Official Records,* Series I, Vol. XII, Occupation of Fredericksburg, Va., Chapter XXIV, 437. Report No. 5, W.W.D. to Colonel Johnson, dated April 20 [1862]. Although the report was written from "Near Port Royal, Caroline County, Va." down the river from Falmouth, it represents the state of affairs in the region resulting from the Union occupation of Falmouth.

181 Donald E. Markle, *Spies and Spymasters of the Civil War* (New York: Hippocrene Books, 1995), 64-65.

182 D.E. Sickles, Brig. Gen. to Gen. Joseph Hooker, 14 March 1862, "Confidential Correspondence Touching Position & c. of the Enemy Near the Rappahannock," General Daniel Sickles Collection Featuring

Sickles' use of African American Scouts in Two Intelligence Reports from the Front Lines, Abraham Lincoln Bookshop (2011), http://www.alincolnbookshop.com/html/new_acquisitions.htm#sickles. General Sickles' camp was in Charles County, Maryland.

183   D.R. Marquis and C.V. Tevis, comp., *The History of the Fighting Fourteenth* (Brooklyn: Brooklyn Eagle Press, 1911), 254. Alfred was also the "faithful and intelligent" servant to Colonel Fowler of the 14th Brooklyn, remaining with the colonel until the end of the war. After the war, Alfred lived in Albany, New York, "where he has a family and is doing well." Both whites and blacks with the surname Peyton lived in Stafford County. No further connection to the county was found; however, Alfred was evidently well familiar with Stafford.

184   P.K. Rose, "The Civil War: Black American Contributions to Union Intelligence," *Studies in Intelligence* (Winter 1998-1999), https://www.cia.gov/library/center-for-the-study-of-intelligence/csi-publications/csi-studies/studies/winter98_99/art06.html.

185   Ibid.

186   John Hennessy, "The Fate of Fredericksburg Determined: President Davis's March 1862 Visit," Fredericksburg Remembered (November 4, 2010), http://npsfrsp.wordpress.com/2010/11/04/the-fate-of-fredericksburg-determined-president-daviss-march-1862-visit/.

187   "William Andrew Jackson," *Anti-Slavery Advocate*, January 1, 1863; "William Andrew Jackson," University of Detroit Mercy Black Abolitionist Archive, University of Detroit Mercy, http://research.udmercy.edu/find/special_collections/digital/baa/item.php?record_id=174&collectionCode=baa.

188   When Jackson's owner, one W.A. Tyler, hired his man out to Davis, he required an $800.00 security be paid in the event that Jackson escaped and was not returned to Tyler. Jackson was aware of this arrangement, and wrote a letter to Davis, "telling him he was sorry to put him to the trouble of paying the money." *Anti-Slavery Advocate*, January 1, 1863. An unsuccessful search for the original letter was made in the "Papers of Jefferson Davis," Rice University, Houston, Texas.

189   Jackson relied on his strong faith. "As for me . . . Jesus is my friend; he has given me grace to conquer, and will bear me safe through with all my undertaking . . . ." "Letter from William A. Jackson," London, November 6, 1862, *The Liberator*, November 28, 1862.

[190] Alan Rice, Dr., "The Abolition Movement and Mill Worker Solidarity," Revealing Histories (2007), http://www.revealinghistories.org.uk/what-evidence-is-there-of-a-black-presence-in-britain-and-north-west-england/articles/the-abolition-movement-and-mill-worker-solidarity.html. Rice states, "In some Lancashire cotton towns, unemployment due to the absence or raw cotton was extreme. For instance, in Bumley during the summer of 1862, 10,000 out of 13,000 operatives were out of work.

[191] Jackson's life seems to have fallen into obscurity. Nothing further appears in the *Liberator*, which printed its last issue on December 29, 1865. It is not known if Jackson was reunited with his family. If he returned to live in Richmond, like most ex-slaves fearing reprisal for providing information to the Union army, he would have purposely desired to remain unknown. Kathy Olmstead, email to author, 7 November, 2011. "After the war ended, the Federal government, in order to protect the postwar lives of its Southern spies, destroyed the records—including those of [Thomas] McNiven and [Elizabeth] Van Lew's activities—that precisely detail the information [Mary Elizabeth] Bowser passed on to General Ulysses S. Grant . . . ." These three individuals were spies at the White House of the Confederacy.

[192] Noel G. Harrison, *Fredericksburg Civil War Sites April 1861-November 1862* (Lynchburg, Virginia: H.E. Howard, Inc., 1995), 69. Harrison gives his source as [Davis?] H. [E.?] Letter, May 5, 1862, "Letters-10," entry 3580, record group 393, National Archives. The Fredericksburg and Spotsylvania National Military Park at Chatham has a transcribed copy of the letter, FRSP Ms. 06651.

[193] Jerrilynn Eby MacGregor, Green Family Chart, email to author, 24 March 2011. The wife was Anna Paige Whittemore. James Lane Green served in Company A, 9th Virginia Cavalry.

[194] David S. Sparks, ed., *Inside Lincoln's Army: The Diary of Marsena Rudolph Patrick, Provost Marshall General, Army of the Potomac* (New York: Thomas Yoseloff, 1964), 249.

[195] "His [Conway's] house and church became stations on the underground railway . . . ." Samuel Atkins Eliot, ed., "Moncure D. Conway (1832-1907)," *Heralds of a Liberal Faith*, Volume IV, Harvard Square Library (2009), http://www.harvardsquarelibrary.org/Heralds/Moncure-Daniel-Conway.php.

196 Moncure Daniel Conway to Mildred Conway March, 14 May 1862, Moncure Daniel Conway Special Collections, Rare Books and Manuscripts, Butler Library, Columbia University.
197 Conway, *Testimonies Concerning Slavery*, 105.
198 Eric J. Mink, "I was a Slave of Major Horace Lacy." Andrew Weaver of the 23rd United States Colored Troops, Slavery and Slave Places (July 30, 2010), http://npsfrsp.wordpress.com/category/slavery-and-slave-places/page/2/. Weaver's service and pension file states he was born March 16, 1845, at "Stafford Co., Chatham Farm, Virginia," the son of Joe and Julia Weaver. Weaver also states that Peter Churchwell "who served in my company [Co. B, 23rd USCT] was raised near me."
199 Raus, 124-125.
200 The term "gateway to freedom" is used currently by the staff at Fredericksburg Spotsylvania National Military Park to describe the exodus of thousands of slaves choosing to self-emancipate themselves during the Union army's occupation of Falmouth and Fredericksburg in the spring and summer of 1862. This "gateway to freedom" opened again when the Union army returned to Falmouth and Stafford County in November 1862 and remained until the middle of June 1863. Like the bridges over the Rappahannock River, the Federal supply depots at Aquia Landing and Belle Plain Landing on the Potomac River were important components of the gateway to freedom.
201 Mills, 167.
202 Noyes, 43.
203 Joshua 6:3, King James Version. "And ye shall compass the city, all ye men of war, and go round the city once. Thus shalt thou do six days." On the seventh day the Israelites were commanded to go around Jericho seven times, and the walls of the city fell.
204 Noyes, 45. A number of African American families named Berryman still live in Stafford County.
205 Henry Clay Work, *The Year of Jubilee* (Chicago: Root & Cady, 1862). The original lyrics were stereotypical African American dialect of the time. It also appeared in "The Shilling Song Book, No.2" (Boston, 1862).
206 Since slaves were viewed as property under the law, the label "contraband" gave the US Army a legal standing to hold slaves as confiscated property of war, and the grounds for not returning them

to their owner. These slaves continued to be the legal property of their Southern owners until January 1, 1863, when the Emancipation Proclamation went into effect.

[207] Photographs of African Americans During the Civil War, Digital ID: cwpb 03854, Library of Congress, Prints and Photographs Division, Washington, DC. The photograph was taken at the Headquarters of the Army of the Potomac in Falmouth, March, 1863.

[208] Mills, 166-167.

[209] "Dick, sketched on the 6th of May, the afternoon of Gen Hookers retreat across the Rappahannock, on return to camp." Photographs of African Americans During the Civil War, Digital ID: cph 3g04219, Library of Congress, Prints and Photographs Division.

[210] Noyes, 44.

[211] Ibid., 43. See also "The Pay to the Colored Fugitives," *New York Tribune*, May 19, 1862. Those employed in the Quartermaster's Department were paid ranging from 25 cents to 40 cents per day plus one ration per day. "The ration to consist of pork and beans, and meal in place of flour or hard bread, when the same can be obtained; beans, vinegar, soup and salt."

[212] "The Ulster Guard on the Rappahannock," *Kingston Argus*, New York, May 7, 1862.

[213] Betty Churchill Lacy, "Memories Of A Long Life," April, 1903, Betty C. Jones, http://homepages.rootsweb.ancestry.com/~elacey/chatham.htm. Lacy was born June 10, 1823. Greenwood was opposite Ellwood, another Lacy owned estate, in Orange County and near the Spotsylvania County line west of Fredericksburg. A local, believed to be Ebenezer McGee, alerted the Union authorities.

[214] "Interesting News at Richmond and Fredericksburg, Va., June 11, 1862," *Washington National Republican*, June 16, 1862. The "Captain" was not named. The cavalry regiments operating at the time were the 1st Pennsylvania, 1st New Jersey, and the 2nd New York. John Hennessy, email to author, 27 October 2010. "I have never seen the unit named, but I'm fairly certain it was the 2d NY cavalry, which was doing most of the outward business hereabouts that summer."

[215] Conway, *Testimonies Concerning Slavery*, 105.

[216] Fredericksburg and Spotsylvania National Military Park, "J. Horace Lacy," *Front Porch Fredericksburg Magazine*, Curator's Corner (January 2001).

[217] Ibid.
[218] Barbara Westabee, interview by author, Falmouth, Virginia, 2005.
[219] Conway, *Testimonies Concerning Slavery*, 124-125.
[220] Noyes, 50.
[221] "Gradual Emancipation—Virginia Free Soil," *The Christian Banner*, Fredericksburg, July 14, 1862, 2/4, micro-film copy at Central Rappahannock Regional Library, Fredericksburg, Virginia.
[222] Benjamin Drew, *The Refugee: or the Narratives of Fugitive Slaves in Canada* (Boston: John P. Jewett and Company, 1856), 76.
[223] Daniel G. Hill, *The Freedom-seekers: Blacks in Early Canada* (Don Mills, Ontario: Stoddard, 1992), 211.
[224] Abigail Tucker, "Digging up the Past at a Richmond Jail," *Smithsonian Magazine* (March 2009), http://www.smithsonianmag.com/history-archaeology/Digs-Devils-Half-Acre.html.
[225] Anthony Burns, letter to Richard Henry Dana, Jr., 23 August 1854, Massachusetts Historical Society.
[226] *Frederick Douglass' Paper*, March 16, 1855, Rochester, New York. Another Virginia born slave, Dred Scott of the noted Dread Scott Decision, died of tuberculosis in 1858. At the time, the disease was colloquially referred to as consumption. It was not until 1869, that tuberculosis became known as a communicable disease.
[227] Reverend Hiram Wilson, letter to Reverend Leonard A. Grimes, 28 July 1862, "Death of Anthony Burns," *The Liberator*, August 22, 1862, Boston.
[228] In 1964, the Archaeological and Historic Sites Board of Ontario (now the Ontario Heritage Foundation) commemorated the life of Anthony Burns with a plaque at the entrance to Victoria Lawn Cemetery. The grave of Anthony Burns has become a focal point on the Niagara's Freedom Trail, a network of sites in the Niagara Region commemorating the struggle for freedom of African Americans and their achievements and contributions as African Canadians. On May 17, 2007, a new school in Stafford County, Virginia, was dedicated as the Anthony Burns Elementary School.
[229] Suzy Hastings, interview by author, 29 August, 2011, St. Catharines, Ontario, Canada. Gardening Angels utilizes developmentally challenged students. Additionally, it partners with the Brain Injury Community Re-entry Association to hire special individuals who have challenges in life.

230 Conway, *Autobiography*, Vol. I, 355.
231 Gwinn family oral history. Eliza and Dunmore reportedly had 19 children. "Some" died when they were very young or in infancy, two older sons were servants for the Conway brothers in the Confederate army, other older sons were employed by Union officers, and nine children went to Yellow Springs. The author was unable to locate any military service records for the Gwinn sons.
232 Conway, *Autobiography*, Vol. I, 358-359.
233 Ibid., Vol. I, 359 n1. It was not unusual for African Americans to change their name in order to escape detection. Williams changed his name from Benjamin to Collin. The author learned about an African American family living in Alexandria after the war whose patriarch was one William Collins. Oral family history suggests he was from Stafford County, Virginia.
234 Conway, *Testimonies Concerning Slavery*, 107.
235 Scott Sanders, "The Conway Colony—A Journey to Freedom," *Yellow Springs News*, February 1, 2001.
236 *Conway House Underground Railroad Network to Freedom Nomination*, National Underground Railroad Network to Freedom Program, National Capitol Region, National Park Service (2004), 21.
237 Zachariah T. Miller to his Parents, 30 May 1862, Helen King Boyer Collection, Georgetown University Library. In his letter from "Headquarters of 61st [Ohio] Regt, Camp near New Creek, Virginia," Miller states that his regiment is not going to Washington, D.C., because of Union problems controlling the Baltimore and Ohio Railroad. The rail line was again disrupted by Lee's campaign into Maryland, which resulted in major battles at Harper's Ferry, West Virginia, and South Mountain and Antietam, Maryland, in September 1862.
238 Cosmelia Hirst, "First Settling of Slaves Here," *Yellow Springs News*, November 8, 1907.
239 Conway, *Autobiography*, Vol. I, 362.
240 *History of the First Baptist Church*, no date or author. Photocopy in Conway Colony File, Conway House Collections, Falmouth, Virginia.
241 Hirst, "First Settling of Slaves Here." The article added, "Mr. Conway has never forgotten his 'people' whom he sent to Yellow Springs. He is still their benefactor."

[242] Ruth Wright, oral history related to Frank White and Lenetta Schools, Yellow Springs, Ohio, 13 June 2003. Grandmother Baber was Bertha Morris Baber b.1874, d.1971.

[243] Conway, *Autobiography*, Vol. II, 349. Conway gives only several lines of this hymn. From these lines, Jim Thomas, an authority and scholar of African American song, identified the hymn with its musical notes.

[244] Hector Sears, Bvt. Capt., Veteran Reserve Corps, Military Commissioner for Stafford County, Reports on Prominent Whites and Freedmen, March-May 1867, Roll 67. *Virginia Freedmen's Bureau Record Group 393*, National Archives, Washington, D.C. James Prior was spelled Pryor in the report.

[245] Walker P. Conway, letter to Margaret Conway, 27 March 1862. This is the same letter in "Orderly and Obedient." Plantation slaves included those who worked in the field, known as "the hoe-people."

[246] The hoe found in 2002 has been conserved and is now in the Conway House Collections.

[247] Jerrilynn Eby, *They Called Stafford Home: The Development of Stafford County, Virginia, from 1600 until 1865*, 156-157. The Rose family ancestral home was Hampstead in Stafford County. Dr. L.B. Rose's father was Alexander Fontaine Rose, an attorney who owned property in Fredericksburg as well as throughout Virginia. Jerrilynn Eby MacGregor, email to author, 13 October 2011. "He [Dr. Rose] was educated at the College of William and Mary and received his medical training at the University of Pennsylvania. L.B. Rose served several terms as mayor of Fredericksburg where he resided after the war."

[248] An acting surgeon was either a contracted civilian doctor employed by the government or an assistant surgeon in the army acting in the capacity of a surgeon. The presence of a military service record for Dr. Rose at the National Archives would seem to indicate the latter. The author did not access the records.

[249] Jean McKee, email to author, 23 October 2005 (Conway House Collections). The 5th US Colored Heavy Artillery was originally organized in Vicksburg, Mississippi, on December 1, 1863, with ex-slaves and assigned to the Department of Tennessee. Four officers and 124 enlisted men were killed and mortally wounded while 697 men died of disease. Richard's name is sometimes spelled on military rolls as Harrot.

[250] Hirst, "First Settling of Slaves Here."

251 Norman Schools, "Moncure Conway (1832-1907)," *Encyclopedia Virginia*, ed. Brendan Wolfe, Virginia Foundation for the Humanities (26 August 2010), http://www.EncyclopediaVirginia.org/Conway_Moncure_Daniel_1832-1907.

252 "First at Gettysburg," *The Richmond Virginian*, August 29, 1915, Richmond, Virginia.

253 d'Entremont, 182, 217.

254 Kathy Olmstead, email to author, 24 March 2005. It is not clear why Peter went by McGwinn instead of Gwinn. The name McGwinn also appears in Yellow Springs among the Gwinn ex-slaves.

255 Peter McGwinn to Peter V.D. Conway, 19 December 1907, Columbia University. "I rejoice to know that my ancestors and my people as a whole had the protecting influence of so great a man [Moncure Conway]."

256 Raus, 110.

257 Ibid., 109.

258 Conway, *Autobiography*, Vol. II, 304.

259 Conway, "Spouting Rock Letters."

260 The threat was caused by the unpredictable movements and successes of Major General Stonewall Jackson's command in the Shenandoah Valley. See Raus, 282n4. Raus cites the *New York Times*, April 22, 1862, giving Fredericksburg as fifty-six miles from Washington and sixty-two miles from Richmond.

261 Samuel Gilpin Diary, 3rd Indiana Cavalry, 16 July 1862, Library of Congress.

262 Raus, 116, 118.

263 Ibid., 108.

264 Noyes, 46-47.

265 One wonders if Dabney chose the Massachusetts coat for the ideas it represented. The author's research on units present at Falmouth and Fredericksburg during the spring and summer of 1862 indicates troops were mainly from states other than Massachusetts. The 13th Massachusetts Infantry was in Falmouth in May, but for only a short period. The cavalry unit Dabney was with could not be identified. It has been suggested that a staff officer supplied the Massachusetts uniform.

266 Marquis and Tevis, 252.

267 The Confiscation Act of 1861 permitted the confiscation of any property, including slaves, being used to support the Confederate insurrection. Slaves were confiscated as "contraband" of war and thus became the property of the US government. Their former owner's claim to them was removed, but the slaves were not freed by this Act.

268 On August 30, 1861, General John C. Fremont issued a proclamation in Missouri which stated that slaves "are hereby declared free." This soon led to Fremont's removal by President Lincoln. Generals David Hunter and John W. Phelps received a similar fate.

269 The location of the barn "near headquarters" likely refers to either General Augur's HQ at Clearview, which later relocated to the Phillips House, or General McDowell's main army HQ at Chatham. No records support a claim that Halsted used his position as a staff officer to procure the use of the Military Railroad, passes, etc. Halsted successfully orchestrated what would appear to be a covert operation.

270 Halsted's wartime experience included capture and imprisonment. Exchanged and released from Libby Prison, he rejoined Augur's command in the Deep South, and recruited ex-slaves for the Corps d'Afrique. In Tennessee, he recruited and organized US Colored Troops. Halsted returned to the theater of war in Virginia and received a slight wound, but remained in the field. He was able to witness the surrender of Lee's army. Halsted moved to Minnesota in 1876, where he became known as the Hermit of Lake Minnetonka. In 1901, he tragically died in a house fire. *Princeton Alumni Weekly*, Vol. 2 (January 11, 1902): 230.

271 Noyes, 30.

272 "Trail To Freedom," Fredericksburg and Stafford, Virginia (2011). www.TrailToFreedom.com.

273 Blight, 198.

274 The original author is unknown. Modern composers have made their own arrangements of the spiritual. The traditional gospel song "Give Me That Old Time Religion" dates from 1873. Forrest Mason McCann, *Hymns & History: An Annotated Survey of Sources* (Abilene, Texas: ACU Press, 1997) 595. McCann attributes the tune back to "English folk origins" and known among the "work songs of African Americans." The Biblical reference is Matthew 14:22-33.

275 Three army corps commanded by Generals McDowell, N.P. Banks, and John C. Fremont, respectively, had been held from the Peninsula

276 Campaign for the purpose of protecting Washington. These were consolidated into the Army of Virginia.
276 Francis Trevelyan Miller, *Photographic History of the Civil War In Ten Volumes* (New York: The Review of Reviews Co., 1911), Vol. 2, 22.
277 Raus, 185. Raus states that ". . . a mass exodus of more than a thousand blacks . . . filled the Chatham Wire Bridge." The Chatham Bridge was destroyed by the retreating Confederates on April 18, 1862. It was rebuilt for the second time by Union Lt. Washington Augustus Roebling as a suspension wire bridge with the labor of ten soldiers and thirty "contrabands." Roebling later built the Brooklyn Bridge which opened May 24, 1883.
278 Samuel Gilpin Diary, 3rd Indiana Cavalry, entry for Tuesday, September 2, 1862.
279 Even with the Union army in Falmouth and Stafford County for nearly five months, the institution of slavery remained somewhat intact locally. As thousands of slaves were making their escape to freedom, two white men of Stafford County entered into a hiring-out contract involving human property. "On or before the first day of January 1863 I promise and bind myself to pay to Barnett Fritter the sum of thirty dollars for the hire of negro man Nace. Given under my hand and seal this 15th day September 1862. R.L. Cooper." Personal collections of Jerrilynn Eby MacGregor and Rick MacGregor, Stafford County, Virginia.
280 W.W. Wright, Engineer and Superintendent US Military Railroad, correspondence to General Herman Haupt, 17 September 1862, *Official Records*, Volume XII, Operations in N. VA., W. VA., and MD. Chapter XXIV, 814-816. John Hennessy, Chief Historian, Fredericksburg Spotsylvania National Military Park, email to author, 6 January 2011. ". . . the exodus into Union lines in Stafford that summer was one of the largest, if not the largest, most concentrated flights to freedom of the war."
281 The Union army returned on November 17, 1862. It remained posted in Stafford until June 15, 1863.
282 Walt Whitman, *Leaves of Grass* (Boston: James R. Osgood and Company, 1881). This is generally recognized as the definitive edition of Whitman's poems.
283 Conway, *Autobiography*, Vol. I, 371-373. "Copperheads" also referred to Northern Democrats who strongly opposed the war and for which they

blamed the abolitionists. The old Methodist hymn is not to be mistaken for *Year of Jubilee* introduced by Christy's Minstrels in 1862.

284. Charyn D. Sutton, "Watch Night," The Onyx Group, Bala Cynwyd, Pennsylvania (December 2000), http://www.wsbrec.org/blackfacts/WatchNight.htm.

285. Joseph Burwell Ficklen to Anna Eliza Fitzhugh Ficklen, 29 December 1862 and 2 January 1863, Alderman Library, University of Virginia. The Ficklen family was comfortably wealthy. Joseph's wife, Anna, apparently resided in Baltimore for much of the war. Ficklen was labeled "conservative union," which meant his political proclivities could change depending on which side occupied Falmouth.

286. George Breck, Lieutenant, Company L, 1st New York Light Artillery, "Letter January 12, 1863," *Rochester Union and Advertiser*. Collections of the Fredericksburg and Spotsylvania National Military Park, National Park Service.

287. Frank White, email to author, 22 March 2010, and Jim Thomas, email to author, 23 March 2010. This traditional spiritual is known today in Stafford County and was sung frequently in the Civil Rights Movement during the 1960s.

288. Fitzgerald, 23.

289. Murray Forbes would seem an especially kind soul who wouldn't begrudge his elderly servant his freedom late in life. He paid to have the stone inscribed and placed on Merrick's grave. Forbes probably also paid for the burial. It is not known if Merricks went back to the Forbes' at some point before he died.

290. Isaac Lyman Taylor, *Campaigning with the First Minnesota: A Civil War Diary*, ed. Hazel C. Wolf (Minnesota History XXV, 1944), 241. After the fighting, Henry found the badly mangled body of his brother and buried him on the field the next morning. Henry's account states, "[Isaac] killed by a shell about sunset July 2nd, 1863. The shell took off the back part of his head, passed out of his back cutting his belt in two—instantly killed. I buried his accoutrements also." Henry inscribed a makeshift board at his brother's head, "No useless coffin enclosed his breast, Nor in sheet nor shroud we bound him, But he lay like a warrior taking his rest, With his shelter tent around him." According to National Park Service records, Isaac Taylor's remains were later interred in the National Cemetery at Gettysburg in the Minnesota Plot, Row B, Grave 12. The headstone on the grave is marked "Unknown."

291 Fitzgerald, 93, and William S. McFeely, *Yankee Stepfather, General O.O. Howard and the Freedmen* (New York, 1968), 41-42. After the war, General Howard was the first commissioner of the Freedmen's Bureau and played an instrumental role in the founding of Howard University.

292 W.L.D. O'Grady, letter to the *New York Sun*, November 28, 1906.

293 Richard Moe, *The Last Full Measure, The Life and Death of the First Minnesota Volunteers* (New York: Henry Holt and Company, 1993), 226. The dust jacket of this book contains a Civil War period photograph of the two brothers Henry and Isaac Taylor.

294 Robert Gould Shaw, *Blue-Eyed Child of Fortune, The Civil War Letters of Colonel Robert Gould Shaw*, ed. Russell Duncan (Athens, Georgia: The University of Georgia Press, 1992), 280-281. Duncan's Introduction, 18, "Shaw's letters tell remarkably little about the institution of slavery and his thoughts about it." Shaw was an officer in the Second Massachusetts Infantry when Governor Andrew offered him a commission as colonel of the 54th Massachusetts. On February 5, 1863, Shaw decided to accept the commission while he was in camp in Stafford County. Colonel Shaw was killed on July 18, 1863, while leading the attack on Ft. Wagner. The 1989 movie "Glory" was based on Shaw's regiment. The 54th Massachusetts itself was never in Falmouth.

295 Dabney, "The Black Scout of the Rappahannock," is described as ". . . having no white blood in his veins." According to the 1880 US Census, Dabney Walker was a Virginia-born mulatto.

296 Edwin C. Fishel, *The Secret War for the Union: The Untold Story of Military Intelligence in the Civil War* (Boston: Houghton Mifflin Company, 1996), 314 and 653n11.

297 Frank Moore, *Anecdotes, Poetry and Incidents of the War: North and South 1860-1865* (New York: Publication Office, Bible House, 1867), 263-264. No official records have documented this story. The original account seems to have appeared in a newspaper article written by a Union officer. Repeated in numerous articles and books, the story is a part of the legend of black intelligence activities during the war.

298 Paula Royster, email to author, 11 September 2010 (Conway House Collections). Lucy's occupation was that of a "washer and ironer." She was originally from Caroline County, Virginia. Lucy died at age 66 in 1880; Dabney died at age 74 in 1885.

299 *Edwin Forbes Civil War Etchings,* ed. William Forrest Dowson (New York: Dover Publications, 1957 and 1985), 78-79.
300 Conway, *Autobiography,* Vol. I, 84. The newspaper was the *New York Tribune,* September 7, 1850.
301 Conway, *The Rejected Stone,* 99.
302 Josiah Marshall Favill, *The Diary of a Young Officer Serving with the Armies of the United States During the War of the Rebellion* (Chicago, Illinois: R.R. Donnelley & Sons, 1909), 205.
303 Ray, 167. See entry for February 1, 1863.
304 J.J. Marks, Rev. D.D., The *Peninsular Campaign in Virginia or Incidents and Scenes on The Battlefields and In Richmond* (Philadelphia: J.B. Lippencott & Co., 1864), 90-92. Marks was chaplain with his regiment in Northern Virginia at the time of his observation, prior to leaving for the Peninsula.
305 Conway, *Testimonies Concerning Slavery,* 45.
306 Conway, *Autobiography,* Vol. I, 238. The assailant of Sumner was Preston Brooks.
307 Church history either glossed over the incident or failed to mention Conway altogether. In June 2006, the First Rappahannock Regional Juneteenth Celebration held opening ceremonies at Conway House. Reverend Robert Hardies and members of All Souls Unitarian Church in Washington, D.C., attended. After 150 years, Reverend Hardies preformed a significant "act of contrition." He formally apologized for the church's dismissal of Moncure Conway and for those church members who "didn't fully possess the courage then to stand up for what was just and what was right."
308 Sarah T. Scott, Letter to John T. Scott, 26 November 1856. Lewis-Scott-Daniel-Greenhow Family Papers, 1787-1908, Accession 21563, Personal Papers Collection, Library of Virginia, Richmond, Virginia.
309 Noyes, 29.
310 George A. Bruce, *The Twentieth Regiment of Massachusetts Volunteer Infantry 1861-1865* (Boston and New York: Houghton, Mifflin and Company, 1906), 218-219.
311 Richard F. Miller and Robert F. Mooney, *The Civil War: The Nantucket Experience Including the Memoirs of Josiah Fitch Murphey* (Nantucket, Massachusetts: Wesco Publishing, 1994), 95.
312 A legalistic interpretation of the Declaration of Independence along with its drafts, leads to the conclusion that the phrase "all men are

created equal" referred only to white men. Thomas Jefferson, *The Papers of Thomas Jefferson, Volume 1: 1760-1776* et al ed. Julian P. Boyd (Princeton, New Jersey: Princeton University Press, 1950), 423-428. All white men had equal rights to own property under English Common Law. This included owning slaves, considered to be property.

[313] Laura E. Richards and Maud Howe Elliott, assisted by Florence Howe Hall, *Julia Ward Howe* (Boston and New York: Houghton Mifflin Company, The Riverside Press, 1915), Vol. I, 193. Mrs. Howe's husband, Samuel Gridley Howe, had been a member of the Secret Committee of Six, which funded the abolitionist John Brown. Julia Ward Howe was the first woman elected to the prestigious American Academy of Arts and Letters.

[314] "Wounding of Stonewall Jackson Trail," Fredericksburg and Spotsylvania National Military Park, National Park Service (2008), http://www.nps.gov/frsp/jacktr.htm.

[315] Murray Forbes Taylor, "Stonewall Jackson's Death," *Confederate Veteran*, Vol. XII, No. 10 (October, 1904): 493. VMI Archives, Preston Library, Lexington, Virginia. Lieutenant Murray Forbes Taylor of Fredericksburg was a nephew of Captain James Fitzgerald Forbes. See also Jennings C. Wise, *The Military History of VMI from 1839 to 1865* (Lynchburg, Virginia: J.P. Bell Company, Inc., 1915), 437.

[316] "Stonewall Jackson Shrine," Fredericksburg and Spotsylvania National Military Park, National Park Service (2009), http://www.nps.gov/frsp/js.htm.

[317] Miller, *Photographic History of the Civil War In Ten Volumes*, Vol. 2, 115.

[318] John Esten Cooke, Moses Drury Hoge, and John William Jones, *Stonewall Jackson: A Military Biography* (D. Appleton and Company, 1876), 485.

[319] Andrew Weaver, Co. B, 23rd USCT, was from Chatham; Charles Sprow, Co. E, 1st Regt. US Colored Cavalry, was a Lacy slave from Spotsylvania; Richard Herod, Co. M, 5th US Colored Heavy Artillery, was from Falmouth; Abraham Tuckson, 23rd USCT (killed July 30, 1864), was from Fall Hill in Spotsylvania County; and Peter Churchwell, Co. B, 23rd USCT, was from Orange County.

[320] George E. Sutherland, "The Negro in the War, A Strong Paper by Major Geo. E. Sutherland," *Milwaukee Sunday Telegraph*, October 7, 1888, microfilm, Wisconsin Historical Society. During the war George

E. Sutherland served as Captain of Company B, 13th US Colored Heavy Artillery.

321 Shirley Hart Alfred, interview by author, Falmouth, Virginia, 3 May 2010. For example, Ms. Alfred pointed out seeing areas where soldiers' graffiti was on the wall near the floor in the hallway of Conway House. Her understanding was wounded soldiers had been laid out across the floor and the graffiti was as high as they could reach. This wall was re-plastered in the 20th century and the graffiti lost. In Moncure Conway's 1904 autobiography, he describes the drawing-room's beautiful wallpaper, since identified as "The Monuments of Paris." He stated the wallpaper did not survive the war without giving the reason. Presumably, it was defaced by the soldiers.

322 Martha Fifield Wilkins, *Sunday River Sketches, A New England Chronicle* (Rumford, Maine: Androscoggin Publications, 1977), 188. Eames is buried in The Sunday River Cemetery, Newry, Maine.

323 Federal Pension Record No. 380984, Daniel Shanahan, Co's F-G-H 20th Mass Inf., National Archives, College Park, Maryland. Shanahan is buried in an unmarked grave in Evergreen Cemetery, Brainerd, Minnesota. His name was mistakenly written down as the pension record of Samuel Shannahan and even further mistaken for William O. Stranahan, Company A, 5th Minnesota Infantry, who deserted on March 7, 1863.

324 "Hung Himself," *Monroe Democrat*, October 6, 1887, Monroe County, Minnesota. Wise is buried in Woodland Cemetery, LaSalle, Michigan. He left behind a wife and two children.

325 The warehouse was built by Basil Gordon, 1768-1847, a Scottish merchant who immigrated to Falmouth as a poor boy and said to be the first man in America to become a millionaire. The second owner was Duff Green, 1792-1854. After 1878, the warehouse became Lightner Store.

326 Jerrilynn Eby MacGregor, "Green Family" Chart, email to author, 19 March 2011(Conway House Collections). Colonel William James Green, 47th Virginia Infantry; at Gaines' Mill on June 27, 1862, he was shot twice while trying to rally disordered troops and fell dead from his horse with the colors still in his hand. Alexander Morson Green, attended Virginia Military Institute without completing, 9th Virginia Cavalry; paroled at Ashland in 1865. James Lane Green, 9th Virginia Cavalry; paroled at Ashland in 1865. Duff Green, Fredericksburg

Artillery; survived the war. Major Charles Jones Green, Virginia Military Institute Class of 1859, 47th Virginia Infantry; wounded five times and survived the war.

[327] Eric J. Mink, "If These Signatures Could Talk," Falmouth Graffiti, Part 1 (October 1, 2010), http://npsfrsp.wordpress.com/category/graffiti/. James Collin's grave number at Andersonville is 3071.

[328] d'Entremont, 17.

[329] William Lloyd Garrison to Andrew Paton, 10 April 1863, Moncure Daniel Conway Archival Collection, Dickinson College, Carlisle, Pennsylvania.

[330] Albert Z. Conner, "Watch For The Morning: Moncure Daniel Conway, Falmouth's Southern Emancipationist," *The Journal of Fredericksburg History*, Vol. 12 (2010): 62-63.

[331] Freedmen's Inquiry Commission, "Final report of the American Freedmen's Inquiry Commission to the Secretary of War," New York City, May 15, 1864. *Official Records of the War of the Rebellion*, Series III, Vol. IV, http://www.civilwarhome.com/commissionreportchapt3.htm.

[332] Marks, 108-110. The quote is from a former slave named Hanson Yerly who lived in Northern Virginia.

[333] Joseph R. Fornieri, ed., *The Language of Liberty: The Political Speeches and Writings of Abraham Lincoln* (Washington, DC: Regnery Publishing, Inc., 2003), 794-795.

[334] Elizabeth Vass Wilkerson, *Diary of Rev. L.C. Vass* (Bloomington, Indiana: Author House, 2008), 4.

[335] Jane Hollenbeck Conner, *Lincoln in Stafford* (Fredericksburg, Virginia: Cardinal Press, 2006), v.

[336] Conway, "Letter from Virginia," 18.

[337] Deuteronomy 5:9 KJV.

[338] Albert Z. Conner, Jr. *A History of Our Own, Stafford County, Virginia* (Virginia Beach, Virginia: The Donning Company Publishers, 2003), 30. The census of 1880 puts Stafford County's population at 7,211; in 1890, at 7,362; and in 1900 at 8,097. Stafford County's population remained close to 8,000 until the 1930s. By the 1940 census, the county was finally showing signs of growth: there were 9,548 residents.

[339] Julian Symons, *Thomas Carlyle: The Life and Ideas of a Profit* (London: Victor Gollancz Ltd., 1952), 61.

340 Conway, *Autobiography*, Vol. I, 394. The house was located in Cheyne Row, Chelsea, London, and now owned by the National Trust.

341 Ibid., 401. Thomas Carlyle was a British author, historian, and philosopher. He was Lord Rector of the University of Edinburgh from 1865-1868 and was awarded the Prussian Order of Merit in 1874. That same year, Carlyle declined the Grand Cross of the Bath from British Prime Minister Benjamin Disraeli. Mrs. Carlyle was Jane Baillie Welsh. After her death on April 21, 1866, Thomas Carlyle confided to Conway, "And so she went on through life—shielding me from all the sharp corners of everyday life—and now—it is all over! . . . I must get at some work—or die." Conway, *Autobiography*, Vol. II, 109. The Letters of Jane Welsh Carlyle have been edited and published in a number of works. Thomas Carlyle died on February 5, 1881.

342 John Hennessy, "Is Not the Negro a Man?" A letter from Stafford, 1862, Fredericksburg Remembered (February 25, 2011), http://fredericksburghistory.wordpress.com/category/freedom.

343 *The American Heritage New Dictionary of Cultural Literacy*, 3d ed., s.v. "franchise," Houghton Mifflin Company, 2005, http://dictionary.reference.com/browse/franchise.

344 Eric Foner, *Reconstruction: America's Unfinished Revolution, 1863-1877* (New York: Harper Collins Publishers, Inc., 1988), 283.

345 The Freedmen's Bureau Online, The Freedmen and Southern Society Project, 1976, http://freedmensbureau.com.

346 "Record Group 393, Part I, Entry 5078 General Orders Issued Vol. II, General Orders No. 77, Headquarters Dept. of Virginia (Maj. Gen. A.H. Terry), Richmond, 6-22-65," *Virginia Freedmen's Bureau Record Group 393*, National Archives, Washington, D.C.

347 Ibid., "Capt. William R. Morse (VRC), Fredericksburg, 2-28-66," Frame 105-7, Roll 44, "Monthly Narrative Reports of Operations and Conditions, Jan.-June 1866."

348 Ibid., "Hector Sears, Stafford Co., 2-16-66," Frame 32-5, and "Hector Sears, Stafford Co., 2-28-66," Frame 60-2, Roll 44, "Monthly Narrative Reports of Operations and Conditions, Jan.-June 1866."

349 Ibid., "James Johnson (F'burg) to Bvt. Brig. Gen. O. Brown, May 31, 1866," Roll 59, "Outrages and Murders."

350 Ibid., "James Johnson to O. Brown, May 1, 1866," Roll 15, "Registered Letters and Telegraphs Received, 1861-1866, 'J.'" A search was made in

the June 29th and June 30th, 1866, *Richmond Examiner* at the Library of Virginia. No article referencing a race riot in Falmouth was found.

351 Ibid., "Hector Sears to O. Brown, Jan. 31, 1867," and "Hector Sears (King George, Stafford, and Acting for Spotsylvania) to O. Brown, Feb. 28, 1867," Roll 46, "Monthly Narrative Reports of Operations and Conditions, Nov. 1866-Apr. 1867."

352 Ibid., "Hector Sears to O. Brown, November 30, 1867," Roll 60, "Narrative Reports of Criminal Cases involving Freedmen, Mar.-Dec. 1867."

353 "Record Group 393, Pt. I, Entry 5080 General Orders of the First Military District Vol. II, General Orders No. 102, HQ First Military Division, Richmond, VA, December 23, 1867," *Virginia Freedmen's Bureau Record Group 393*, National Archives.

354 Ibid., "James Johnson to O. Brown, Feb. 29, 1868," and "Hector Sears to O. Brown, May 30, 1868," Roll 60, "Narrative Reports of Criminal Cases involving Freedmen, Mar.-Dec. 1867."

355 Job 33:6, KJV.

356 Moncure Daniel Conway, *The Golden Hour* (Boston: Ticknor and Fields, 1862), 81, 115, and 121.

357 Moncure Daniel Conway, letter to Ellen Dana Conway, 19 September 1875, Archives and Special Collections, Dickinson College, Carlisle, Pennsylvania.

358 John Hennessy, "The Wound Inflicted: Memorial Day, Reconciliation, and the Rebuke of Fredericksburg's African-American Community," Fredericksburg Remembered (January 11, 2011), http://fredericksburghistory.wordpress.com/2011/01/11/the-wound-inflicted-memorial-day-reconciliation-and-the-rebuke-of-fredericksburgs-african-american-community/.

359 Evan Morrison Woodward, Major, *Our Campaigns; The Second Regiment Pennsylvania Reserve Volunteers*, ed. Stanley W. Zamonski (Shippensburg, Pennsylvania: Burd Street Press, 1995), 68.

360 The photograph is a tintype, a mode of photography used into the later part of the 19th century.

361 Conway, *Testimonies Concerning Slavery*, 4.

362 Norman Schools, *Union Church and Cemetery National Register Nomination*, National Park Service, Washington, DC, 2008.

363 Stafford County Deed Book Vol. 26-A (1868), 509. While the current trustees strive to uphold the deed's stipulations regarding the physical

stewardship of the land and church structure, they do not agree with, abide by, or condone other stipulations within the 1868 deed that are now outdated, inapplicable, illegal, or discriminatory. The deed may also be seen at http://www.falmouthunionchurch.org/history/deed.htm.

[364] John White, Servant, "A Brief History of the Union Branch of the True Vine," no date (Conway House Collections). The name is based on Biblical scripture found in John 15: 5, KJV. "I am the vine, ye are the branches." Members were "officially inducted" up till 1944. Since then, membership has been voluntary.

[365] A "Certificate of Corporation" of the UBTV was recorded in 1903 in Stafford County Deed Book 10, 562. The "Charter of the UBTV Incorporated" was duly recorded by the Commonwealth of Virginia State Corporation Commission in Richmond, on August 7, 1905.

[366] "Reports on Prominent Whites and Freedmen, March-May 1867," Roll 67, Report from Hector Sears for Stafford, King George, and Spotsylvania, June 3, 1867, Frame 446-9, *Virginia Freedmen's Bureau Record Group 393*, National Archives, Washington, D.C.

[367] The lot was forfeited back to John Moncure as according to a deed of 1873, "the said Moncure having permitted the said Curtis to hold possession and reside there upon the said Lot from the 14th day of November 1840" until her death c.1873 "and no rent or payment has been exacted by the said Moncure during the said period."

[368] J.R. Kosch, *History of White Oak Primitive Baptist Church 1789-1989* (1989), 14 and 17. Copy in possession of Frank White, White Oak, Virginia.

[369] Frank White, telephone conversation with author, January 2011. Local Black oral history suggests the Freedmen's Bureau was "thought" to be connected.

[370] Ephesians 6: 5-9, KJV. "Servants, be obedient to them that are your masters, with fear and trembling, in singleness of your heart, as unto Christ; Not with eyeservice, as menpleasers; but as the servants of Christ, doing the will of God from the heart; With good will doing service, as to the Lord, and not to men; Knowing that whatsoever good thing any man doeth, the same shall he receive of the Lord, whether he be bond or free. And, masters, do the same things unto them, forbearing threatening: knowing that your Master also is in heaven; neither is there respect of persons with him." Here the domestic

relationship of the ancient world is between that of employee and employer.

[371] Frank White, interview by author, White Oak, March 2010. Mr. White's father made an attempt to locate descendants of the church members in Alexandria without success. He concluded the church failed and the members from Stafford were absorbed into other black churches in Alexandria. They did not return to Stafford County.

[372] Guild, Introduction.

[373] Murray Forbes died July 30, 1863. The whites in the photograph may be Union veterans revisiting the town. The Forbes House no longer stands in Falmouth. It was disassembled piece by piece and reassembled in another part of Stafford County. The original site of the Forbes House is now used as a parking lot. During the 20th century, the house was known as the Brown House.

[374] Marion Brooks Robinson, interview by author, Falmouth, Virginia, March 2009. "Bill Butler Road was named after him. My father once showed me the foundation of Butler's home in what is now Clearview."

[375] The exception was Mt. Olive Baptist Church, founded in 1818, in the Roseville area of Stafford County.

[376] Jim Thomas, email to author, 1 May 2011(Conway House Collections). Thomas further states, "There were also songs with secret codes to celebrate their good feelings following such a meeting like 'Come out the Wilderness' and 'His name so sweet.'"

[377] Frank White, email to author, 2 May 2011 (Conway House Collections). Orange County is the second county west of Falmouth.

[378] Fitzgerald, 112.

[379] "The African American Image in Virginia," Resource Library, Traditional Fine Arts Organization, Inc., Arizona, http://www.tfaoi.com/aa/8aa/8aa451.htm.

[380] Stafford County Deed Book TT, 576.

[381] Stafford County Deed Book UU, 63.

[382] Guild, *Black Laws of Virginia*, 179. See 1867-1870 Constitution. Article VIII, Section 3. In accordance with the citizenship and equal protection (Reconstruction) clauses in the 14th Amendment to the US Constitution, the Virginia General Assembly was to provide "a uniform system of public free schools, and for its gradual, equal, and full introduction into all counties of the state by 1867, or as much earlier as practical." Due to a substantial amount of time passing before the full

implementation of this act by the General Assembly, African American education fell upon the African American church.

383 Stuart Jones, "A Historical Study of Public Education in Stafford County, Virginia, from 1865 through 1965" (PhD diss., American University, 1970), 23 and 76. Jones states there were five white schools and two colored schools in Falmouth in 1884.

384 Frank White, email to author, 19 November 2010 (Conway House Collections). The highest grade offered to black children in Stafford County was the seventh grade until 1939, when Stafford Training School (now the Rowser Building) was built. Stafford County had two white high schools at that time, both accredited. Stafford Training School had four graduating classes, 1943, 1944, 1945, and 1946. The school was never accredited, so Stafford sent black children to Walker Grant High School in Fredericksburg. The last Stafford student to graduate from Walker Grant was in 1960. In 1959, Stafford Training School had its name changed to H.H. Poole High School, which was accredited by the time the 1961 class graduated. Another class graduated in 1962. In September of that year, the entire 11th and 12th grade classes were transferred from H.H. Poole to integrate the all white Stafford High School.

385 Herbert Brooks, interview by author, Falmouth, Virginia, 2 November 2009. St. Clair Brooks was well regarded by the black residents. Referred to as the unofficial mayor of Falmouth, he probably did more than any single individual to raise the level of race relations within the town during a time of segregation and prejudice.

386 "Sears, Stafford Co., 3-31-66," Roll 44, "Monthly Narrative Reports of Operations and Conditions, Jan.-June 1866," and "Sears, Stafford and King George Co., 8-31-66," Frame 297-8, Roll 45, "Monthly Narrative Reports, Jul.-Oct. 1866," *Virginia Freedman's Bureau Record Group 393*, National Archives, Washington, D.C.

387 Ruth Coder Fitzgerald, "The Barnes House," *Historic Falmouth Towne and Stafford County, Incorporated Newsletter*, Vol. 7, No. 2 (1987): 2. The article gives Falmouth resident, Mrs. Randolph H. Brooks (deceased), as a source. Also, Kirby Kendall, Jr., interview by author, Falmouth, Virginia, 2 November 2010. Mr. Kendall's grandmother, Annie Payne Musselman, related the story of the school to him.

388 Eby, *They Called Stafford Home*, 321-322; "Daniel Lucas Dead," Fredericksburg *Free Lance*, November 15, 1904. Bettie was the youngest of the Barnes sisters.

389 The house was sold to the Melchers of Belmont. It has had several owners since, but today the house is still called the Barnes House. An oil on canvas portrait exists (c.1830) of Harrison B. Barnes (Conway House Collections). Barnes briefly served in Company I, 47th Virginia Infantry, which was raised in Stafford County during the Civil War.

390 Blake Dickinson, "Mason affair results in severe embarrassment for Moncure Conway," *House Divided*, Dickinson College, Carlisle, Pennsylvania (2008), http://hd.housedivided.dickinson.edu/node/14735. "Moncure Conway sent a letter to James Murray Mason, a Confederate emissary to Britain, in which he declared his authority (derived from the leading American abolitionist) to negotiate a lasting peace with the Confederacy based on a mutual agreement to emancipate Southern slaves. As Conway had no such authority to do so, the affair was a crushing embarrassment when the correspondence was published. The political fallout added to Conway's disillusionment and caused him to remain estranged from his native country, and he remained in England for years to come."

391 Today, the home of the South Place Ethical Society is in Conway Hall, named in honor of Moncure Conway. It is located in Red Lion Square, London, England. Conway Hall was one of the few buildings left standing in that area during the Blitz.

392 Conway, "Letter from Virginia," 1-4. The original in his handwriting contained a notation on the upper corner of the first page, "Anthology for Meditation at Camden." The letter's 25 pages written to his wife were evidently for his own "meditation" upon returning to England. Camden was a part of London.

393 Conway, *Autobiography*, Vol. II, 301.

394 Conway, *Autobiography*, Vol. I, 220-222. The "young lady" was FitzGerald's fiancé, Charlotte Taylor, who in 1871 married Rear Admiral Robley D. Evans. Charlotte tried to learn the details of FitzGerald's death. He was wounded in the morning's fighting on May 3rd. A fellow officer could not relate the full truth that, after being hit by a shell while being evacuated in the afternoon, there was not much left of FitzGerald to bury. Charlotte seemingly closed this sad chapter in her life. The author found no mention of Gerald FitzGerald or Moncure

Conway in her letters or correspondence after her marriage. Family descendents had no prior knowledge of FitzGerald before the author's contact. Charlotte is buried alongside Rear Admiral Evans in Arlington National Cemetery.

395   Lydia Crain, "Falmouth, A Virginia Village in the 'Forties' from a Child's Point of View."
396   Conway, *Testimonies Concerning Slavery*, 11-12.
397   Ibid., 13. See "Then I Laid My Burden Down" and the testimony of a slave against the state of Virginia.
398   Brooks, interview, 2 November 2009.
399   Conway, *Testimonies Concerning Slavery*, 52-53.
400   Chester Rogers, interview by author, 22 May 2011, Falmouth, Virginia.
401   Conway, *Autobiography*, Vol. I, 28.
402   Conway, *Testimonies Concerning Slavery*, 53. Conway relates his conversation with an old slave who names Lucas as "Big Jim" and Captain O'Bannon as "Cap'n B."
403   Genesis 4:7 KJV.
404   Marion Brooks Robinson, interview by author, Falmouth, Virginia, March 2010. Ms. Robinson recalled that in her childhood, "On one of my many visits Miss Nannie pointed out the place in the stables where he [Lucas] had been buried." The grave has never been moved.
405   Historical and Archeological Committee, Citizens to Serve Stafford, "Falmouth Folklore As told by Marion Brooks Robinson," *Foundation Stones of Stafford County, Virginia* (Fredericksburg, Virginia: The Fredericksburg Press, Inc., 1991), 104-105. Falmouth's residents perhaps referred to Jack O'Bannon as an immigrant because of his Irish name and the repugnance of his brutality. Janet Edson, "Carlton" (unpublished brochure, Fredericksburg, Virginia, 2010). Ms. Edson states Bryan O'Bannon was the first of the family to arrive in Virginia from Ireland at some time before 1720. John Maurice O'Bannon was born in 1800 in the area of Fauquier and Rappahannock Counties.
406   Wayne Burton, interview by author, Falmouth, Virginia, February 2009.
407   Historical and Archeological Committee, *Foundation Stones*, 105.
408   Herbert Brooks, interview, 2 November 2009; Edson, "Carlton." Ms. Edson states John Maurice O'Bannon married Harriet Ann Corbin in 1830 and they purchased Carlton in 1837. Two older children, both boys, married and left Falmouth. John Maurice O'Bannon died in

1870. "No one has been able to determine where John was buried, but one of the daughters intimated that they did not want him to be placed near them for eternity." Harriet O'Bannon's death is recorded as 1891, on a modern marker placed over her grave. Nannie died in 1935 and Ellen died in 1937. After their deaths, the estate became derelict until purchased by Dr. E. Boyd and Ruth Graves in 1942. A photograph, in the possession of a family member, shows Ellen and Nannie in their long dresses, on the back porch of Carlton.

409 Chester Rogers, interview, 22 May 2011.

410 This lot may have been on the north side of Washington Street and the west side of Falls Run. Falmouth's lot numbers have changed several times over the years. To a large extent the original lot numbers remain lost.

411 Virginia Legislative Petitions, "Henry Minor," Reel 187, Box 238, Folder 100, Library of Virginia. Thomas Seddon was born 1779 and died 1831.

412 Julia Marie Heflin, "Valley View," *Works Progress Administration Historical Inventory: Photographs*. (Richmond, Virginia, Works Progress Administration, c.1936). Central Rappahannock Regional Library, Fredericksburg, Virginia.

413 Frank White, email to author, 8 December 2010 (Conway House Collections). Brooke is also known as Brooke Station.

414 "Peter Booker," *Jefferson County Journal*, Adams, New York, May 24, 1882.

415 The Fredericksburg and Spotsylvania National Military Park and area historians are currently working on identifying as many names as possible of the freedom seekers who entered the Union lines at Fredericksburg, Falmouth, and Stafford County during the "Gateway to Freedom" in 1862 and again in 1863.

416 "Peter Booker," *Jefferson County Journal*, Adams, New York, June 14, 1882.

417 "A Reminiscent Letter," *Jefferson County Journal*, Adams, New York, February 15, 1898.

418 Ibid. Major Sidney Jones Mendell and his family moved to Iowa in the fall of 1866. In 1909, he died in Morgan Township, Franklin County.

419 "Probable Fatal Shooting," *Fredericksburg Star*, April 16, 1884.

420 "Died From His Injuries," *Fredericksburg News*, April 24, 1884. Dr. Lawrence Ashton was the attending physician. He married Ann

Amanda "Nannie" Green, sister of Alexander Morson Green, making him Robert's uncle. Dr. Ashton lived in the old Dunbar House, previously owned by Miss Anna Dunbar (see "A Kiss").

421 Brooks, interview. In this area "Graves of Negroes" appears on the "Scheel Map." Eugene C. Scheel, *Stafford County Historical Map*, Stafford County Historical Commission, 2003. The cemetery has been recorded by the Stafford Cemetery Committee. The deep ravines with creek beds leading down from Stafford Heights to the Rappahannock River were locally known as "guts." Each probably had its own name, now lost to time.

422 Conway, *Testimonies Concerning Slavery*, 44-45.

423 Conway, *Autobiography*, Vol. I, v-vi.

424 Moncure Daniel Conway to Gretchen Simson, 29 January 1907, Archives and Special Collections, Otto G. Richter Library, University of Miami. Gretchen was the wife of sculptor Theodore Spicer Simson who created a bronze bust of Conway. The bust resides at Dickinson College in Carlisle, Pennsylvania. The Jamestown Exposition in 1907 marked the 300th anniversary of the founding of Jamestown.

425 Andrew Carnegie, "Moncure D. Conway Lover of Truth," *New York Times*, April 25, 1908. Conway's funeral service was held in New York City. His ashes are buried in Kensico Cemetery in Valhalla, New York.

426 Cosmelia Hirst, "First Settling of Slaves Here," *Yellow Springs News*, November 8, 1907.

427 Luke 4:6-7 KJV.

428 On October 19, 2006, in honor of Moncure Conway, a new school was dedicated as Conway Elementary School in Stafford County.

429 US Federal Census 1860, Slave Schedules. Before the Civil War, Green and Ross lived at Shepherd's Green on Potomac Creek and after the war, on Ridgeway Farm. Both were in Stafford County. Alexander Morson Green died January 19, 1904, and is buried at Effingham in Prince William County, Virginia. Nancy Ross died January 8, 1924, and is buried in the Ross Family Cemetery in Stafford County.

430 Indian War Widow Pension Claim No. 16878, William C. Ross, Company K, 9th Cavalry, War Department, June 19, 1924, National Archives, College Park, Maryland.

431 Cheyenne and Arapaho Indian Agency, Indian Census Rolls, Microcopy Number M595 roll 27, 46 and M595 roll 28, 32. See also Record

of Deaths for Cheyenne Indian Tribe since May 7, 1892. National Archives Southwest Region, Ft. Worth, Texas.
432 Dennis Collins, *The Indians' Last Fight or the Dull Knife Raid*, (Girard, Kansas: Press of the Appeal to Reason, 1915), 208-209.
433 *The El Reno American*, January 21, 1915, obituary for W.C. Ross.
434 "Find a Grave," William Carter Ross, Memorial 42576283, Walking Dead (October 1, 2009), http://www.findagrave.com/.
435 "Grows More Interesting," *The New York Age*, January 11, 1917, New York. The name appearing in the paper was given as, "(Mrs.) Mary B. Owe . . . , Falmouth, Va."
436 James Lucas, interview by author, July 2010. The surname Rowser may be a change or corruption of the surnames Rowzee or Rowzey. Rowzee was also an old white surname in Stafford County. Uncle Jim may have been the "James Rowzey" who was one of the three original trustees of Little Shiloh Baptist Church.
437 For location of the Pollock Farm see Jerrilynn Eby, *They Called Stafford Home*, (1997), 250, 270-274. See also Homer D. Musselmam, *47th Virginia Infantry*, (Lynchburg, Virginia: H.E. Howard, Inc., 1991). The "Regimental Roster" list William G. Pollock as "b. July 29, 1829. Farmer in Stafford Co. Enl. 5/18/61 in Co. A as Lt. Present on all rolls through 12/31/64 final roll. S.O.#11/8, 4/21/63 leave. S.O.245/7, 10/23/64 leave. Promoted to Capt. 12/19/64. G.O.128, 11/25/62 detailed for court. On 1/7/65, Capt. Pollock applied for 60 day furlough. The examining officer stated he was greatly debilitated as a result of chronic diarrhea and unfit for duty. Died April 7, 1865 in Stafford Co. bur. Traveler's Rest Cemetery, Stafford Co."
438 L. Reginald Lucas, "Application for Consideration of Naming to Wall of Honor," City of Fredericksburg, (undated, 2006 or 2007).
439 Brooks, interview, 2 November 2009. Anthony Burns' sister, a slave owned by Charles Suttle, was kept as a "breeding-woman."
440 Ibid. St. Clair Brooks deceased, Herbert Brooks' father, was the witness who passed down the account in oral history.
441 Paula Royster, email to author, 2 April 2009 (Conway House Collections).
442 Raus, 107.
443 Kendall, interview, 2 November, 2010.
444 Brooks, interview, 2 November 2009. Sarah E. Coppedge (born 1818, died 1890) was Mr. Brooks' great grandmother.

445 Ibid.
446 Ibid. Mr. Brooks learned how to swim in this manner.
447 Fitzgerald, 227.
448 Robinson, interview, March 2010.
449 Melchers died in 1932. His wife deeded the house and estate to the Commonwealth of Virginia in 1942. Today, Mary Washington University administers the Belmont estate. The University interprets Melchers' life in Falmouth and his body of work. The house, grounds, and Melchers' studio are open to the public.
450 The frame house was moved to Falmouth from another location sometime between 1880 and 1887. Additions were made by Fannie's father, Willie P. Roots.
451 Fannie would have been 14 years old. The girl appears to be Fannie when compared with her photograph. A second possibility is the girl may be Fannie's sister, Mary.
452 "Long-Established Roots," *Free Lance-Star*, June 11, 1997, Fredericksburg, Virginia.
453 Guild, *Black Laws of Virginia*, 180. See 1870 Chapter 259 of the Criminal Code.
454 Frank White, interview by author, Falmouth, Virginia, April 2010.
455 Brooks, interview, 2 November 2009.
456 Robinson, interview, March 2010.
457 Students from the Falmouth Colored School were doubled up with students at Union Branch School (black) on Hollywood Farm Road in White Oak "down near Wildcat Corner." The Union Branch School was started by the Union Branch of the True Vine. The following year, the students attended Leeland School, which had previously been a white school but was determined to be too small and old for the white students, who were given a new school building. In 1939, the Stafford Training School opened for black students.
458 Robert Burton, interview by author, Falmouth, Virginia, October 2009.
459 Deuteronomy 3:27, KJV.
460 Roger J. Poindexter, Jr., telephone conversation with author, 25 March 2010; Stafford County Deed Book 359, 60-61, April 12, 1979. In 1979, Mt. Pisgah was renamed the Glad Tidings Revival Center. It closed its doors in 1987, the year that Reverend Poindexter died. The building subsequently was abandoned. A church known as Bethesda Baptist may have been on or near the site of Little Shiloh about 1920.

The author has found no information about this church other than it had an association with White Oak Church in White Oak. The Stafford County Cemetery Committee has found no visible evidence of any associated graveyard at the site.

461 Robinson, interview, March 2009. Ms. Robinson related, "Her [Helen's] family had stayed on after the war." The extended Brooks family in Falmouth was very large and included many children.

462 Melchers also made an oil painting of this same work in charcoal. The painting has background added which is identifiable to that in the Geneva Brooks House in Falmouth. Mammy Helen is known to have lived at this house. Both the painting and charcoal rendition reside at Belmont, Geri Melchers Home and Studio, Falmouth, Virginia.

463 Brooks, interview, 2 November 2009; Robinson interview, March 2009. Members of the Brooks family remain displeased about the incident today. Moncure Conway's uncle cohabitated (marriage being illegal) with a mulatto woman and they lived together as husband and wife in the "Stafford woods." George Washington Conway was buried in a Black cemetery near Stafford Court House. "The white folks came and dug him up in the middle of the night and buried him at Aquia Church."

464 An example of reversing the door occurs on the second story bedchambers at Weston Manor, Historic Hopewell Foundation, Inc., Hopewell, Virginia.

465 Louellen "Whitefeather" Silver, interview by author, White Oak, Virginia, February 2010. Ms. Silver was Fannie's longtime friend and confirmed the purpose of the blue paint. Fannie's house is now a part of the Belmont estate. The use of "haint blue" was not restricted to Falmouth; it is known in other parts of the South as well. Folklore suggests African Americans in the rural South painted their mailboxes blue to keep away bad news.

466 Robinson, interview, March 2009.

467 Brooks, interview, 2 November, 2009. Mr. Brooks provided the quote for Julia Russell.

468 Falmouth Baptist Church (white), Mt. Pisgah "Colored" Church, Mrs. Ellis Store (white), and Wheeler's Market (black).

469 Thomas Jefferson, *Notes on the State of Virginia*, ed. William Peden (Chapel Hill: University of North Carolina Press, 1954), 138.

470 The author was present when Herbert Brooks told this to the members of his Sunday school class at Falmouth Baptist Church in 2011. Frank

White, African American living in Stafford County, related to the author that his father made dried apples by placing slices on the low tin roof of an outbuilding, left for three days.
471 Lawrence Wheeler, telephone conversation with author, July 2009.
472 Gloria Payne Chittum, interview by author, Falmouth, Virginia, September 2009. Ms. Chittum related that animals including fowl were raised in those days for food and not for pets. Being as children are, they made pets of the animals.
473 Elaine Thompson, African American historian, interview by author, 13 November 2010, George Mason University.
474 White, telephone conversation with author, November 2010.
475 Linwood Bourne, Jr., interview by author, 19 February 2012, Falmouth, Virginia. Linwood Bourne, Sr., operated the AMOCO station until 1978. The station was raised to make way for a new bank building.
476 Charles Emery Stevens, *Anthony Burns: A History*, 167-168.
477 Site visit by author, 12 July 2011. Very little visual evidence exists. The author's estimation of the number of graves is based on using unobtrusive ground penetrating testing, which was hampered by thick undergrowth. The burials are arranged in rows. An extensive survey is needed to confirm the exact number of graves.
478 Kirby Kendall, Jr., interview, 2 November 2010, and Janet Edson, telephone conversation with author, 5 May 2011.
479 Conway, *Testimonies Concerning Slavery*, 10.
480 *Union Church and Cemetery National Register Nomination* (2008), 11.
481 Ibid., 5.
482 I Corinthians 15:51-52; I Thessalonians 4:16-17, KJV.
483 Fitzgerald, "African-American History of Stafford County," Brochure. "In the late 1600s slaves were brought into the sparsely settled Rappahannock Valley, primarily to serve as agricultural laborers." The Civil Rights Movement as we know it today started with the Freedom Riders in 1961. On September 5, 1961, two young sisters entered the all-white Stafford County Elementary School. This was the first desegregation of schools in the Fredericksburg area. Falmouth was not directly involved.
484 Conway, "Letter from Virginia," 13.
485 Richards and Elliott, Vol. I, 306. This entry in Julia Ward Howe's journal was made sometime between January and May, 1871 (some of her entries omit the specific date during that period).

BIBLIOGRAPHY

Books

Beale, Jane Howison. *The Journal of Jane Howison Beale, Fredericksburg, Virginia 1850-1862.* Fredericksburg, Virginia: Historic Fredericksburg Foundation, Inc., 1995.

Blight, David W. *A Slave No More, Two Men Who Escaped to Freedom Including Their Own Narratives of Emancipation.* Orlando, Florida: Harcourt, Inc., 2007.

Bruce, George A. *The Twentieth Regiment of Massachusetts Volunteer Infantry 1861-1865.* Boston and New York: Houghton, Mifflin and Company, 1906.

Brydon, G. MacLaren. *A Sketch of the Colonial History of St. Paul's, Hanover, & Brunswick Parishes King George County, VA. 1916.* Library of Virginia, 1 volume, 136 leaves typescript (accession number 19756).

Burtis, Mary Elizabeth. *Moncure Conway 1832-1907.* New Brunswick, New Jersey: Rutgers University Press, 1952.

Child, William. *A History of the Fifth Regiment, New Hampshire Volunteers, in the American Civil War, 1861-1865.* Bristol, New Hampshire: R.W. Musgrove, 1893.

Collins, Dennis. *The Indians' Last Fight or the Dull Knife Raid.* Girard, Kansas: Press of the Appeal to Reason, 1915.

Conner, Albert Z., Jr. *A History of Our Own, Stafford County, Virginia.* Virginia Beach, Virginia: The Donning Company Publishers, 2003.

Conner, Jane Hollenbeck. *Lincoln in Stafford.* Fredericksburg, Virginia: Cardinal Press, 2006.

Conway, Moncure Daniel. *The Golden Hour.* Boston: Ticknor and Fields, 1862.

———. *Moncure Daniel Conway, Autobiography, Memories, and Experiences*, Two Volumes. Cambridge: Houghton, Mifflin and Company, The Riverside Press, 1904.

—. *The Rejected Stone, or Insurrection vs. Resurrection in America*. Boston: Walker, Wise, and Company, 1861.

—. *Testimonies Concerning Slavery*. London: Chapman and Hall, 1864.

Cooke, John Esten, Moses Drury Hoge, and John William Jones. *Stonewall Jackson: A Military Biography*. D. Appleton and Company, 1876.

Darter, Oscar H. *Colonial Fredericksburg and Neighborhood in Perspective*. New York: Twayne Publishers, 1957.

Dawes, Rufus Robinson. *Service with the Sixth Wisconsin Volunteers*. Marietta, Ohio: E.R. Alderman & Sons, 1890.

d'Entremont, John. *Southern Emancipator, Moncure Conway: The American Years, 1832-1865*. New York Oxford: Oxford University Press, 1987.

Devine, T.M., Ph.D. ed. *A Scottish Firm in Virginia 1767-1777 W. Cuninghame and Co*. Scottish History Society, Edinburgh: Clark Constable, 1984.

Douglass, Frederick. *Narrative of the Life of Frederick Douglass, An American Slave*. Boston: Anti-Slavery Office, 1845.

Drew, Benjamin. *The Refugee: or the Narratives of Fugitive Slaves in Canada*. Boston: John P. Jewett and Company, 1856.

Eby, Jerrilynn. *Laying the Hoe, A Century of Iron Manufacturing in Stafford County, Virginia*. Westminster, Maryland: Willow Bend Books, 2003.

—. *They Called Stafford Home: The Development of Stafford County, Virginia, from 1600 until 1865*. Bowie, Maryland: Heritage Books, Inc., 1997.

Favill, Josiah Marshall. *The Diary of a Young Officer Serving with the Armies of the United States During the War of the Rebellion*. Chicago, Illinois: R.R. Donnelley & Sons, 1909.

Fishel, Edwin C. *The Secret War for the Union: The Untold Story of Military Intelligence in the Civil War*. Boston: Houghton Mifflin Company, 1996.

Fitzgerald, Ruth Coder. *A Different Story, A Black History Of Fredericksburg, Stafford, and Spotsylvania, Virginia*. Morris Plains, New Jersey: Unicorn Publishing House, 1979.

Foner, Eric. *Reconstruction: America's Unfinished Revolution, 1863-1877*. New York: Harper Collins Publishers, Inc., 1988.

Forbes, Edwin. *Civil War Etchings*. Edited by William Forrest Dowson. New York: Dover Publications, 1957 and 1985.

Fornieri, Joseph R., editor. *The Language of Liberty: The Political Speeches and Writings of Abraham Lincoln*. Washington, D.C.: Regnery Publishing, Inc., 2003.

Gates, Theodore B. *The Ulster Guard and the War of the Rebellion*. New York: Benj. H. Tyrrel, 1879.

Goolrick, John T. *The Story of Stafford, A Narrative History of Stafford County, Virginia*. Fredericksburg, Virginia: Cardinal Press, Inc., 1976.

Guild, June Purcell, L.L.M. *Black Laws of Virginia, A Summary Of The Legislative Acts Of Virginia Concerning Negroes From Earliest Times To The Resent*. Lovettsville, Virginia: Willow Bend Books, 1996.

Harrison, Fairfax. *Landmarks of Old Prince William*, Volumes I and II. Baltimore, Maryland: Gateway Press, Inc., 1987.

Harrison, Noel G. *Fredericksburg Civil War Sites April 1861-November 1862*. Lynchburg, Virginia: H.E. Howard, Inc., 1995.

Haynie, Miriam. *The Stronghold, A Story of Historic Northern Neck of Virginia and Its People*. Richmond, Virginia: The Dietz Press, Incorporated, 1959.

Hening, William Waller. *Laws of Virginia*. Richmond: Franklin Press, 1820.

Hill, Daniel G. *The Freedom-seekers: Blacks in Early Canada*. Don Mills, Ontario: Stoddard, 1992.

Historical and Archeological Committee, *Foundation Stones of Stafford County, Virginia*. Fredericksburg, Virginia: The Fredericksburg Press, Inc., 1991.

Historical and Archeological Committee. *Foundation Stones of Stafford County, Virginia* Vol. II. Fredericksburg, Virginia: The Fredericksburg Press, Inc., 1992.

Jefferson, Thomas. *Notes on the State of Virginia*. Edited by William Peden. Chapel Hill: University of North Carolina Press, 1954.

Jefferson, Thomas. *The Papers of Thomas Jefferson, Volume 1: 1760-1776*. et al edited by Julian P. Boyd. Princeton, New Jersey: Princeton University Press, 1950.

Kosch, J.R. *History of White Oak Primitive Baptist Church 1789-1989* (1989). Publisher unknown. Copy in possession of Frank White, White Oak, Virginia.

Mann, J. William. *Bells and Belfries*. Fredericksburg, Virginia: Published by the author, 1993.

Markle, Donald E. *Spies and Spymasters of the Civil War*. New York: Hippocrene Books, 1995.

Marks, J.J., Rev. D.D. *The Peninsular Campaign in Virginia or Incidents and Scenes on The Battlefields and In Richmond*. Philadelphia: J.B. Lippencott & Co, 1864.

Marquis, D.R. and Tevis, C.V., compilers. *The History of the Fighting Fourteenth*. Brooklyn: Brooklyn Eagle Press, 1911.

Mays, David F. *Edmund Pendleton 1721-1803*, Two Volumes. Harvard Press, 1952.

McCann, Forrest Mason. *Hymns & History: An Annotated Survey of Sources*. Abilene, Texas: ACU Press, 1997.

Miller, Francis Trevelyan. *The Photographic History of The Civil War In Ten Volumes*. New York: The Review of Reviews Co., 1911.

Miller, Richard F. and Robert F. Mooney. *The Civil War: The Nantucket Experience Including the Memoirs of Josiah Fitch Murphey*. Nantucket, Massachusetts: Wesco Publishing, 1994.

Mills, J. Harrison. *Chronicles of the Twenty-First Regiment, New York State Volunteers*. Buffalo, New York: Gies and Co. Printers and Bookmakers, 1887.

Moe, Richard. *The Last Full Measure, The Life and Death of the First Minnesota Volunteers*. New York: Henry Holt and Company, 1993.

Montlezun, Baron de. *Voyage Fait dans les Annees 1816 et 1817, de New-Yorck a la Nouvelle-Orleans, et de L'Orenoque Au Missippi, par les Petites et les Grandes-Antilles*. Paris: Librarie de Gide Fils, 1818.

Moore, Frank. *Anecdotes, Poetry and Incidents of the War: North and South 1860-1865*. New York: Publication Office, Bible House, 1867.

Morison, Samuel Eliot, and Henry Steele Commager, William E. Leuchtenburg. *The Growth of the American Republic: Volume 1*. Seventh Edition. New York: Oxford University Press, 1980.

Musselman, Homer D. *47th Virginia Infantry*. Lynchburg, Virginia: H.E. Howard, Inc, 1991.

Norris, Robert O., Jr., introduction to *The Stronghold, A Story of Historic Northern Neck of Virginia and Its People*, by Mariam Haynie, xvi. Richmond, Virginia: The Dietz Press, Incorporated, 1959.

Noyes, George F., Capt. U.S. Volunteers. *The Bivouac and the Battlefield; Or Campaign Sketches in Virginia And Maryland*. New York: Harper & Brothers, Publishers, 1863.

Raus, Edmund J., Jr. *Banners South, A Northern Community at War.* Kent, Ohio: The Kent State University Press, 2005.

Ray, William. *Four Years with the Iron Brigade, The Civil War Journal of William Ray, Company F, Seventh Wisconsin Volunteers.* Edited by Lance Herdegen and Sherry Murphy. Cambridge: Da Capo Press, 2002.

Rice, Howard C. Jr. and Anne S.K. Brown, editors. *The American Campaigns of Rochambeau's Army, 1780, 1781, 1782, 1783.* Providence: Brown University Press, 1972.

Richards, Laura E. and Maud Howe Elliott, assisted by Florence Howe Hall. *Julia Ward Howe.* Boston and New York: Houghton Mifflin Company, The Riverside Press, 1915.

Sanborn, F.B. *The Life of Henry David Thoreau: Including Many Essays Hitherto Unpublished, and Some Accounts of His Family and Friends.* Boston: Houghton Mifflin Company, 1917.

Shaw, Robert Gould, Colonel. *Blue-Eyed Child of Fortune, The Civil War Letters of Colonel Robert Gould Shaw.* Edited by Russell Duncan. Athens, Georgia: The University of Georgia Press, 1992.

Sparks, David S., editor. *Inside Lincoln's Army: The Diary of Marsena Rudolph Patrick, Provost Marshall General, Army of the Potomac.* New York: Thomas Yoseloff, 1964.

Stanton, Robert, introduction to *Underground Railroad*, National Park Service Handbook 156, with essays by Larry Gara, Brenda E. Stevenson, and C. Peter Ripley. Washington, D.C.: US Department of the Interior, 1998.

Stevens, Charles Emery. *Anthony Burns: A History.* Boston: John P. Jewett and Company, 1856.

Symons, Julian. *Thomas Carlyle: The Life and Ideas of a Prophet.* London: Victor Gollancz Ltd., 1952.

Taylor, Isaac Lyman. *Campaigning with the First Minnesota: A Civil War Diary.* Edited by Hazel C. Wolf. St. Paul, Minnesota: Minnesota History XXV, 1944.

United States War Department. *War of the Rebellion, A Compilation of the Official Records of the Union and Confederate Armies,* 128 Volumes. Washington, D.C.: Government Printing Office, 1881-1902.

White, Wyman S. *The Civil War Diary of Wyman S. White.* Edited by Russell C. White. Baltimore: Butternut and Blue, 1993.

Whitman, Walt. *Leaves of Grass.* Boston: James R. Osgood and Company, 1881.

Wilkerson, Elizabeth Vass. *Diary of Rev. L.C. Vass*. Bloomington, Indiana: Author House, 2008.
Wilkins, Martha Fifield. *Sunday River Sketches, A New England Chronicle*. Rumford, Maine: Androscoggin Publications, 1977.
Wills, Anita. *Notes And Documents of Free Persons of Color*. Raleigh, North Carolina: Lulu Publishing Company, 2003.
Wise, Jennings C. *The Military History of VMI from 1839 to 1865*. Lynchburg, Virginia: J.P. Bell Company, Inc., 1915.
Woodward, Evan Morrison, Major. *Our Campaigns; The Second Regiment Pennsylvania Reserve Volunteers*. Edited by Stanley W. Zamonski. Shippensburg, Pennsylvania: Burd Street Press, 1995.

Articles and Manuscripts

Besant, Annie. "A Leaf on a Grave." MC 1999.6, Box 3, Folder 4 *(TS)*, Archives and Special Collections, Dickinson College, Carlisle, Pennsylvania.
Carnegie, Andrew. "Moncure D. Conway Lover of Truth." *New York Times*, April 25, 1908.
Chamerovzow, Louis Alexis. "The Slave's Underground Railroad to Freedom." *Edinburgh Series of Anti-Slavery Tracts*, No. 1. Samuel J. May Anti-Slavery Collection, Cornell University, Ithaca, New York.
Conner, Albert Z. "Watch For The Morning: Moncure Daniel Conway, Falmouth's Southern Emancipationist." *The Journal of Fredericksburg History*, Vol. 12 (2010): 62-64.
Conway, Moncure Daniel. "Letter from Virginia," October 1875. Moncure Daniel Conway Special Collections, Rare Book and Manuscripts, Butler Library, Columbia University, New York, New York.
Crain, Lydia. "Falmouth, A Virginia Village in the 'Forties' from a Child's Point of View." *Fredericksburg Free Lance*, March 15, 1898. Micro film, Virginiana Room, Central Rappahannock Regional Library, Fredericksburg, Virginia.
Edson, Janet. "Carlton." Unpublished brochure, Fredericksburg, Virginia, 2010.
Evans, Larry. "Freedom meant something different to black people." *Free Lance Star*, Fredericksburg, Virginia, August 14, 1976.

Felder, Paula S. "The Falmouth Story, A View from the Twentieth Century." Virginiana Room, Central Rappahannock Regional Library, Fredericksburg, Virginia.

Fitzgerald, Ruth Coder. "The Barnes House." *Historic Falmouth Towne and Stafford County, Incorporated Newsletter*, Vol. 7, No. 2 (1987): 2.

Fredericksburg and Spotsylvania National Military Park. "J. Horace Lacy." *Front Porch Fredericksburg Magazine*, Curator's Corner (January 2001). Fredericksburg, Virginia.

Gilpin, Samuel. Samuel Gilpin Diary. E.N. Gilpin papers, 1861-1911, Library of Congress Manuscript Division, Washington, D.C.

Hirst, Cosmelia. "First Settling of Slaves Here." *Yellow Springs News*, November 8, 1907.

"Hung Himself." *Monroe Democrat*, October 6, 1887. Monroe County, Minnesota.

"Historic Resources at the Falls of the Rappahannock River," Department of Planning and Community Development, City of Fredericksburg, Virginia (2001).

History of the First Baptist Church. Yellow Springs, Ohio. No date or author. Photocopy in Conway Colony File, Conway House Collections, Falmouth, Virginia.

Johnson, John Janney. "Fredericksburg's Early Entrepreneurs." *Fredericksburg Times* (October, 1995): 20-24.

Jones, Stuart. "A Historical Study of Public Education in Stafford County, Virginia, from 1865 through 1965." Ph.D. diss., American University, Washington, D.C., 1970.

Lucas, L. Reginald. "Application for Consideration of Naming to Wall of Honor," City of Fredericksburg (undated, 2006 or 2007). Copy in Falmouth Black History File, Conway House Collections, Falmouth, Virginia.

Ogata, Kerry. "African American Women and Medicine: Expanding Interpretations of Colono Ware." Master's thesis, Department of Anthropology, University of South Carolina, Columbia, 1995.

Parrish, Shirley Virginia. "The Fur and Skin Trade of Colonial Virginia." Master thesis, Department of History, Old Dominion University, Norfolk, Virginia, 1972.

Princeton Alumni Weekly, Volume 2 (January 11, 1902): 230. Seeley G. Mudd Manuscript Library, Princeton University, Princeton, New Jersey.

Sanders, Scott. "The Conway Colony—A Journey to Freedom." *Yellow Springs News*, February 1, 2001.

Shelton, W.G., Jr. "Religion in America, Churches of Olde Falmouth Towne." Printing by the author (1987). Copy in Union Church File, Conway House Collections, Falmouth, Virginia.

Smith, Margaret L. "1720 Falmouth, Va." Garden Club of Falmouth, Virginia (1922). Reprinted in the first half of the twentieth-century.

Stine, Linda France, Melaine A. Cabak, and Mark D. Groover. "Blue Beads as African-American Cultural Symbols." *Historical Archeology, Journal for the Society for Historical Archaeology*, Vol. 30 (3rd quarter 1996): 49-75.

Sutherland, George E. "The Negro in the War, A Strong Paper by Major Geo. E. Sutherland." *Milwaukee Sunday Telegraph*, October 7, 1888, microfilm, Wisconsin Historical Society.

Taylor, Murray Forbes. "Stonewall Jackson's Death." *Confederate Veteran*, Vol. XII, No. 10 (October, 1904). Virginia Military Institute Archives, Preston Library, Virginia Military Institute, Lexington, Virginia.

Teasdale, Charles. Charles Teasdale Diary. Company E, 14th Brooklyn NY State Militia. Unpublished. Privately owned in New York. Excerpts in 14th Brooklyn File, Conway House Collections, Falmouth, Virginia.

Washington, John. "Memorys of the Past." Papers of John Washington *(TS)* 1984. Manuscript Division, Library of Congress, Washington, D.C.

Work, Henry Clay. *The Year of Jubilee*. Chicago: Root & Cady, 1862.

Yacovone, Donald. "A Covenant with Death and an Agreement with Hell." The Massachusetts Historical Society (2007).

Documents

Charles County Will Book AH9 (1788), 489-94. Charles County Court House, LaPlata, Maryland.

Cheyenne and Arapaho Indian Agency. Indian Census Rolls, Microcopy Number M595, rolls 27 through 32. National Archives Southwest Region. Ft. Worth, Texas.

Falmouth Trustees Minutes Book, 1764-1868. Simpson Library, Special Collections, Mary Washington University, Fredericksburg, Virginia.

Federal Pension Record No. 380984. Daniel Shanahan. Co's F-G-H—20th Mass Inf. National Archives, College Park, Maryland.

Schools, Norman. *Conway House Underground Railroad Network to Freedom Nomination* (2004). National Underground Railroad Network to Freedom Program, National Capitol Region, National Park Service, Washington, D.C.

Schools, Norman. *Union Church and Cemetery National Register Nomination*, Falmouth, Stafford County, Virginia (2008). National Park Service, Washington, D.C.

Stafford County Deed Book 10. Stafford Court House, Stafford, Virginia.

Stafford County Deed Book 26-A (1868). Stafford Court House, Stafford, Virginia.

Stafford County Deed Book 359. Stafford Court House, Stafford, Virginia.

Stafford County Deed Book TT. Stafford Court House, Stafford, Virginia.

Stafford County Deed Book UU. Stafford Court House, Stafford, Virginia.

Virginia Freedmen's Bureau Record Group 393. National Archives, Washington, D.C.

Virginia Historic Landmarks Staff. *Clearview National Register Nomination*, Stafford County, Virginia (1975). National Park Service, Washington, D.C.

Works Progress Administration Historical Inventory: Photographs. Richmond, Virginia. Works Progress Administration, c.1936. Central Rappahannock Regional Library, Fredericksburg, Virginia.

Letters

Breck, George, Lieutenant, Company L, 1st New York Light Artillery. Letter, 12 January 1863, published in *Rochester Union and Advertiser*.

Buchanan, William. Letter to Zachariah Vowles, Esquire, 19 January 1811. Conway House Collections, Falmouth, Virginia.

Burns, Anthony. Letter to Richard Henry Dana, Jr., 23 August 1854. Massachusetts Historical Society, Boston.

Conway, Moncure Daniel. Letters to Andrew Ingalis Clark, Tasmania, 11 October 1883—2 December 1905. Tasmania Library Special and Rare Book Collection, University of Tasmania, Australia.

Conway, Moncure Daniel. Letter to Ellen Dana Conway, 19 September 1875. Moncure Conway. Archives and Special Collections, Dickinson College, Carlisle, Pennsylvania.

—. Letter to Mildred Conway March, 14 May 1862. Moncure Daniel Conway Special Collection, Rare Books and Manuscripts, Butler Library, Columbia University.

—. Letter to Gretchen Simson, 29 January 1907. Archives and Special Collections, Otto G. Richter Library, University of Miami, Coral Gables, Florida.

Ficklen, Joseph Burwell. Letters to Anna Eliza Fitzhugh Ficklen. Manuscripts Room, Alderman Library, University of Virginia, Charlottesville.

Garrison, William Lloyd. Letter to Andrew Paton, 10 April 1863. Moncure Daniel Conway, Archives and Special Collections, Dickinson College, Carlisle, Pennsylvania.

Miller, Zachariah T. Letter to his Parents, 30 May 1862. Zachariah T. Miller Papers, Helen King Boyer Collection, Georgetown University Library, Washington, D.C.

Morton, Charles E., Lt. Letters to his Mother and Father printed in the *Newburgh Journal*. Albert Z. Conner Collection, Stafford, Virginia.

O'Grady, W.L.D. Letter to *New York Sun*. "To the editors of the Sun," 28 November 1906.

Scott, Sarah T. Letter to John T. Scott, 26 November 1856. Lewis-Scott-Daniel-Greenhow Family Papers, 1787-1908, Accession 21563, Personal Papers Collection, Library of Virginia, Richmond, Virginia.

Unknown Civilian. Letter to My darling Will, 8 May 1862. Lewis Leigh Collection, Box 30, US Army Military History Institute, Carlisle, Pennsylvania.

Wilson, Reverend Hiram. Letter to Reverend Leonard A. Grimes, 28 July 1862. "Death of Anthony Burns." *The Liberator*, August 22, 1862, Boston.

WEB SITES

Conway, Moncure Daniel. "An Ancient And A Modern Compromise." *House Divided*. Dickinson College, Carlisle, Pennsylvania (2007). http://hd.housedivided.dickinson.edu/node/668 (accessed 23 September 2011).

Costa, Tom. "Runaway Slaves and Servants in Colonial Virginia." *Encyclopedia Virginia*. Edited by Brendan Wolfe. Virginia Foundation for the Humanities (January 18, 2012). http://encyclopediavirginia.org/Runaway_Slaves_and_Servants_in_Colonial_Virginia (accessed 25 January 2012).

Costa, Tom, and the Rector and Visitors of the University of Virginia. "The Geography of Slavery in Virginia." University of Virginia, Charlottesville (2005). http://www2.vcdh.virginia.edu/gos/index.html (accessed 13 July 2010).

Culpepper Minute Men Patriots. "Marking Revolutionary War Patriots' Graves." National Society, Sons of the American Revolution (2011). http://www.cmmsar.com/graves.html (accessed 18 June 2004).

Dickinson, Blake. "Mason affair results in severe embarrassment for Moncure Conway." *House Divided*. Dickinson College, Carlisle, Pennsylvania (2008). http://hd.housedivided.dickinson.edu/node/14735 (accessed 19 May 2011).

Eliot, Samuel Atkins, Ed. "Moncure D. Conway (1832-1907)." *Heralds of a Liberal Faith*. Volume IV. Harvard Square Library (2009). http://www.harvardsquarelibrary.org/Heralds/Moncure-Daniel-Conway.php (accessed 8 June 2009).

"Find a Grave." William Carter Ross, Memorial 42576283. http://www.findagrave.com/ (accessed 6 May 2011).

Fitzgerald, Ruth Coder. "African-American History of Stafford County." Stafford County Tourism Brochure. Library Point, Central Rappahannock Regional Library (2002). http://librarypoint.org/african_american_history_of_stafford_virginia (accessed 4 December 2010).

Freedmen's Inquiry Commission. "Final report of the American Freedmen's Inquiry Commission to the Secretary of War." New York City, May 15, 1864. *Official Records of the War of the Rebellion*, Series III, Volume IV. Washington, D.C., 1900. http://www.civilwarhome.com/commissionreportchapt3.htm (accessed 9 March 2011).

Hennessy, John. "Is Not the Negro a Man?" A letter from Stafford, 1862. Fredericksburg Remembered (February 25, 2011). http://fredericksburghistory.wordpress.com/category/freedom (accessed 2 March 2011).

—. "The Fate of Fredericksburg Determined: President Davis's March 1862 Visit." Fredericksburg Remembered (November 4, 2010). http://npsfrsp.wordpress.com/2010/11/04/the-fate-of-fredericksburg-determined-president-daviss-march-1862-visit/ (accessed 31 October 2011).

—. "The Wound Inflicted: Memorial Day, Reconciliation, and the Rebuke of Fredericksburg's African-American Community," Fredericksburg Remembered (January 11, 2011). http://fredericksburghistory.wordpress.com/2011/01/11/the-wound-inflicted-memorial-day-reconciliation-and-the-rebuke-of-fredericksburgs-african-american-community/ (accessed 27 June 2011).

King, Jr., Martin Luther. "Letter from a Birmingham Jail." African Studies Center, University of Pennsylvania. Philadelphia, Pennsylvania (2010). http://www.africa.upenn.edu/Articles_Gen/Letter_Birmingham.html (accessed 8 October 2011).

Lacy, Betty Churchill. "Memories Of A Long Life." April, 1903. Betty C. Jones. http://homepages.rootsweb.ancestry.com/~elacey/chatham.htm (accessed 9 August 2011).

Mink, Eric J. "I was a Slave of Major Horace Lacy." Slavery and Slave Places. National Park Service, Fredericksburg and Spotsylvania National Military Park. http://npsfrsp.wordpress.com/category/slavery-and-slave-places/page/2/ (accessed 28 September 2010).

—. "If These Signatures Could Talk." Falmouth Graffiti, Part 1 (October 1, 2010), National Park Service, Fredericksburg and Spotsylvania National Military Park. http://npsfrsp.wordpress.com/category/graffiti/ (accessed 1 October 2010).

Rice, Dr. Alan. "The Abolition Movement and Mill Worker Solidarity." Revealing Histories Remembering Slavery, Manchester, United Kingdom (2007), http://www.revealinghistories.org.uk/what-evidence-is-there-of-a-black-presence-in-britain-and-north-west-england/articles/the-abolition-movement-and-mill-worker-solidarity.html (accessed 1 November 2011).

Rose, P.K. "The Civil War: Black American Contributions to Union Intelligence." Intelligence Agency Library, Washington, D.C. https://www.cia.gov/library/center-for-the-study-of-intelligence/csi-publications/csi-studies/studies/winter98_99/art06.html (accessed 22 July 2009).

"Route of the French Army Wagon Train from Annapolis, Maryland, to Yorktown, Virginia, in 1781." Expedition Particuliere Commemorative Cantonment Society, Mount Vernon, Virginia (2010). http://xenophongroup.com/mcjoynt/wagon.htm (accessed 18 January 2012).

Schools, Norman. "Moncure Conway (1832-1907)." *Encyclopedia Virginia*. Edited by Brendan Wolfe. Virginia Foundation for the Humanities (August 26, 2010). http://www.EncyclopediaVirginia.org/Conway_Moncure_Daniel_1832-1907 (accessed 20 December 2010).

Sickles, D.E., Brig. Gen. to Gen. Joseph Hooker, 14 March 1862. "Confidential Correspondence Touching Position & c. of the Enemy Near the Rappahannock." General Daniel Sickles Collection Featuring Sickles' use of African American Scouts in Two Intelligence Reports from the Front Lines. Abraham Lincoln Bookshop, Chicago, Illinois (2011). http://www.alincolnbookshop.com/html/new_acquisitions.htm#sickles (accessed 21 April 2011)

"Slave Holdings Listed in Falmouth 1815 Personal Property Tax List." Mary Washington University, Fredericksburg, Virginia. http://departments.umw.edu/hipr/www/Falmouth/1815pp/falmouth1815pp.htm (accessed 28 June 2010).

"Stonewall Jackson Shrine." National Park Service, Fredericksburg and Spotsylvania National Military Park (2009). http://www.nps.gov/frsp/js.htm (accessed 21 October 2011).

Sutton, Charyn D. "Watch Night." The Onyx Group. Bala Cynwyd, Pennsylvania (December 2000). http://www.wsbrec.org/blackfacts/WatchNight.htm (accessed 8 June 2010).

"The African American Image in Virginia." Resource Library, Traditional Fine Arts Organization, Inc., Arizona. http://www.tfaoi.com/aa/8aa/8aa451.htm (accessed 21 December 2010).

The American Heritage New Dictionary of Cultural Literacy, Third Edition. Houghton Mifflin Company (2005). Dictionary.com. http://dictionary.reference.com/browse/franchise (accessed 3 August 2011).

The Emancipation Proclamation, January 1, 1863. Transcript. National Archives, Washington, D.C. http://www.archives.gov/exhibits/featured_documents/emancipation_proclamation/transcript.html (accessed December 2010).

The Freedmen's Bureau Online. The Freedmen and Southern Society Project, 1976. http://freedmensbureau.com (accessed 22 November 2010).

"The Washington-Rochambeau Revolutionary Route." National Park Service (2003). http://www.nps.gov/revwar/pdf/Significance%20Report-Screen.pdf (accessed 31 January 2012).

"Trail To Freedom." Fredericksburg and Stafford, Virginia (2011). www.TrailToFreedom.com (accessed 19 June 2010).

Tucker, Abigail. "Digging up the Past at a Richmond Jail." *Smithsonian Magazine* (March 2009). http://www.smithsonianmag.com/history-archaeology/Digs-Devils-Half-Acre.html (accessed 3 July 2011).

"William Andrew Jackson." University of Detroit Mercy Black Abolitionist Archive. University of Detroit Mercy, Detroit, Michigan. http://research.udmercy.edu/find/special_collections/digital/baa/item.php?record_id=174&collectionCode=baa (accessed 1 November 2011).

"Wounding of Stonewall Jackson Trail." National Park Service, Fredericksburg and Spotsylvania National Military Park (2008). http://www.nps.gov/frsp/jacktr.htm (accessed 21 October 2011).

INDEX

A

A Call for Unity, published letter, 60
A Declaration of the Causes and Necessity of Taking Up Arms, 11
A Leaf on a Grave, eulogy, 72
A Lesson in Politeness, newspaper article, 220
A Mule Driver, sketch, 164
A Sight in Camp in the Daybreak Gray and Dim, poem 149
Abel, 216
Abolitionist, also abolitionists, xvii, xxiii, 25, 40, 45, 48, 51-52, 55, 61, 69-71, 81, 89- 90, 102, 107-108, 111, 136, 166, 169, 177-178, 208, 216, 225, 271, 276
Adam, 113
Adams, New York, 220-222
Africa, 21, 238
African, 2, 10, 13, 29, 47, 52, 73-74, 161, 194, 216, 238
African American Church, 26, 149, 203-204, 258
African Americans, xvii-xviii, xxi, xxiv, 2, 6, 12, 16, 23, 25-26, 31-33, 75-76, 78, 85, 88, 101-103, 105, 109, 114-115, 117, 130, 136, 147, 150, 158, 164, 171, 175, 185-186, 188, 190-194, 196, 198, 200, 202-207, 214, 232-233, 238-239, 243, 245, 248, 255-256, 258-260, 263, 289

Africans, xxiii, 248, 255
Alabama, 3, 60, 72
Alexander, Peter, 251, 256, 280, 287
Alexander, William, Earl of Stirling, 218
Alexandria, Virginia, 7, 113, 193, 199, 201
Amelia Street, Falmouth Towne, 8
America, 7, 71, 73, 79, 108-109, 120, 177-178, 187-188, 203, 208-209, 227, 290
American forces, 16
American Academy of Arts and Letters, 239
American Anti-Slavery Society, 48, 51
American Colonization Society, 65
American Freedmen's Inquiry Commission, 179
American Revolutionary War, also American Revolution, 11-13, 16, 19, 21, 24, 32, 142
An Ancient and a Modern Compromise, sermon, 72, 228
Andersonville Prison, 176
Anglican, 24, 31, 262-263
Anglican Church, 262
Animas City, Colorado Territory, 228
Ann Street, Falmouth Towne, 8
Annie, servant woman, 110
Ans-chis, Cheyenne-Arapaho woman, 229, 230p, 232
Antebellum Period, xviii, 26, 44, 67, 164

Anthony, Susan B., 71
Antioch College, 128-129, 132
Appomattox Court House, 136, 182, 235
Aquia Creek, 8, 146
Aquia Landing, 55, 138, 145-147
Arlington National Cemetery, 113, 284
Army of Northern Virginia, 131, 136, 148, 156, 160, 182
Army of the Potomac, 102, 146, 159, 163, 174
Army of Virginia, 147
Ashford, Mina Schoonover, 232
Ashton, Dr. Lawrence, 224
Atlanta, Georgia, 205
Augur, Brigadier General Christopher C., 140
Aurelius, Marcus, 229

B

Babcock, John C., 160
Ball, Reverend R.A., 123
Baltimore & Ohio Railroad Station, 130
Baltimore, Maryland, 27, 130-131, 137, 270-271, 275
Banks, Henry, fugitive slave, 123
Baptist, 24-25, 31, 48, 56, 198, 201, 237
Barnaby, slave, 63
Barnes family, 208, 282-283
Barnes House, 208, 282
Barnes, Balsora, 208
Barnes, Bettie, 208
Barnes, Fannie, 208
Barnes, Harrison Brockenbrough, 208
Barnes, Lucy, 208
Barnes, Margaret, 208

Battle Hymn of the Republic, 180
Battle of Antietam, 75, 148
Battle of Bull Run, 77, 102
Battle of Chancellorsville, 76, 170
Battle of Fredericksburg, 148, 155, 167, 169, 175
Battle of Manassas, also First Manassas, 77
Battle of Second Manassas, 147
Battle of Spotsylvania Court House, 176
Battle of the Crater, 113
Battle of the Wilderness, 176
Beale, Jane Howison, 19
Belle Isle Prison, Richmond, 174
Belmont, 214, 233, 239-241, 282, 284, 288
Besant, Annie, 72, 291
Bethlehem Primitive Baptist Church, 200-201, 293
Betty, negro woman, 61
Bible, 38, 58-59, 113, 181, 198, 248
Bill Butler Road, Falmouth, 203
Billy, slave, 63
Black Church, 152, 205-206
Black Codes, 186
Black Dispatches, 105
Black school, 206-207, 242
Black Scout of the Rappahannock, 141-142, 160
Blood Money, poem, 42-43
Bloodhound Law, 41p caption
Blue Ridge Mountains, 3-4
Booker, Peter, 220-223
Boston, 7, 45, 48, 54, 56, 64, 108, 124-125, 129, 149, 175, 177
Boston Post Road, 7
Bourne, Linwood, 260

Bourne's AMOCO station, 260
Bouvier, Jacqueline Lee, 99
Bouvier, Lt. John Vernou, 99, 100p
Breck, Lt. George, 153
Brentsville, Virginia, 110
Bridgewater Mills, 224
Britain, 72, 109, 291
British, 8-9, 16, 108, 177-178, 187
British Crown, 11
British Methodist Episcopal Church, 123
Brooke family, 19
Brooke, Susannah, 19
Brooke, Virginia, 219-220, 287
Brooklyn, New York, 107
Brooks family, 245-247, 287
Brooks, Marion, 217, 245
Brooks, St. Clair, 207, 242, 246, 284
Brooks, Wes, 217
Brown v. Board of Education, 239
Brown, Brevet Brigadier General Orlando, 192
Brown, Judy, 206
Bryden, G. MacLaren, 14
Buchanan, Andrew, 21
Buchanan, William, 21
Buffalo soldiers, 228, 231
Bureau of Colored Troops, 171
Bureau of Military Information, 160
Bureau of Refugees, Freedmen, and Abandoned Lands, 190
Burns, Anthony or Tony, 42, 48, 49p, 51, 54-57, 60, 123-126, 201, 261
Burnside, Major General Ambrose E., 159-160
Bush arbor, 204-205

Bussell, Benjamin, 19
Butler Road, Falmouth, 203, 259
Butler, Bill, 202
Butler, Elizah, free black, 94, 203
Butterfield, Major General Daniel, 160
Byrd, Sallie, 237-238, 281

C

Cady's Gut, 225, 281
Cain, 52, 216
Cambridge Street, Falmouth, 206
Cambridge, Massachusetts, 211
Canaan, 121
Canada, 44, 46-47, 64, 124, 145
Canadian Valley, Oklahoma, 232
Capital of the Confederacy, 146, 190
Captain Duff Green, 110
Captain Jack O'Bannon, 28, see also John "Jack" Maurice O'Bannon
Captain John Dow, 6
Captain John Smith, xxiii, 2, 30
Captain Pickett, 33-35
Carlton, 214-218, 258, 261-262
Carlyle, Jane Welsh, 187-188
Carlyle, Thomas, 187-188, 291
Carnegie, Andrew, 227-228, 291
Caroline County militia, 21
Caroline County, Virginia, 171, 193, 289
Caroline Street, Falmouth Towne, 8, 202
Carter, Charles, 9
Carter, Landon, 9
Carter, Robert, 8-9
Carter Street, Falmouth Towne, 9
Cartice, Dorie (Dora Curtis), 200
Catholics, 211
Catlett's Station, 103

Cedar Mountain, 147
Cemetery Gardening Angels, 126
Center for African American
    Genealogical Research,
    Inc., 238
Central Intelligence Agency, 103
Channing, William Henry, 79, 268
Charles Towne, South Carolina, 7
Charleston Harbor, 75
Charleston, South Carolina, 160
Chase, Secretary Salmon P., 78,
    267, 270
Chasseurs, 84-85
Chatham, xviii, 17, 18-19, 18p,
    65-67, 106, 112-113, 119, 149,
    169, 182, 225
Chatham Bridge, 8
Chesapeake Bay, 1, 13, 62
Chicago, 114
Christ, Jesus, Savior, 31, 53, 77,
    111, 149, 170, 263, 293-294
Christian, 56, 59, 150, 152, 237,
    293-294
Christianity, 25, 56, 59, 152, 207
Christians, 18-19, 74, 263
Christmas, 158-159
Christmas Day, 72, 291
Christmas Eve, 152
Christy's Minstrels, 114
Church Hill, 24, 263
Church of England, 31
CIA's Studies in Intelligence, 103
Cincinnati, Ohio, 64, 68, 79,
    81, 111
Circular 10, Freedmen's Bureau, 192
City of New York, ship, 108
City of Refuge, 123

Civil Liberty, 266
Civil Rights Act of 1964, 239
Civil Rights Movement, 264
Civil War, xviii, xxi, 11, 21, 26, 35,
    68, 70-71, 77, 102, 104, 108,
    111, 114-115, 134, 137, 142,
    145, 148, 155, 178, 182, 185,
    188, 190, 194-196, 198-199,
    202-203, 205-208, 214-215,
    217-220, 226, 228, 235-238,
    247, 255, 258, 263, 265, 275,
    280, 282-284, 293
Clark, Elder John, 57, 60p
Clarks, 256
Clearview, 21-22, 22p, 30p, 214
Clothes-Line Telegraph, 160-161, 163
Coalter, Hannah Jones, 65-66, 65p
Cohasset, Massachusetts, 88
Collins, James, 176
Colonial, xvii, 8, 31, 259
Colonial Period, 3, 5, 247
Colonialism, 39
Colono Ware, 2-3
Color, painting, 239-240, 240p
Colored church, 243, 281
Colored School, 207-208
Columbia, American goddess of
    Liberty, 189
Columbus, Ohio, 131
Commonwealth of Virginia,
    27, 275
Compensated Emancipation
    Act, 145
Compromise of 1850, 42
Comte de Rochambeau, 16
Concord, Massachusetts, xv, 46
Confederacy, 171, 177, 182, 219

Index

Confederate Army, 68, 76, 81, 110, 112, 118, 135, 148, 156, 159, 175-176, 228, 265, 275
Confederate forces, 85, 105-106, 146-147
Confederate President Jefferson Davis, 105-106, 219
Confederate Provisional Congress, 219
Confederate States, 152, 178, 208, 236
Confederate States of America, 72, 105, 109
Confederate White House, 106-107
Confederates, 75, 84, 103, 110, 150
Confiscation Act of 1861, 143
Congress, Confederate, 219
Congress, United States, 42, 78, 88, 107, 194
Constitution of the United States, 16, 51, 70, 72, 107, 116, 214
Contraband, 103, 105p, 114, 120-121, 140, 143-144, 159, 221
Contrabands, 96-97, 121, 141-142, 146-147, 158, 222, 271
Conway Colony, 131, 273, 275
Conway family, 45, 126, 134
Conway Hall, Dickinson College, 291
Conway House, xviii-xix, 31, 38, 68, 81, 89-90, 126-127, 127p, 133-135, 168, 174, 194, 228, 275-276
Conway, Ellen Dana, 69p, 71
Conway, Gordon & Garnett National Bank, 137
Conway, Margaret E., Mrs. W.P., 38p, 81, 90, 136

Conway, Mildred, 69, 81
Conway, Moncure Daniel, xvii, xix, xxi, xxiii-xxiv, 11, 27-28, 31, 33-38, 39p, 40-42, 44-46, 48, 51-52, 54-55, 64, 66, 68-72, 75, 77-78, 81, 86-87, 89, 91p, 102, 111-112, 119-120, 126, 129-131, 133-134, 138, 142, 147, 150, 166, 177-179, 182-183, 185, 187-188, 195, 197, 203, 208-211, 213-216, 225-228, 227p, 250, 258, 262, 265, 268-269, 272-273, 275-277, 279, 290-292
Conway, Peter Vivian Daniel, "PVD," 136, 137p
Conway, Valentine, 70
Conway, Walker P., 28, 38, 52, 53p, 81, 134, 136, 138, 208, 227, 273-275
Coon, Ham, 256
Coppedge, Sarah, 238
Copperheads, 150
Cotton famine, 108
Court of Appeals, Virginia, 66
Crain, Lydia, 28-29
Cross, Biblical, 248, 262
Crow Wing County, Minnesota, 175
Crow's Nest, 37
Crutchfield, Albert, 224
Cuba, 87
Culpeper County, Virginia, 6, 147
Cuninghame and Company, 9, 11
Cuninghame, William, 11
Custer, Brigadier General George Armstrong, 176

D

Dabney, black scout, 140-142, 144, 160
Daily Dispatch, Richmond newspaper, 110
Dana, Miss Ellen Davis, 68
Daniel, Dr. John Moncure, 37
Daniel, Justice Peter Vivian, 136
Daniel, lad slave, 61
Daniel, Margaret Eleanor, 37-38
Danville, Virginia, 110-111
Davenport, slave, 21
Davis, Jefferson, Confederate President, 105-109, 219
Davis, Major H. E., Jr., 109
Davis, Theodore R., special artist, 156
Dawes, Captain Rufus Robinson, 98, 155
Dayton, Ohio, 131
De Baptiste, George, 13
De Baptiste, John, 13-15
Decker, Lt. James Nelson, 82-83, 83p, 95
Declaration of Independence, United States, 37, 40, 51, 142, 178
Declaration of the Rights of Man and of the Citizen, France, 178
Department of Virginia, Freedmen's Bureau, 190
Devil, 73, 77, 96
Devlin, Pvt. Patrick, 95
Dick, freed slave, 115, 116p
District of Columbia, 127-128, 146
Divine Idea, 168-169, 265
Dixie, song, 99
Dolly, slave, 215
Doswell, J. Temple, 105-106
Douglas Street, Fredericksburg, 236-237
Douglass, Frederick, 61, 102, 103p
Dragon, ship, 13
Dred Scott Decision, 136
Duff Green Warehouse, 176
Duke, a black man, 114, 115p
Dunbar House, 68
Dunbar, Miss Anna, 68, 70, 273
Dusty Bull, 229, 230p

E

Eames, Edwin H., 174
East, the, 125, 129, 267
Easter Day, 223
Easter Hymn, 262
Easton, Pennsylvania, 81, 111, 139p caption, 274
Egypt, 121
Egyptians, 121
El Reno Cemetery, Canadian County, Oklahoma, 232
El Reno, City of, 232
Ellwood, home, 68
Emancipation Proclamation, 31, 130, 148, 150, 152-153, 184p, 208
Emerson, Ralph Waldo, 40, 40p, 228, 265
England, 3, 71, 94, 177, 187, 208-209, 255, 290
Englishmen, 108
Episcopalians, 24
Equality, xxiv, 16, 43, 177-179, 189, 292
Essex County, Virginia, 121, 284
Europe, 3, 9
European, 2, 248

INDEX

Europeans, 9
Eustaces, Mr. and Miss, 81
Evil spirits, 248
Exeter Hall, London, 209
Exodus, 75

F

Fair Ideal America, 168, 212
Fairhaven, Massachusetts, 107
Fall Hill, home, 19, 92
Falls, 1-4, 8, 23, 31, 223, 255
Falls Run, 216-217, 284
Falmouth Anglican Church, 262
Falmouth Baptist Church (old site), 243
Falmouth bottom, 238
Falmouth Bridge, 106, 223-224, 259
Falmouth cemetery, 94
Falmouth Colored School, 242, 243p, 283
Falmouth Elementary School, 242
Falmouth Ferry, 11, 13
Falmouth Station, 147
Falmouth Towne, 9
Farmer's Bank, Fredericksburg, 191
Father (Heavenly), 44, 293
Father Abraham, 172, 182
Fauquier Court House, Virginia, 10
Federal Period, 16
Federal troops, 87, 99, 130, 194
Ficklen family, 214, 239
Ficklen, Joseph B., 153, 200
Ficklen, William F., 223
Ficklen's Bridge, 223
Ficklen's Hill, 85
Fifteenth Amendment, 185
First African Baptist Church, Boston, 149-150

First Anti-Slavery Baptist Church, Yellow Springs, 131
First Congregational Unitarian Church, Cincinnati, 72, 111
First Constitutional Convention, 12, 16, 169
First Unitarian Church, Washington, D.C., 52
FitzGerald, Gerald, 210-211, 211p, 212
Fitzhugh home, 112
Fitzhugh, William, Esq., 18
Favill, Lt. Josiah Marshall, 165
Florida, 72
Forbes House, 92-93, 202, 202p
Forbes, Captain James Fitzgerald, 170-171
Forbes, Dave, David Sterling, 93
Forbes, Edwin, special artist, 115, 164
Forbes, Kate, 92
Forbes, Murray, 33, 92, 154, 170
Forbes, Sallie, 92-93, 155, 170
Forlorn Hope, 175
Forres, Scotland, 19
Fort Delaware, 119
Fort Pulaski, Georgia, 219
Fort Sumter, South Carolina, 75, 167
Fort Supply, Oklahoma Territory, 229
Fort Wagner, South Carolina, 160
Fortune, Timothy Thomas, 232
Founding Fathers, 41, 168, 276
Fourth of July, 51, 120
Fowler, Colonel Edward Brush, 142
Framingham, Massachusetts, 51
Frances, slave, 81
Franchise, sketch, 189
Fraternity, 178-179

Fredericksburg, 96, 98, 103, 105-106, 111-113, 118-120, 137-138, 140, 144-148, 156 159-163, 166-169, 176, 191-194, 196, 199-200, 208, 210, 214, 219, 236, 244-245, 255, 275
Fredericksburg Artillery, 136, 235
Fredericksburg Star, newspaper, 201, 223
Fredericksburg Station, 147
Free States, 131, 146, 272
Freedmen, 189, 191-193, 207
Freedmen and Southern Society Project, 190
Freedmen's Bureau, 191, 191p, 194
Freedom seekers, 123, 128-131, 133, 138, 143-144, 146, 174
Freedom's Eve, 152
Fremont, Major General John C., 79
French allies, 16
French army, 11
French Expeditionary Force, 11
French Revolution, 178
French troops, 11
Front Royal Gazette, newspaper, 56-57
Fugitive Slave Act of 1793, 136, 145
Fugitive slave church, 124
Fugitive Slave Law, 41-42, 48, 51, 56, 125, 145, 209
Fur and skin trade, xxiii, 3

G

Garrison, Fanny, 150
Garrison, William Lloyd, 51, 51p, 74, 108, 150, 177, 265
Garrison, William Lloyd, Jr., 150

Gateway to freedom, xviii-xix, 75, 113, 144, 147, 174, 180
General Order No. 77, Virginia Freedmen's Bureau, 190
General Order No. 102, Virginia Freedmen's Bureau, 193, 199
Genesis, 113
Georgetown, 64, 127-129, 133, 171, 267, 269, 275
Georgia, 7, 205, 219
Gerald FitzGerald. Killed in Battle on the Rappahannock, May, 1863, poem, 212
Gettysburg, 136, 155, 159
Ghana, 238
Ghanaian, 2
Glasgow, Scotland, 9, 11
God, 17, 43, 52-53, 57-60, 73, 77, 88, 98, 111, 125, 133, 150, 152, 169-170, 179-182, 243, 263, 265, 271, 293-294
God of Battles, The, 171
Goochland County, Virginia, 219
Goosey Goose, 259
Gordon Street, Falmouth, 223
Gordon, Eliza, 222
Gordonsville, Virginia, 105
Gore, Officer, 224
Grandmother Baber, 132
Grant, General Ulysses S., 76
Graveyard Convention, 14-15
Gray, Salley Johnson, 220
Great Britain, 71, 108, 145, 177, 209, 290
Great Coastal Road, 7
Great Lakes, 3
Green, Adam, slave, 21

Green, Alexander Morson, 111, 224, 228, 229p
Green, Charles Jones, 110
Green, Duff, 110-111, 192, 199, 228
Green, Duff McDuff, 110
Green, Duff, Jr., 110
Green, James Lane, 110, 193
Green, Long Duff, 110
Greenwood, home, 117
Grimes, Reverend Lenard G., 124
Grinnell, Moses, 131
Guinea Station, Virginia, 171
Gunn family, 255-256
Gunn, Eva, 248
Gwinn, Alfred, 134, 135p
Gwinn, Dunmore, 70, 126-128, 128p, 129, 131-132, 132p, 135, 137, 168, 267
Gwinn, Eliza, 126-129, 128p, 131-132, 132p, 135, 137, 168, 267
Gwinn, Evaline, also Evelyn, 70, 71, 71p, 132
Gwinn, Nancy Butler, 81, 135
Gwinn, Peter, 137, 275

H

Haint, 248
Haint blue, 248
Haiti, 138
Haitian Bureau of Emigration, 138
Halsted, Major George B., 142, 143p, 144, 146
Harpers Weekly, newspaper, 156-157, 107, 189
Harris Light Cavalry, 83, 95
Harrison's Landing, Virginia, 146
Hartford, Connecticut, 107

Harvard Divinity School, Cambridge, 211
Heaven, 43, 59, 77, 131, 133, 172, 179, 263
Herod, Elizabeth, 135
Herod, Richard, 135-136
Heslin, Pvt. John, 96
Hill, Confederate Lieutenant General Ambrose Powell, 162, 171
Hill's corps, 162
Hiring-day, 44
Historic Port of Falmouth Park, 207
Hogtown, 5
Holmes, General Theophilis, 105
Holy Lord, 248
Hooker, Major General Joseph, 160-163
Howard, Abram, 27
Howard, Major General Oliver Otis, 158-159, 190
Howe, Julia Ward, 169-170, 169p, 207, 265
Humstead, Charles, slave, 36
Humstead, Peter, slave, 37
Hunter, James, 12
Hunter's Iron Works, 12, 32
Hush arbor, 204, 260
Hush harbor, 203-204

I

Idea, the, 168
Illinois, 155
Independence Day, 120
Indiana, 140
Indians, 175, 228, 285
Industrial Revolution, 32
Ireland, 95, 255, 277
Irish, 217

Irish Brigade, 158
Ironing, painting, 246, 246p
Ironside Baptist Church, 205-206
Island of St. Kitts, 13

J

Jack, mulatto slave, 61
Jack, Negro slave, 61
Jackson, Confederate Lieutenant General Thomas Jonathan "Stonewall," 162, 170-171
Jackson, William Andrew, 106-107, 107p, 108-109
James River, 146, 219
James, slave, 18
Jamestown Exposition, 227
Jamestown, Virginia, xxiii, 2
Jefferson County Journal, newspaper, 220, 222
Jefferson County Regiment, 220
Jefferson, Thomas, 258
Jericho, 113
Jesus, 43, 53, 72-73, 203, 293
Jews, 121
Jim Crow, 238-239
Jim, African American scout, 103
Jim, slave, 63
Job, 194
Johnson, Confederate General Joseph, 106
Johnson, Enoch, 223-224
Johnson, James, Superintendent, 192
Johnson, Manuel, 219-220
Johnson, York, 200-201
Jones, Cadwallader, 3
Jordon, 85, 88, 144, 147
Jubilee 113-114, 151
Judas, 43

Judgment Day, 86

K

Kelly's Ford, Virginia, 164
Kiff, Pvt. Josiah, 96
King and Queen County, Virginia, 61
King Carter, 9
King Charles II, 7
King George County, Virginia, 9
King Street, Falmouth, 8, 19
King, Brigadier General Rufus, 106
King, Dr. Martin Luther, Jr., 60
King, James, African American boy, 193
King's Highway, 7- 8, 11-12
King's Street, Falmouth Towne, 8
Kingdom Coming, song, 114
Ku Klux Klan, 239

L

Lacy, Betty Churchill Jones, 65, 68, 111-112, 112p, 117
Lacy, James Horace, 65, 67-68, 67p, 112-113, 117-119, 225
Ladd, Pvt. Charles, 97
Lady Spotswood, 68
Lafayette College, 139p caption
Lancashire, England, 108-108
Lancaster County, Virginia, 62
Land of Freedom, 145-147, 150
Lawson, Tom, 223-224
League of Nations, 226
Lears or Leavis, Charles H., 200
Lee Monument, Richmond, Virginia, 265
Lee, Captain Jessie M., 229
Lee, General Robert E., 76, 105, 148, 162-163, 146, 182, 265

Leopoldville, Congo, Africa, 21
Letter from a Birmingham Jail, 60
Letter from Virginia, 209-110, 277
Lewis, Fielding, 13
Libby Prison, Richmond, 174
Liberia, 65
Liberty, 74, 178-179, 195
Lincoln, President Abraham, 78-79, 80p, 81, 108, 140, 145-146, 148, 180, 182, 189-190, 268
Little Miami River, 131
Little Shiloh Baptist Church, 206-207, 236, 243-244, 245p
Liverpool, England, 108
Lockwood house, Adams, New York, 221
London, xxiv, 108, 182, 209, 277, 290-291
London Emancipation Society, 108
Long family, 255-256
Long, Lucy, 223
Longstreet, Confederate Lieutenant General James, 162
Lord, 53, 59, 96, 150, 153, 155, 179, 181, 263, 293
Lord Fairfax, 9
Lord Rector of Edinburgh University, 187p caption
Loring, Commissioner Edward, 51
Louisiana, 72, 219
Lucas family, 255-256
Lucas, Annie Duncan, slave, 208
Lucas, Big Jim, 216, 218, 262
Lucas, Charles H., 193
Lucas, Daniel, 208
Lucas, James, 242, 254p
Lucas, L. Reginald, 236
Lucas, Maria, 236p

Lucas, Nathaniel, 193
Lucas, Rev. Cornelius S., "Pap Lucas," 207, 235, 236p, 237
Lucas, William, slave, 11
Lucy, slave, 21-22
Lumpkin, Robert, 123
Lumpkin's slave jail, 123

M

Macy's Department Store, New York, 256
Madison, James, 41
Maine, 79
Major Hawks, Wells J., Confederate officer, 171
Mann, Horace, 129
March, Professor Francis Andrew, 139p caption
Mars' Monc, 90
Mary, mother of Jesus, 43
Mary, no surname, 232-233
Marye's Heights, 167
Maryland, 9, 37, 130-131, 138, 270
Mason, George IV, 41, 178
Mason, James Murray, 41, 41p, 209
Massachusetts, 46, 51, 64, 88, 107, 109, 130, 141-142, 141p, 166
Massachusetts Regiment, 2nd, 210
Massachusetts Volunteer Infantry, 20th, 167-168, 174
Massachusetts Volunteer Infantry, 54th, 160
Maury, Colonel Abraham, 19
Maury, Elizabeth Brayne "Betsey," 19
Mayfield, Fredericksburg suburb, 244
McClellan, Major General George B., 146
McClellan's army, 120

McDowell, Major General Irvin, 89, 102-103, 106-107, 119
McDowell's army, 86, 120
McGuire, Dr. Hunter, 171
McGwinn, Peter, 137
Melchers, Corinne, 239-241
Melchers, Gari, 214, 233-234, 239, 246
Memorial Day, 196
Memorys of the Past, 88, 94
Mendell, Captain, Major Sidney J., 220-223
Merricks, Osborne, 153-155, 154p, 201, 247
Methodist, 24, 38, 133, 151, 198, 269
Michigan, 175
Michigan Brigade, 176
Michigan Cavalry, 5th, also Fifth, 176
Michigan Volunteer Infantry, 7th, 175
Middle Peninsula, 62
Mills, John Harrison, 115
Minnesota, 175
Minnesota Infantry, 1st, 155
Minor, Henry, 218-219
Miss Ophelia, 71
Mississippi, 72
Moncure, John, 200
Monroe and Berry Store, Falmouth, 257p, 259
Monroe Democrat, newspaper, 175
Montross Gallery, New York, 233
Monument Avenue, Richmond, Virginia, 265
Morris, Juda, 224
Morson, Dr. Hugh, 200-201
Morton's Ford, Virginia, 176
Moses, 58, 131, 244

Moses, slave, 12
Moxley, James, 193
Mr. Green, 109-110
Mr. Stark, overseer, 18
Mrs. Mendell, 222
Mt. Pisgah Church, 243-244, 244p, 259
Mud March, 160
Murphy, Orderly Sergeant Josiah Fitch, 168
Murphy, Pvt. John, 96

N

Nancy, child slave, 61
Nast, Thomas, special artist, 189
National Academy of Design, 239
National Baptist Convention, 205
National Cemetery, Fredericksburg, 194, 196
National Union League, 189
Native American, 2, 175, 229
Native Americans, 2-3, 30, 255
Natt, slave, 6
Ned, slave, 6
Negro Battle Hymn, 189
Negro race, 178
Negro suffrage, 109
Nell, African princess, 29
Nelson, Mary L., "Lottie," 237
New England, 56, 76, 125
New England Anti-Slavery Society, 150
New Hampshire, 93
New Jersey, 142
New Jersey Cavalry, 1st, 113
New Jerusalem, 198
New Mexico, 229
New South, 178
New Testament, 58, 263

INDEX

New World, 190, 248
New Year, 148, 150-152, 233
New Year's Day, 44
New Year's Eve, 150, 152
New York, 82, 96, 108, 110, 140, 153, 220, 222, 233, 291
New York City, 107, 291
New York Daily Tribune, newspaper, 42
New York Cavalry, 2nd, 83, 95-96, 140
New York Infantry, 35th, 220
New York Infantry, 51st, 148
New York Infantry, 57th, 165
New York Infantry, 76th, 113
New York Infantry, 88th, 158
New York Light Artillery, 1st, 153
New York State Militia, 20th, 99
New York State Militia, 21st, 101
New York State Volunteers, 21st, 97
New York State Volunteers, 26th, 138
New York Sun, newspaper, 158
New York Times, newspaper, 166, 233
Nigerian, 2
North America, 67
North Carolina, 56, 175
North Carolina Infantry, 18th, 170
North, the, 41, 45, 56, 62-63, 65, 72, 74, 77, 114, 135, 146, 165, 167, 179, 181, 270
Northern Neck, Virginia, 9, 62
Northerners, 41, 81
Northland, 129
Northumberland County, Virginia, 62
Norton, Pvt. Thomas, 96
Noyes, Captain George F., 113, 116-117, 140, 142, 144, 167

NY State Militia, 14th Brooklyn Chasseurs, 84, 142

O

O Captain! My Captain!, poem, 183
O'Bannon, John "Jack" Maurice, also Captain Jack O'Bannon, 215-217, 225, 262
O'Bannon, Miss Ellen, 217-218
O'Bannon, Miss Nannie, 217-218
O'Grady, W.L.D., 158
Oberlin College, Ohio, 56, 124
Oberlin Evangelist, publication, 56
Odham's AMOCO station, 260
Oh Freedom, traditional spiritual, 153
Ohio, 56, 64, 71-72, 111, 129, 131-132, 134, 136, 138, 168, 270, 273, 275
Old Dominion, 153
Old Eliza, see also Eliza Gwinn, 90
Old Uncle Berryman, 113-114
Onesimus, 59
Orange County, New York, 82
Orange County, Virginia, 68, 171, 176, 204
Oswego Commercial Times, newspaper, 107

P

Page Street, Falmouth Towne, 9
Page, Mann, 9
Pap Lucas, see also Cornelius S. Lucas, 237
Parallel, 49th, 65
Paris, 227, 291
Paris Peace Convention, 226
Parker, Alice, slave, 139p
Parker, James, slave, 81, 138, 275

Parker, Theodore, 45-46, 45p, 265
Paul, apostle, 58, 60
Payne family, 15
Payne, Burley, 15
Payne, Gloria, 259
Payne, Nelson, 246
Peninsula Campaign, 91
Peninsula, the, 120
Pennsylvania, 81, 111, 155, 165
Pennsylvania Cavalry, 1st, 96
Penny, Justice J.W., 221
Pentecostal, 244
Peter, Saint, 113
Petersburg, Virginia, 113, 174, 176, 182
Peyton, Alfred, 103
Philadelphia, 11, 21, 27, 151
Philemon, 59
Phillip, slave, 18
Phillips, Wendell, 48, 50p, 265
Piedmont of Virginia, 2
Pilgrim's Progress, 198
Pleyal's Hymn, 95
Poindexter, Reverend Roger J., 244
Pollock family, 235
Pollock, Captain John Gray, 235
Pollock, Captain William G., 235
Pompey, African American boy, 116
Pool, James, 206
Pool, Thomas, 206
Pope, Major General John, 146-147
Port of Falmouth, 4, 154
Potomac Creek, 8
Potomac Path, 7
Potomac River, 62, 138, 146, 209
Potomac Trail, 7
Pratt, John Lee, 225
Presbyterians, 24
President John F. Kennedy, 99

Prince Street, Falmouth Towne, 8
Prince William County, Virginia, 10
Prior, James, 81, 134, 200
Prior, Sallie, 223
Prominent Whites and Freemen, 134, 200
Promised Land, 121, 131, 145-146, 244
Prophet Bill, 77-78
Providence, Rhode Island, 108
Provost Marshal, 93, of Falmouth, 109

Q

Quaker, 129
Quakers, 61

R

Radical Republican Party, 194
Raleigh, Sir Walter, 40
Rapidan River, 176
Rappahannock Forge, 12
Rappahannock River, xvii-xviii, xxiii, 2-4, 6, 9, 11-13, 17, 19, 21, 23, 31, 37, 39, 62, 66, 85-86, 88, 90, 92, 106, 113, 122, 141-142, 147, 149, 159, 160-161, 167-169, 175, 206-207, 210, 212-213, 225, 235, 242, 255, 263, 278
Rappahannock Valley, 3
Ray, Pvt. William, 97, 165
Raymond Street, St. Catharines, Canada, 126
Rebel Negro Pickets, 156, 156p
Rebels, 87, 95, 102, 141, 160
Rebs, 97
Reconstruction, 185, 189, 200, 204-205, 210
Redpath, James, 138

Republic, 73, 188, 195
Republicans, 148
Revolutionary burying-ground, 14, 263
Revolutionary War, 11-13, 16, 19, 24, 142
Richmond County, Virginia, 62
Richmond, Fredericksburg, and Potomac Railroad, 138, 146
Richmond, Virginia, 48, 54, 75-76, 91, 106-108, 110, 118, 120-121, 123, 138-140, 146, 162, 174, 176, 190, 192-193, 199, 219, 265, 275
River Road, Falmouth, 8, 242, 252p caption, 256
Robert Wheeler's Store, 259
Robinson, Fielding, 201
Robinson, James, 11
Rochester, New York, 53
Rocky Mountains, 125
Rolling Roads, 5p caption
Roots family, 255-256
Roots, Fannie, "Miss Roots," 240-241, 241p, 248, 250p
Roots, Reuben, 249
Roots, Willie P., 237, 240
Rose, Dr. Lawrence B., 135
Ross, Alexander Morson, 229
Ross, Margaret M., "Maggie," 229
Ross, Mary, 228, 231p
Ross, Nancy, 111, 224, 228
Ross, Robert, 223-224
Ross, William Carter, 228-229, 230p, 231p, 232
Rowser family, 255-256
Rowser Road, also Rowser Lane, Falmouth, 233, 242

Rowser, James, "Uncle Jim," 233, 235p
Rowzey, James, 206
Royal Governor, 68
Ruggles, Confederate General, 118
Rumford, home, 235
Russell family, 225, 255-256
Russell, John W., 225
Russell, Julia, 251p, 256, 256p

S

Sabot Hill, home, 219
Saint Christopher Island, 13
Salisbury Prison, North Carolina, 175
Sally, child slave, 61
San Diego, 137
Sand beach, Falmouth, 207
Satan, 73, 77, 133, 279
Savannah, Georgia, 7
Scotland, 9, 11, 19, 94, 255, 277
Scots, 9
Sears, Bvt. Capt. Hector, VRC Military Commissioner, 134, 191-193
Secessionists, 166
Second Battle of Reams Station, 174
Second Inaugural Address, 180
Second Regiment Pennsylvania Volunteers, 196
Second Wisconsin Infantry, 100
Seddon family, 218
Seddon farm, 219
Seddon, James Alexander, Confederate Secretary of War, 218-220
Seddon, Thomas, 219
Shanahan, Daniel, 174-175

Shaw, Captain and later Colonel Robert Gould, 160
Shaw, Effie, 160
Sheffield Daily Telegram, newspaper, 108
Shenandoah Valley, 75, 147
Shiloh "Old Site" Church, Fredericksburg, 245
Shiloh Baptist Cemetery, also Shiloh Church Cemetery, Fredericksburg, 236, 245
Sickles, Brigadier General Daniel, 103
Sixth Sub District, Virginia Freedmen's Bureau, 191-192
Slave Code, 190
Slavery, xvii, xxiv, 2, 7, 16, 29-30, 32, 35, 51-52, 54, 56, 66, 70, 73-74, 77-81, 88, 98, 108-109, 111, 114, 123-125, 131, 133, 138, 145-146, 164-166, 169, 171, 176-177, 180-181, 187, 190, 195, 199, 201, 203-204, 206, 209, 211, 216, 219-220, 226, 228, 237, 260-261, 264, 272, 277
Smithsonian Institution, 78
Sojourner Truth, 51
South Carolina, 7, 72, 75, 160, 166
South Place Chapel, London, 209
South, the, 61, 63, 72, 74, 76-77, 94, 102, 104, 113, 121, 124, 141, 167, 177-179, 181, 185-186, 188-189, 203, 219-220, 234, 238, 260, 265
Southern, xvii, xxiii, 20, 25, 52, 74, 76, 78, 93, 99, 109, 121, 130, 132, 164, 175, 177, 180, 186, 225, 228, 239, 248

Southerner, 67, 178-179
Southerners, 41, 51, 81, 265
Spirit, the Holy Spirit, 53, 243, 293
Spotsylvania County, Virginia, xviii, 65, 123, 160, 171, 191, 193
Spout Hill, 223
Sprague, Governor William, 108
Springfield, Ohio, 134
St. Catharines, Ontario, Canada, 123, 125-126
Stafford County Citizens' Alliance, 241
Stafford County Court, 28
Stafford Court House, 160, 199
Stafford County, Virginia, xvii, 18-19, 27-28, 37, 46, 48, 52, 62, 64, 99, 111, 119, 123, 145, 153, 165-166, 171, 174, 178, 182, 185, 191-193, 199, 201, 203-207, 215-216, 218- 220, 223, 227-228, 235, 239, 242, 264, 275
Stafford Heights, 99, 120, 148
Standing Twenty, 229
Stanton, Elizabeth Cady, 71, 290
Stanton, Edwin M., Secretary of War, 107, 179, 267
State of Virginia, 67, 111, 190
Steal Away, song, 203
Stone, Justice F.B., 193
Stone, Officer, 224
Stone, The Honorable Thomas, 37
Stonewall Brigade, 21
Sub District of Alexandria, 19th Division, Virginia Freedmen's Bureau, 193
Sub District of Richmond, 14th Division, Virginia Freedmen's Bureau, 193

Sumner, Senator Charles, 79, 166, 270
Sumner's Corps, 148p
Supreme Court of the United States, 136, 239
Susannah, sloop, 6
Sutherland, Captain George E., 171
Suttle, Charles Frank, 48, 51, 54

T

Tackett, Charles, 219
Taylor, Henry, 155
Taylor, Isaac, "Ike," 155, 159
Taylor, Jane, 201
Teamsters' Duel, sketch, 157, 157p
Teasdale, Pvt. Charles, 84
Temperance Hall, London, 108
Terry, Major General A.H., 190
Testimonies Concerning Slavery, book, xxiv, 178, 187, 262, 273
Texas, 72
The Abolitionist Hymn, 17
The Age, New York newspaper, 232-233
The Christian Banner, Fredericksburg newspaper, 120-121
The Globe, newspaper, 232
The Golden Hour, book, 81, 195
The Liberator, Boston newspaper, 51, 108-109, 124
The President of the United States, 81, 150
The Union Branch of the True Vine, 199-201, 293
The Washington National Republican, newspaper, 117

There's a Meeting Here Tonight, song, 203
Thistle Mill, 19
Thompson, George, 108
Thoreau, Henry David, 46-47, 47p, 51, 64, 265
Thoreau, Sophia, 47
Thornton, Francis IV, 19
Thornton, Mildred W., 19
Tidewater, 4
Train Ride to Freedom, 71, 131-132, 267
Transcendentalist Movement, 168
Transcendentalists, 52, 168
Travelers' Rest, 63
Treaty of Paris, 16
Tribune, New York newspaper, 86, 111
Trustees of Falmouth, 5, 9, 16, 23
Tubman, Harriett, 123
Turner, Helen, also Mammy Helen, 245-247, 246p, 247p
Twelfth Baptist Church, Boston, 124

U

Ulster Guards, 20th NYSM, 99
Uncle Jim, painting, 233, 234p
Uncle Tom's Cabin, book, 71
Uncle, elderly slave, 216
Underground Railroad, 61-65, 129, 145, 203, 260
Union, the, 72, 79, 83, 107, 120, 171, 180-181, 189
Union army, 75-76, 81-82, 84-85, 87-88, 96, 102, 106, 111-113, 115, 120, 127, 138, 143-144, 146, 148, 155-156, 159, 161, 169-170, 174-175, 196, 216

Union camp, 88, 156-157
Union Church, 24-26, 24p, 48, 56, 94, 155, 175, 198-199, 201, 233, 239, 242, 263
Union Church Cemetery, 14, 153, 194, 225, 242, 247, 263
Union forces, 104, 146, 217
Union Street, Falmouth, 233
Union troops, 85-86, 89, 92, 106, 114, 120, 139, 147, 160
Unitarian, 69
Unitarians, 52, 166, 268
United Daughters of the Confederacy, 236
United Nations, 226
United States, xix, 16, 81, 109, 123, 145, 150-151, 185, 190, 194-195, 205, 208, 219, 291
United States Colored Troops, 160, 171
United States Colored Troops, 3rd, 11, 173p
United States Colored Troops, 23rd, 113
Universalist, 265
Universalist Church, Richmond, Virginia, 54
University of Virginia Law School, 219
Upper South, 9
US Army, 143, 190
US Burial Corps, 194
US Cavalry 9th, 228
US Cavalry 10th, 228
US Colored Heavy Artillery, 5th, 136
US Constitution, 51
US Government, 175, 194
US Military Railroad, 147

US Pension Office, 175
US Regular Artillery, 85
US Route 1, Falmouth, 206, 256, 258-260
US Route 17, Falmouth, 258
US Sharpshooters, 85, 91
US Sharpshooters Regiment, 2nd, 84, 87, 92-93, 93p
Ute Campaign, 228

V

Valley View, also Valley View Farm, 219-220
Vass, Elizabeth, 19, 20p, 21, 182
Vass, James, 19-20, 28, 182
Vass, Lachlan C. II, 21
Vass, Lachlan C. III, 21
Vass, Reverend Lachlan C., 21, 182
Victoria Lawn Cemetery, St. Catharines, Canada, 125
Virginia Cavalry, 9th, 82, 111
Virginia Colony, 9, 68
Virginia Declaration of Rights, 178
Virginia Freedmen's Bureau, 134, 190-191
Virginia Gazette, newspaper, 11
Virginia General Assembly, xxiii, 4, 9, 13, 23, 27, 202, 263
Virginia Herald, Fredericksburg newspaper, 18, 27
Virginia Historical Society, 206
Virginia Infantry, 27th, 21
Virginia Infantry, 47th, 235
Virginia Legislature, 215, 225
Virginia Military Institute, 228
Virginia Supreme Court, 65, 67
Virginian, 45-46, 51, 140, 177

Virginians, 265, 292
Voting Rights Act of 1965, 239
Vowles, Zachariah, Esquire, 21

W

Wales, 95, 255
Walker, Dabney, ex-slave, 160-164
Walker, James M., 110
Walker, Lucy Ann, ex-slave, 160-163
Wallace, Judge, 214
War Between the States, 12, 236
Warrenton, Virginia, 41
Washington Peace Conference, 219
Washington Street, Falmouth, 101p, 208, 237-238, 241, 256, 258
Washington, D.C., 55, 75, 78, 88-90, 102-103, 113, 137-138, 140, 142, 145-147, 163, 166, 171, 201, 210-212, 222, 267-268, 270, 275
Washington, General, 12
Washington, George, 13, 19, 32, 40
Washington, John, xviii, 85, 87-88, 89p, 94, 97, 146, 174, 216, 263
Washington, Martha, 224
Washington, Mary, 223
Watch Night, 150-152
Water Cure, 131
Waud, Alfred R., special artist, 157, 191p caption
Weaver, Andrew, xviii, 113
Webster, Daniel, 42, 140
Weller, Pvt. George, 96
West Africa, 2
West African, 7, 248
West Cambridge Street, Falmouth, 9

West Indies, 13
West Virginia, 131
West, the, 131, 147
West, William W., 57
Westmoreland County, Virginia, 62
Wheeler family, 255-256
Wheeler, Robert, 256, 257p, 259
Wheeler's Market, 259
Wheeler's Store, 259
When I Can Read My Title Clear, hymn, 133
White House, 79
White Oak Church, 200-201
White Oak, Virginia, 200
White, First Sergeant Wyman S., 84, 87, 92-93
White, W. Henry, agent, 111
Whitman, First Lt. George Washington, 148
Whitman, Walt, 42, 42p, 48, 148, 182-183, 290
Whittemore, John M., 110
Williams, Aunt Nancy, 45-46, 129
Williams, Benjamin, 45-46, 64
Williams, Collin, 64, 129
Willow Street, Falmouth, 135, 202-203
Wilson, Reverend Hiram, 124
Windham, hymn, 95
Winnie, slave, 61
Wisconsin, 97
Wisconsin Volunteers, 6th, 98, 155-156
Wisconsin Volunteers, 7th, 165
Wise, Edward, 175, 176p
Wolverines, 176
World War I, 214

World War II, also Second World War, 185, 255
Wright, W.W., Engineer and Superintendent, 147

Y

Yankee, 69-70, 82, 87, 95, 110, 170
Yankees, 101, 217, 87
Yanks, 87
Year of Jubilee, hymn, 151
Year of Jubilee, song, 114
Yellow Springs News, newspaper, 227, 132
Yellow Springs, Ohio, 71, 129, 131-132, 134, 136, 138, 267, 273, 275
Yorktown, Virginia, 11, 16

Z

Zion Baptist Church, St. Catharines, Canada, 123, 125
Zion, boy ex-slave, 144-145

CPSIA information can be obtained at www.ICGtesting.com
Printed in the USA
LVOW102110041212

310091LV00002B/368/P

9 781475 908107